Researching and Applying Metaphor

THE CAMBRIDGE APPLIED LINGUISTICS SERIES
Series editors: Michael H. Long and Jack C. Richards

This series presents the findings of recent work in applied linguistics which are of direct relevance to language teaching and learning and of particular interest to applied linguists, researchers, language teachers and teacher trainers:

In this series:

Researching and Applying Metaphor

EDITED BY

Lynne Cameron
University of Leeds

and

Graham Low
University of York

CAMBRIDGE
UNIVERSITY PRESS

PUBLISHED BY THE PRESS SYNDICATE OF THE UNIVERSITY OF CAMBRIDGE
The Pitt Building, Trumpington Street, Cambridge CB2 1RP, United Kingdom

CAMBRIDGE UNIVERSITY PRESS
The Edinburgh Building, Cambridge CB2 2RU, United Kingdom
40 West 20th Street, New York, NY 10011–4211, USA
10 Stamford Road, Oakleigh, Melbourne 3166, Australia

First published 1999

Typeset in Sabon 10.5/12pt   CE

A catalogue record for this book is available from the British Library

Library of Congress Cataloguing in Publication applied for

Printed in the United Kingdom at the University Press, Cambridge

ISBN 0 521 64022 9 hardback
ISBN 0 521 64964 1 paperback

Contents

Contributors

David Block, Institute of Education, University of London, UK

Lynne Cameron, School of Education, University of Leeds, UK

David D. Clarke, Dept. of Psychology, University of Nottingham, UK

Martin Cortazzi, School of Education, University of Leicester, UK

Alice Deignan, School of Education, University of Leeds, UK

Raymond W. Gibbs, Jr, Dept. of Psychology, University of California at Santa Cruz, United States

Richard Gwyn, Health Communication Research Centre, School of English, Communication and Philosophy, Cardiff University, Wales, UK

Lixian Jin, Dept. of Human Communication, de Montfort University, Leicester, UK

Graham Low, English as a Foreign Language Unit, University of York, UK

James Mahon, Dept. of Philosophy, Duke University, Durham, North Carolina, United States

Gerard Steen, Dept. of Discourse Studies, University of Tilburg, The Netherlands

Zazie Todd, Dept. of Psychology, University of Leicester, UK

Acknowledgements

The editors, authors and publishers are grateful to the composers and publishers who have given permission for the use of copyright material identified in the text.

Dylan, B. & Levy, J. *Hurricane* © 1975 Ram's Horn Music on pp. 105–115.

Conventions

The following typographic conventions have been adopted:

ON THE PAGE	CONVENTION	FUNCTION
Metaphor	Bold type	The word is being used as a linguistic example.
Metaphor	Italics	Indicates emphasis, a technical term, or a published title. Rating scale values like *Strongly agree* are italicised to distinguish them from the author's opinion or direct quotations. Latin expressions, like *per se*, are also in italics.
'Metaphor'	Single inverted commas	The word is being highlighted, generally to indicate a degree of distancing by the author.
"Metaphor"	Double inverted commas	The word is a quotation. Statements or questions which are presented as parts of imaginary or possible conversations are also in double inverted commas.
METAPHOR	Capitals	Part of a 'proposition' (e.g. METAPHORS ARE OBJECTS) held to underlie a surface utterance
Topic, Vehicle	Capital T or V	Topic or Vehicle as technical terms (i.e. the component terms of a metaphor)

Series editors' preface

Metaphor, or the means by which one thing is described in terms of something else, has been described as a central tool of our cognitive apparatus. It is central to our understanding of how language, thought and discourse are structured. Consequently the study of metaphor has been of interest to scholars in a wide range of disciplines, including linguistics, psychology, philosophy and literature. While the role of metaphor in language has been a focus of considerable interest in linguistics and other fields since the pioneering work of Lakoff and Johnson and has been the focus of several thousand journal articles, it has received much less attention within applied linguistics. The present book therefore provides a valuable introduction to and overview of the field of metaphor studies while focussing particularly on issues likely to be of significance to students and practitioners of applied linguistics.

The papers in the book cover a wide range of issues in metaphor research, including approaches to metaphor theory, the nature of metaphorical language, metaphor as process and product, teachers' and learners' use of metaphors in conceptualizing their work and investigative methods in metaphor research. A number of different contexts for metaphor use are illustrated, including academic discourse, second language teaching, first language use, dictionary compilation and work with the seriously ill. Fascinating examples are given of how metaphors shape the description of many topics in discourse and how much of our experience of life is described in metaphoric terms. The book also proposes a research agenda for applied linguistic studies of metaphor, one which seeks to explore the role of metaphor in contexts of language use (rather than semiotically or systemically) and to determine the role metaphor plays in human interaction.

The papers in this collection however are of interest not only in terms of their contributions to the study of metaphors in use but also for their research methodology. Throughout the book the need for a variety of research approaches is stressed and the advantages and limitations of different research procedures discussed. Researching and Applying Metaphor will hence be of interest to readers in a wide variety of disciplines, since it raises many issues relevant to linguistics, educational theory and applied linguistics. Through its inclusion in the Cambridge Applied Linguistics Series we hope it will contribute to a more rigorous and systematic research of metaphor in applied linguistic contexts.

Michael H. Long
Jack C. Richards

Preface

The aims of the book

Metaphor in one form or another is absolutely fundamental to the way language systems develop over time and are structured, as well as to the way human beings consolidate and extend their ideas about themselves, their relationships and their knowledge of the world. Metaphor is, as a direct consequence, important to psychologists, sociologists, scientists, humorists, advertising copywriters, poets, literary commentators, philosophers, historical linguists, semantics researchers and even syntacticians. It is also of considerable importance to applied linguists, but, curiously, what can only be described as an explosion of research activity over the past twenty or so years, in a whole series of different disciplines, seems largely to have passed applied linguistics by. The result is that, while psychologists and philosophers have developed fairly coherent approaches to the topic of metaphor, it is still very unclear what we even mean by an applied linguistic approach.

Our primary aim is to help rectify this situation. Although the title *Researching and Applying Metaphor* is certainly intended to indicate that the focus of the book is on applied linguistic problems, it is also designed to flag as clearly as possible the fact that our major interest lies in research. We want to promote and encourage more good-quality research into metaphor, but to do this we need to begin to create an informed discussion within 'the applied linguistics community'. This book is accordingly addressed primarily to applied linguists who have already undertaken some empirical research into metaphor, or who are thinking of doing so.

The term 'applied linguistics' can have a variety of meanings, from the narrow senses of 'second language acquisition' or 'language teaching', to the broader senses of 'applying linguistic knowledge to any real-world situation', or conversely, 'researching any real-world situation where language is used'. The one unifying factor in the above senses tends to be the 'purposeful use of language', so we have concentrated on the idea of researching 'metaphor in use'. This is, we feel, very much in line with Honeck, who, reviewing the state of metaphor research in 1980, remarked that what was needed was to go beyond semantics and develop a contextual approach which involved "a delicate integration of word-sense, syntactic form, pragmatic context, speaker-listener relationship, and goals, over time" (Honeck, 1980: 42). The papers in this book consider metaphor in use within a range of different contexts: the teaching and learning of foreign languages; first language use by and with children; language use by the seriously ill and those caring for them; language use in second language acquisition theory, in dictionaries and academic essays. Between them, they demonstrate how a complex phenomenon such as metaphor can be, and needs to be, researched using multiple methods of investigation.

Metaphor need not by any means be restricted to language, and recent research has demonstrated the important role played by metaphor in thought, behaviour and pictorial representation. However, to date most applied linguistics *has* been concerned primarily with the nature or impact of language in one form or another and this is, perhaps inevitably, the concern of the papers in this volume. The general perspective of the book may be described as broadly cognitive, in the sense of being person-oriented (and at times social-group-oriented) rather than system-oriented, but the overriding focus on discourse and metaphor-in-use means that the authors are frequently talking about matters other than the sort of conceptual structures made so well known by Lakoff and Johnson (1980). Despite the strong claims made by this strand of metaphor theory, the nature and strength of links between metaphor and thought are still only partly understood. Several papers in the book explore how metaphor in language may reveal patterns of thought in individuals and in groups. We have aimed in this area to proceed with caution, while remaining excited about possibilities. One particular possibility for future research is to explore whether and how patterns of thought may be changed through deliberate changes in metaphor use.

Each author writing about data collection and analysis has been asked to discuss not just their findings, but their research methodology, decisions they made in the research process, and the limitations of their particular approach. We hope that readers will find in this book critically evaluated applications of recent developments in metaphor theory which can be drawn on to inform their own applied linguistic work, and that the interaction of research with theory in applied linguistic contexts will in turn contribute to the development of the field of metaphor studies.

The structure of the book

Researching and Applying Metaphor is divided into four sections. We have chosen to abandon the standard 'Introduction' format of a list of the major research traditions linked to a summary of a number of recent papers. Interested readers can find excellent accounts in Ortony (1993) and Gibbs (1994). Instead, we have constructed for the first section three very different, but inter-connected, introductory chapters which address the reader as potential researcher, rather than as passive absorber of other people's conclusions. In Chapter 1, Lynne Cameron begins by discussing at a general level how an applied linguistic perspective on metaphor might differ from the perspectives of other types of researcher. She then homes in on the central question of the way in which an applied linguistic approach impacts on how one might usefully envisage the basic components and levels involved in metaphor: what are often called Topic and Vehicle. In Chapter 2, Ray Gibbs takes a rather different kind of overview; he distils years of experience of researching psycholinguistic aspects of figurative language and proposes, for the first time, a set of easy-to-work-with, good-practice metaphor research guidelines. Chapter 3 moves from overview to detail; Graham Low picks up several of the general points made in Chapters 1 and 2 and explores aspects of validating metaphor studies, focusing in particular on the need for a measure of lateral thinking and for taking a discourse perspective, even where the study involves manipulated texts.

Section II moves from theory towards the collection and analysis of data, and contains three papers proposing major realignments in particular areas. James Mahon shows the importance of reporting and using theory accurately; by using statements in the *Rhetoric* as well as the *Poetics*, Mahon shows not just that the standard view of Aristotle on metaphor is inaccurate, but that Aristotle in fact held a surprisingly modern view of metaphor. Gerard Steen takes up the question of levels of analysis broached by Cameron in her introductory chapter and offers both a taxonomy of dimensions on which analysis is needed, and examples of the taxonomy in use on the text of a popular song. Cameron is concerned to show how research on metaphor in spoken discourse involving children indicates that we need to restrict or modify several of the generally accepted ways of describing and analysing metaphor in order that data can be adequately analysed.

Section III contains three studies that employ naturally occurring data. David Block explores how SLA researchers employ metaphor to valorise or stigmatise particular views about the research process and by implication define the boundaries of the research community. Martin Cortazzi and Lixian Jin focus on metaphors used by language teachers to conceptualise their work as teachers and explore how this can at times contrast with metaphors used by learners. Finally, Alice Deignan looks at how recently developed corpus-analysis techniques can be used to address a number of applied linguistic problems, but considers too some of the limitations that present themselves to this important new methodology.

Section IV contains three papers that rely on elicited data. Richard Gwyn is concerned to show how, in situations of serious illness, both sufferers and those surrounding the sufferer develop and use metaphors as coping techniques. Low explores the opposite situation from that described by Deignan: how best to derive teaching guidelines in a common EAP situation where no valid corpus exists. In the last paper, Zazie Todd and David Clarke consider the question of how to explore the ways in which adults perceive metaphor in children's speech, and to do so develop a method that is systematic yet which remains context-sensitive.

The origins of the book

The genesis of *Researching and Applying Metaphor* was a three-day seminar of the same name, sponsored jointly by the British Association of Applied Linguistics and Cambridge University Press, which took place at the University of York in January 1996. The papers in Sections II, III and IV were all originally presented at the seminar, but have been substantially revised for this book. The three papers in Section I have been specially written. Our thanks are due not just to BAAL, CUP and the long-suffering authors of the papers in the book, who stoically put up with endless harassment by the editors, but also to those who presented papers which were equally interesting, but which focused on topics or methods which did not fit neatly into the format of the book. Without the contribution of all, this book could never have been produced.

PART I

KEY ISSUES IN METAPHOR RESEARCH

1 Operationalising 'metaphor' for applied linguistic research

Lynne Cameron

The history of figurative language ... [is] more of a conglomeration of discontinuities than a coherent progression toward resolution of common problems. (Honeck, 1980: 37)

A starting point: metaphor as a phenomenon of language in use

Metaphor is a device for seeing something in terms of something else. (Burke, 1945: 503)

A general type of description of metaphor often seems to be the only level at which theorists and researchers of different persuasions can agree, with similar 'definitions' found in many key publications (Kittay, 1987; Black, 1979; Gibbs, 1994; Lakoff & Johnson, 1980). Once past this level of generality, disagreement develops in a mire of conglomerated detail, and intending researchers may find themselves reeling as they approach the published literature in order to select an appropriate theoretical and analytic framework for a study.

In this chapter, I attempt to impose some order on this confusion by addressing various aspects of the question of how to operationalise the concept of metaphor for research of an applied linguistic nature. As applied linguists, we are concerned with language use in real-life situations, particularly problematic ones. In general terms, the applied linguistic researcher is aiming to reveal and understand underlying processes of language learning or use, and perhaps to evaluate intervention in them.

The various papers in this volume illustrate research procedures that often start from the identification of metaphor as linguistic product in text or discourse, and then move to making inferences about the role of metaphor in language in use:

- inferring about mental representations of states or events from language evidence (e.g. Block in Chapter 7 and Gwyn in Chapter 10);

- inferring about changes in mental representations and/or behaviour from language evidence (e.g. Cortazzi and Jin in Chapter 8);
- inferring about metaphor in the learning of English as a foreign language (e.g. Low in Chapter 11).

In each of these studies, the research works with and from *language in use*, and this gives rise, I would argue, to two key meta-theoretical implications. The first is that applied linguistic metaphor theory and research will be concerned with the linguistic as meshed with the social and with the cognitive. As Clark (1996) points out, if we take a *purely cognitive* approach or a *purely socio-cultural* approach to language use and, by extension, to an aspect of language use such as metaphor, we do not get pictures that are differently but equally valid; rather, we get partial and inaccurate pictures, since it is precisely the interaction between the cognitive and social in language use that produces the language and behaviour that we observe and research. What we need is a view of language in use which prevents a one-sided or compartmentalised approach, by allowing the social and cognitive to be integral parts of theory and analysis of data. Language in use in human interaction, as I have suggested elsewhere (Cameron, 1997a), can usefully be considered as a complex, dynamic system in which language resources – both forms of language and skills in using language – are employed in particular contexts to achieve interactional goals under particular processing demands. Language as text, in the sense of the language as words actually used as well as the linguistic system that can be abstracted from it, then becomes an 'emergent' feature of interaction between language as resource and discourse contexts. Operationalising metaphor (or other concepts) for applied linguistic purposes requires that account is taken of resources (language and cognitive), interactional goals and processing demands at each point of theory development and research.

The second important meta-theoretical consequence of treating metaphor as a phenomenon of language in use is the need to place constraints on the theoretical frameworks used for empirical research, by requiring them to be congruent with what is known of the processing of metaphor. Such a constraint may sound quite innocuous and uncontroversial, but its application would, I suspect, clear the ground of much metaphor theory that, while of technical interest, will not transfer directly to empirical work.

In the next section, I explore the outcomes for metaphor research of constraining analytic frameworks as suggested above. In the third section, I argue that the application of such constraints to current and historical theories of metaphor in fact highlights the need for new, applied linguistic frameworks for studying metaphor in use. A historical overview points to two key areas for development in the theory of metaphor: the need to go beyond the Information Processing paradigm and the need to re-establish a language focus in metaphor research. In the fourth section, aspects of operationalising metaphor are considered in more detail. The concluding section brings together key aspects of such frameworks that have been identified in the chapter.

Levels of analytic frameworks for metaphor

One immediate result of adopting a language-in-use approach to metaphor is that language users become an integral part of the research picture, and answers to many questions about metaphor identification and description *must* take them into account. Sometimes theoretical descriptions of how metaphor works appear to be isolated from user-related evidence. A good example would be theories of metaphor comprehension, sited within traditions of non-applied linguistics or philosophy based on formal logic, which explain metaphor comprehension as a 2- or 3-step process including, as one of the steps, the accessing of a literal meaning (e.g. Kittay, 1987; Winner, 1988). Such theories, which do not take into account temporal, contextual, neurological or other processing factors, are at odds with the results of many empirical studies that show clearly that processing metaphorical meaning often takes no longer than processing literal meaning (see Vosniadou, 1989, or Chandler, 1991, for fuller discussion and references). At the very least, disjunctions between theory and processing results should suggest that studies at one or other level are not subtle enough. A recent paper by Giora and Fein, for example, points to the need to distinguish degrees of familiarity in metaphors processed by subjects. They claim that subjects are more likely to process familiar metaphors directly, while less familiar metaphors are more likely to invoke the literal meaning of the metaphor (Giora & Fein, 1996). Such empirical results serve as a reminder that theory can be over-general and that theoretical frameworks must be selected to fit the level of detail and the type(s) of metaphor and discourse under investigation. I suggest, however, that we should go further and require that theoretical frameworks be congruent with processing evidence.

In setting up a requirement of theory-processing congruence, I follow the neuroscientist David Marr, who first raised the issue in connection with the study of vision (Marr, 1982). Marr's research demonstrated how a delineation of levels of explanation could lead to the development of more adequate and valid theory and processing models. Since then, the importance of separating levels of analysis has been discussed in relation to other mental phenomena, including language (Jackendoff, 1992), consciousness (Dennett, 1991) and analogical reasoning (Palmer, 1989; Gentner, 1989). For applied metaphor research, we can make a distinction between a *theory level of analysis* and a *processing level of analysis*, placing a requirement of congruence between the two.[1] A third level, the neurological, can also be distinguished. In metaphor studies, neurological research is likely to have much to contribute to the development of congruent frameworks, but work is still in its very early stages.

Level 1, the theory level, is the level at which theoretical analysis and categorisation of metaphor takes place, and where a central concern is the identification of metaphor: "what may or may not be analysed as a metaphor" (Steen, 1994: 24). Work at this level is driven by the concern to produce adequate and elegant theoretical accounts that are coherent within the particular logic chosen, as, for example, when Kittay (1987) sets out a semantic field theory account of metaphor, based on a relational theory of meaning. At this level too, the implications of metaphor as a discourse task can be considered, by analysing demands placed on users and receivers.

Level 2 relates to on-line processing by individuals engaged in production or interpretation tasks: how concepts are activated when lexical items in a metaphor are made sense of, how an interpretation of metaphor is reached, how metaphor can organise conceptual structures in long-term memory, how processing of metaphor can change conceptual structures and/or provide new meanings for lexical items. In the original work on levels by Marr, such processing was seen only as individual and internal; from a language-in-use perspective we would want to set such processing within its discourse context (Cameron, 1996), and include the effect of social interaction on processing.

The level at which metaphoricity is determined will influence the evidence required for metaphoricity, and the type of data that will count as evidence. Clarification of the distinction between 'theory' and 'processing' levels will help in the critical evaluation of existing theories of metaphor; the validity of theory-level accounts can be evaluated by how far they take adequate account of what is known

---

[1] The original labels for Levels 1 and 2 are "computational" and "algorithmic" (Marr, 1982). Kittay uses "conceptual" and "psychological" (Kittay, 1987). I have chosen, until more satisfactory labels can be found, to use "theory" and "processing"; I am aware, however, that this labelling is not unproblematic, since, for example, theorising is carried out for both levels.

LEVEL 1 THE THEORY LEVEL

Concerns

Metaphor identification.

Categorisation of metaphor types.

The goals and the logic of the production, interpretation and noticing of metaphor in discourse as processing tasks.

LEVEL 2 THE PROCESSING LEVEL

Concerns

The activation of concepts, as constructed through interaction between individuals and their socio-cultural environment, in the processing of metaphorical language in discourse.

How an interpretation of metaphor is reached; how a particular metaphor comes to be used.

The structuring of conceptual domains through metaphor; conceptual change through encounters with metaphor.

LEVEL 3 THE NEURAL LEVEL

Concerns

Neural activity that brings about metaphor processing at Levels 2 and 1.

Figure 1   Levels of analysis and representation of metaphorical language

about processing. Levels of metaphor analysis are summarised in Figure 1.

Operationalising metaphor for a research study requires the researcher to establish appropriate theoretical frameworks that define and categorise the phenomena of concern, and that, having constrained what is counted as evidence, further constrain how that data can be analysed. The framework in Figure 1 is expanded further in Chapter 6, where it is used to explore the question of identification procedures for one particular discourse context. In the next sections of this chapter, I show how a requirement of congruence between levels of analysis and representation can constrain details of frameworks for operationalisation of metaphor. At this stage, the following general points relevant to researching metaphor are highlighted:

• The researcher needs to be clear, and explicit, as to whether operationalising 'metaphor' is being done at theory level or at processing level.

- At whichever level the operationalisation is being carried out, the researcher needs to check that the analytic framework will satisfy constraints from lower and higher levels.
- Different types of metaphor may require different theoretical frameworks.
- Analytic frameworks may need to be multi-dimensional to account for different aspects of metaphor, such as language form, familiarity or discourse role.

Keeping in mind the need to aim for congruence in frameworks, I now move to examine some of the key literature in metaphor studies from a language-in-use perspective.

Metaphor, language and thought

Researchers need to decide early in the research process whether metaphor is being considered as a phenomenon of language, or of thought, or both, and to consider the implications of that decision. In this section, I first take a broad historical perspective on metaphor studies, noting that scholars have long focused on the cognitive aspects of metaphor, not just on the linguistic features. Furthermore, metaphorical language has often been studied in particular contexts of use, thus connecting the cognitive with the socio-cultural. However, this multiple perspective seems to have been lost for part of this century, first as a result of many metaphor theorists in linguistics and philosophy relying on formal logic as a basis for argumentation, and later as cognitive psychologists have worked within an information-processing paradigm with its central analogy of the mind/brain as computer. I show how researching metaphor pushes this epistemological base to its limits in the need to take account of language, thought and interaction, and suggest that a closer focus on language in metaphor research is needed.

Metaphor, language and thought: a historical overview

That metaphor is a mental phenomenon, sometimes manifested in language, sometimes in gesture or in graphic form, seems currently uncontroversial. Claims for the cognitive nature of metaphor that were, less than twenty years ago, seen as new and dramatic, are now taken as obvious. This is testimony to the work that has been done in those twenty years by key figures in the field. It may be, though, that the recent cognitive shift in metaphor studies, rather than leading us in totally new directions, is taking us back to an on-going concern with the interaction between the mental and the linguistic. Throughout history, the cognitive nature of metaphor weaves a constant thread through shorter-term concerns with other aspects. What is new about the current cognitive trend is the strength of certain claims about metaphor and thought, and the breadth that can be brought to metaphor studies by recent developments in psychology and language processing.

Examination of the writings of Aristotle on metaphor produced in the 4th century B.C. (see also Mahon, in Chapter 4) reveals an essentially cognitive view of metaphor as the substitution in discourse of one idea for another to produce new understanding. Moreover, when Aristotle discusses metaphor in the particular discourse genre of political rhetoric, employed to achieve particular interactional goals, he offers a socially contextualised view of metaphor in use. The history of metaphor theory shows that this early concern to address metaphor in use continued, for example in the writings of Vico and Tesauro in the 17th/18th centuries (discussed by Cooper, 1986; Eco, 1984). It seems to be in this century that the cognitive dimensions of metaphor have been downplayed, as metaphor theory increasingly became the concern of linguists and philosophers working through formal logic and operating on the assumption that language was a static, decontextualised system. Metaphor was relegated by some, such as Searle (1979), from linguistics altogether, seen as irrelevant to the formal study of language, and/or pushed into the area of pragmatics, where the meaning of metaphor is to be inferred from the literal sense of the words. Thus, in 1980, Lakoff and Johnson could write,

... metaphor is typically viewed as characteristic of language alone, a matter of words rather than thought or action. (Lakoff & Johnson, 1980: 3)

The fact that some of the metaphor theory produced without explicit consideration of the cognitive or socio-cultural dimensions is actually quite useful in research derives, I would suggest, from theorists' covert consideration of the creativity and constraints arising from use, context and processing.

The shift in metaphor studies back to a more overtly cognitive position, prompted by Lakoff and Johnson's (1980) book *Metaphors We Live By*, arose from the perception of inadequacies of formal logic-based approaches, and the need to take account of new findings about the psychology of categorisation, including prototype theory. However, there is still considerable variation in what is meant by 'cognitive', as it is used in Cognitive Psychology (Gibbs, 1994), Cognitive Linguistics (Lakoff, 1987a) and Relevance Theory

(Sperber & Wilson, 1986). In a recent article on idioms, Kövecses and Szabó (1996) contrast a "traditional" approach to idioms, that separates the language system from the conceptual system, with a "cognitive" approach, that sees language and conceptual systems as operating interactively. Their cognitive semantics approach considers the effect of conceptual resources on the generation and comprehension of idioms, offering explanations for the systematicity of idioms in the language, and implications for the accessing of the meaning of idioms. However, their work demonstrates the limitation of a cognitive view that does not take into account the dynamics of human mental processing and the goal-oriented nature of interaction in context.

Within cognitive psychology, the information-processing paradigm dominates thinking and research into the workings of the human brain. In the broader arena of cognitive science, such Artificial Intelligence approaches may predominate, but other approaches are also available (Eysenck & Keane, 1995). Eysenck and Keane (1995: 3) use the term 'cognitive' in a broader sense as related to "the understanding of the mind".

Beyond an Information-Processing paradigm

It is important to realise the extent of the influence of the IP paradigm in cognitive psychology, and thus in related metaphor research, in order to evaluate the advantages and limitations of a narrow cognitive approach to researching metaphor. The work of Gibbs, for example (Chapter 2; 1994), has developed our understanding of different types of processing of figurative language, but even this work is contextually limited by the psychological tradition of laboratory experiments, and can be usefully supplemented with consideration of everyday metaphor as being sited within goal-directed interaction in context.

The major limitations of the IP paradigm, however, derive from the inadequacy of its underlying mind/brain ~ computer analogy (Rose, 1993; Lowe, 1996). One development has been to replace the analogue computer in this underlying analogy with parallel distributed processors (PDP), which operate in ways more similar to the function of the human brain. In this scenario, the mind/brain ~ computer analogy remains, but produces a connectionist model of human processing, in which information is represented by the activation of networks of pathways between nodes. Work in, or close to, metaphor studies has made use of connectionist models of mental processing (Chandler, 1991; Holyoak & Thagard, 1989; Gentner,

1989), and this will be discussed in more detail later in the chapter. However, even with this updating, the IP paradigm is still for some seen as basically inadequate because human beings do not process *information* but *meaning*, making use of imagination, prior experience and beliefs and judgements (Lowe, 1996; Rose, 1993). PDP may be a better metaphor for the mind/brain, but it is still *only a metaphor*; neurons are essentially different from nodes in a connectionist network and memories are different from activated networks. Work such as that of Rose (1993) and Schank (1982) on the dynamic and on-the-spot construction of memory and meaning in processing, and the work of Barsalou (1987) on the contextual dependence of activated concepts, indicate that a constructivist view of understanding and other mental processes may provide a more adequate model. A particularly exciting development in this area of cognitive science, which also serves to emphasise how the complexity of the human brain passes beyond that of a connectionist metaphor, concerns the idea of theory-based concepts. This work is revealing how individuals conceptualise, classify and store information from their experience in ways that structure such information, both internally and in relation to other world knowledge, through explanatory "theories" (Ross & Spalding, 1994; Carey, 1985; Keil, 1979, 1983). When theory-based concepts are activated in discourse processing, comprehension is facilitated by the use of the explanatory relations linking the features of the concepts.

The links between metaphor and thought have been tightened even further by George Lakoff and others, in the proposal that the conceptual system is not only involved in the processing of metaphor, but that thought is itself structured metaphorically, and that the systematicity of metaphor on the surface of language merely reflects underlying conceptual structure in which something is understood, stored and processed in terms of something else (Lakoff, 1987a). This 'strong' cognitive view has been disputed by Quinn (1991) and others (e.g. Steen, 1994) who prefer a weaker view on the metaphorical nature of thought; for a discussion the reader is referred to Gibbs (1994). While my personal preference is for a broad, weaker view, we include in this volume several papers that build on the stronger view, such as those by Block (Chapter 7) and Gwyn (Chapter 10).

Re-emphasising language in metaphor research

The recent emphasis on cognitive aspects has, I would suggest, led to an unwarranted lack of interest in the *language* of metaphor, and applied linguistics researchers have a key role to play in developing understanding of how language resources are put to work in the use of metaphor in discourse.

It would be difficult today to discuss metaphor as *merely* a matter of language, but there are remnants of such a view scattered around in the literature. Simple, surface definitions of simile, for example, still may include as a necessary and sufficient condition the presence of the word **like** between two noun phrases. Such a surface-level definition can confuse discussions of the relation between metaphor and simile, that can be clarified once it is made clear that, cognitively speaking, a metaphor may underlie a simile (Kittay, 1987). To quote Aristotle, again in cognitive mode:

Metaphors will of course also be similes, and similes are metaphors that invite explanation.   (*Rhetoric*, transl. Lawson-Tancred, 1991: 2)

The fact that metaphor is more than language does not mean that language form is irrelevant to the study of metaphor. The recent trend of reducing all metaphors to the form of A IS B, in order to focus concern on conceptual content has, as I discuss in more detail below, under-emphasised the potential effect of form on processing and understanding, and an applied linguistic dimension to metaphor study will hopefully restore and renew interest in language form at word, clause, sentence and discourse levels.

In addition, language form needs to be seen as inter-dependent with language in use, and this often means language in use in interaction. Research into metaphor use in various types of interaction, such as conversation, classroom discourse, interviews (Gwyn, in Chapter 10), needs analytic frameworks that are sensitive to interactional effects (see for example, Drew & Holt, 1988; Cameron, submitted for publication). Vygotskyan notions of the interactive nature of the relation of language and thought, and "the social formation of mind" (Kozulin, 1990; Wertsch, 1985; Rogoff, 1990), can be used to construct theory-level frameworks for metaphor that integrate the socio-cultural and the cognitive (Edwards, 1997; Cameron, 1996). While the application of these ideas to metaphor is not taken further here, the possibility of a broader 'cognitive' approach to language use, and thus to metaphor, which makes use of constructs such as explanation-based concepts and social interactionist accounts of their development, holds much promise for the future of metaphor research.

In this section, I have tried to show why it is important for the researcher to be clear about whether research is focusing on metaphor in language or in thought when setting up analytic frameworks. Theoretical clarity is also needed in the relation assumed between language and thought, as this will underlie inferences that are made between linguistic evidence and thinking. In the next section, I look more closely at levels of analysis and description in the frameworks set up for metaphor research, and the requirements that researchers should place on them.

The nature of metaphor in language in use

In this section, I set out some of the key concepts and considerations in the operationalisation of metaphor, using as a starting point the general description of metaphor with which the chapter began:

Metaphor is a device for seeing something in terms of something else.
(Burke 1945: 503)

In labelling the components of a metaphor, the first *something* is often labelled the 'Topic' (occasionally the 'Tenor'), and the 'Vehicle' is the label given to the *something else*, a use that derives from Richards (1936) and Perrine (1971), and that has become more or less conventional, although Black (1979) suggested the alternative terms "primary subject" and "secondary subject". I first deal with the nature of the Topic and Vehicle. Burke's statement implies an anomaly of some sort between Topic and Vehicle, and the possible nature of that anomaly is the second area for discussion. The third part of this section reviews the act of *seeing in terms of*, or the resolution of the anomaly between Topic and Vehicle in a metaphor in the process of understanding. Again, this resolution can be described both at a theoretical level and in terms of real-time psycholinguistic processing, and it is important to remain alert to the implications of working at a particular level of description.

As Steen (in Chapter 5) points out, there are limitations to a Topic-Vehicle approach to describing metaphor. It is, however, fruitful for many types of study and has been shown to have some reality in real-time psycholinguistic processing (Steen, 1992; Cameron, 1997b).

I shall approach the operationalisation issue by asking the following three questions:

Q1 *What kinds of things are the Topic and Vehicle in metaphor?*

Q2 *What degree/kind of difference is needed between the Topic and Vehicle for metaphor identification?*

Q3 *How is the Topic 'seen in terms of' the Vehicle?*

Q1   *What kinds of things are the Topic and Vehicle in metaphor?*

The bases of current cognitive views of metaphor stem from considering the Topic and Vehicle not just as surface forms but rather as underlying systems of semantic and contextual information. It is worth noting that, although the same label is often applied to both lexical item and underlying concept, this can present potential problems.

Take the following example, from Low (in Chapter 11): **this paper thinks**. Low's conceptual analysis of the metaphor goes beyond the surface forms, to identify the underlying metaphoric structure as:

THIS PAPER IS A PERSON

(CONCEPTUAL) TOPIC	paper
(CONCEPTUAL) VEHICLE	a person

An analysis that works with surface forms would have:

This paper thinks

(SURFACE) TOPIC	**this paper**
(SURFACE) VEHICLE	**thinks**

The conceptual analysis has already made inferences from language to thought that involve generalisations, and that might need some form of justification.

I will consider alternative proposals for the underlying conceptual systems of Topic and Vehicle, but first I want to deal with the surface language forms of the Topic and Vehicle terms. From an applied linguistic viewpoint, one wants to consider language items not in isolation, but within their discourse context, as part of a longer text and as integral to the use of language for particular interactional goals. The discourse context may be spoken or written. Researching metaphor in its discourse context has several implications for the study of metaphor that are often not taken into account in research or theory stemming from linguistics, psychology and philosophy, and these will be expanded on throughout this volume.

TOPIC AND VEHICLE AS SURFACE DESCRIPTORS

As lexical items, Topic and Vehicle may be drawn from any word class and may range in scale from morpheme, e.g. parts of compound nouns as in **bookworm** (author's data), through word, phrase and sentence to unit of discourse, as in poem or allegory (Cooper, 1986: 195). A somewhat dated but extensive grammatical categorisation of the lexical items in metaphors was carried out by Brooke-Rose (1958), using as database a corpus of poetry. Steen (in Chapter 5) begins the production of an up-dated linguistic checklist for metaphor.

In the metaphor literature, exemplar metaphors around which theory is built typically have Topics and Vehicles which are both nominal (i.e. nouns or noun phrases), as in **Juliet is the sun**. Furthermore, metaphors used in constructing tests of comprehension or explication in empirical studies are also frequently nominal; an example would be **weeds are the measles of the garden**, cited in Evans and Gamble (1988). Empirical evidence, however, suggests that verb metaphors may be more common than nominal metaphors in many types of discourse (Steen, in Chapter 5; Cameron, 1997b). The widespread use of Lakoff and Johnson's general underlying form of metaphor, A IS B, to substitute for a range of surface forms (Lakoff & Johnson, 1980) helps perpetuate the myth of the nominal metaphor as the most common or typical.

Aside from word class, many of the examples upon which metaphor theory is constructed have other typical features that may be misleading. Topic and Vehicle terms in exemplar metaphors are usually both explicit and are connected within a unit that is a clause or a phrase:

Encyclopaedias are goldmines   (Ortony, 1979b: 353)

Gibbs (in Chapter 2) discusses one alternative syntactic form – the xyz metaphor – but Topics and Vehicles can be linked in metaphors of many syntactic forms, within and beyond the phrase and clause:

Modifier–head (adjective + noun; adverb + verb etc)	*lollipop* trees
Subject–verb	the trees *took* the fire and *hid* it
Verb–object	we can *build* our understanding
Verb phrase–prepositional phrase etc.	you have to stick *to your guns*

(Examples from author's data: Vehicle terms in italics)

A further way in which metaphors in discourse often deviate from the typical examples is in the absence of explicitly stated Topic terms. The non-explicit Topic must be recovered in processing from clues in the surrounding text and context. An example would be:

you've had *an awfully good innings* (= you've had plenty of time using the computer)   (Author's data)

Making sense of the unstated Topic reference does not seem to necessarily place an extra processing burden on the receiver

(Cameron, 1997b), and, again, a goal-directed, context-based view of processing would explain this more easily than an information-processing view.

Using isolated, nominal, clause-length metaphors as typical exemplars in theory-building may also be misleading, in downplaying the frequently observed systematicity of Vehicle choice, which is widespread in all types of discourse. Just as **Juliet is the sun** in its original discourse context is one of a series of related metaphors, so metaphor Vehicles often occur in networks within a text or across texts. This surface systematicity can be seen at various levels:

Local systematicity Within a particular text, related Vehicles may occur that develop an extended metaphor across several aspects of the Topic.

Global systematicity Across texts from a range of discourse types and content, semantically linked Vehicles may occur, producing systems and layers of metaphors. Some such systems seem to reflect fundamental underlying ways of thinking, and these are variously labelled "basic metaphors" (MacCormac, 1985) and "root metaphors" (Pepper, 1935).

Between these two we may place:

Discourse systematicity Within language use in specific discourse communities, related Vehicles may be drawn on. An example of this phenomenon would be the use of terms from spoken language to talk about literacy activities in school classrooms:

> What is the writer *telling* us?
> The story *talks about* racoons.
> The next question *says* . . .   (Author's data)

It is likely that processing is assisted by systematic use of lexis, and it should thus be taken into account in Level 2 frameworks and upwards into theory at Level 1. Such systems of surface Vehicle terms, which in use are likely to be overlapping and partial (see Deignan, in Chapter 9), are held to provide the linguistic evidence for the "conceptual metaphors" of Lakoff and Johnson (1980), and thus for inferences about the interaction of metaphor and thought.

TOPIC AND VEHICLE AS UNDERLYING CONCEPTUAL SYSTEMS

Examination of the surface forms of Topic and Vehicle cannot be taken very far before cognitive issues arise, and when metaphor has been seen as simply a matter of form or renaming, we are likely to find over-simplified theory supporting the view; Mahon, in Chapter 4, makes a similar point when discussing how Aristotle's comments about metaphor have been misrepresented. As suggested earlier, writers on metaphor through the centuries have consistently seen the Topic and Vehicle terms of metaphor as the surface forms of under-lying systems of conceptual information, but with variation in the content and organisation of these systems. Aristotle held that the Vehicle term in the discourse carried with it *endoxa*, the shared opinions of the speech community. In this century, Black's extension of the notion has had a major impact on the development of metaphor theory. He first wrote of the Vehicle as a "system of associated commonplaces" (Black, 1962) and later as an "implication complex" (Black, 1979). The Topic term, too, was seen as belonging to a system of relations (*ibid.*, 1979: 28), so that, for Black, a metaphor acts to juxtapose two conceptual systems.

Important distinctions still exist across different theories of meta-phor, even when Topic and Vehicle are taken as conceptual domains underlying lexical items. One simple but useful contrast that can be made is between metaphor theory that takes these domains to be abstract systems, held to exist for *all users* of the language in the culture of a particular speech community, and metaphor theory that works with domain systems, held to exist, or be activated, in the minds of *individual users* of metaphorical language (Gibbs, Chapter 2, on products and processes). When operationalising metaphor, it is important to be explicit about which you are working within, and to justify inferences made from one to the other.

Within the first 'universal' group can be sited work that tries to account for metaphor through semantic field theory or componential semantics (e.g. Cohen, 1977; Sternberg, Tourangeau & Nigro, 1979). Recent work in linguistics (e.g. Sperber & Wilson, 1986) has blurred the clear line that was earlier drawn between semantics and prag-matics, and this in turn has influenced theoretical views of Topic and Vehicle systems. Approaching metaphor from within the discipline of philosophy, Kittay (1987) has made an important contribution, constructing a relational theory of meaning which augments semantic field theory with pragmatics in order to develop a theory of metaphor identification and interpretation. The lexical fields of Topic and Vehicle serve to identify underlying content domains, and the rela-tions of contrast and affinity that organise the lexical fields serve to articulate the content domain (1987: 225). In Kittay's theory, inter-pretation of a metaphor then involves the transfer of relations between the semantic field of the Vehicle and that of the Topic (further developed in Section 4.4). Moreover, Kittay addresses the earlier concerns of this chapter with theory/processing congruence by explicitly placing her work at Level 1 and acknowledging that it cannot serve for Level 2 purposes. In Chapter 6, I attempt to draw on Kittay's theoretical work to set up Level 2 frameworks.

In Lakoff and Johnson's (1980) "conceptual metaphor" (further developed in Johnson, 1987, and Lakoff, 1987a), the Vehicle domain is held to be a conceptual system mapped, at least partially, on to the conceptual system of the Topic domain – with the crucial additional hypothesis that the underlying conceptual domains are themselves metaphorically structured and stored as such in long-term memory. In other words, metaphor does not just link conceptual systems when encountered, but, in some fundamental way, metaphor constructs, or "motivates and constrains" (Gibbs, 1994: 7), concepts, and when a linguistic metaphor is encountered, pre-existing systems are activated (Glucksberg, 1995). This hypothesis has received some empirical support, in particular from the work of Gibbs and his colleagues (full references can be found in Gibbs, 1994). Lakoff and Johnson identify conceptual metaphor through analysis of Topic–Vehicle relations in collected examples of conventionalised metaphors found in the language of native speakers. They then generalise from the surface language items to inferred systems of thought. The weak point of such analyses lies in the directness of the inferencing from language use to claims about thought structures. By starting instead from the nature of concepts and mental representations, metaphor analysis can make use of several promising ways of viewing Topic and Vehicle domains as complex knowledge representations, rather than as sets of features (Keil, 1979; Neisser Ed., 1987; Sternberg Ed., 1994; Vosniadou & Ortony Eds., 1989). This is a Level 2 orientation, and the advantage to employing it is that Topic and Vehicle terms in discourse (like any other terms) are allowed to activate mental structures that are variously described as schemata, scripts, frames and mental models (see e.g. Ross & Spalding, 1994; McNamara, 1994). Common to all of these four concepts is the idea that domains may not be taxonomically organised, as some formal theories require, but rather, in real human minds working in real contexts of language use, they may be thematically structured, containing organised information about related entities, actions, events and language. Work on exemplar-based thought and memory (summarised in Medin & Ross, 1989) suggests that what is activated may not be abstract, but linked to specific earlier encounters. Gibbs (in Chapter 2) mentions the activation of images in processing Topic and Vehicle, and I can see no reason why such sensory memories should stop with sight; metaphor Topics and Vehicles may activate memories of smell and taste too. Furthermore, research on speech processing emphasises the flexibility and range of activation in the human mind; for example, on hearing **trombone**, connections with **bone** are activated, as well as more musical schemata (Shillcock, 1990). Since the Vehicle term is by definition anomalous in the on-going discourse in some way, it may well prompt wider activation across several potentially relevant domains of knowledge. The work of Barsalou (1987, 1989) on concept stability and *ad hoc* categories suggests that conceptual domains are not stable and stored in memory, but rather are created in processing, and influenced by recent experience and other contextual factors.

Although 'connectionist' models are subject to the criticisms detailed earlier, they do contribute a useful analogy for concept activation as the spreading of impulses along pathways between nodes. As pathways are activated, so patterns of activation are created, which can be seen to represent conceptual domains. Chandler (1991) has attempted to produce a connectionist metaphor of metaphor processing, and much work has been carried out in the field of artificial intelligence using such PDP networks to solve analogical problems (e.g. Holyoak & Thagard, 1989). The connectionist analogy is useful in an applied context to the extent that it suggests other important properties of the activation of concepts:

- Activation of mental representations will *spread* through various types of motivated links (e.g. sound resemblance, exemplar memory, sensory memory, contextual information).
- Spreading activation is controlled (i.e. concept domains are bounded) when no pathways are found from certain nodes.
- Because of spreading activation, the mind can successfully process partial information.
- Gradability is inherent in the activation, because pathways can be differentially strengthened through multiple links.

Recent interest in explanation-based concepts can be extended to the activation of Topic and Vehicle domains. Encountering a metaphor would result in the activation of domains *and* of explanatory theories within those domains. So, encountering the **sun** in **Juliet is the sun** would activate not just features of **the sun**, but other relational information that links those features, such as the sun as centre of the solar system acting as centre of gravity for other planets that thus revolve around the sun.

'Domains' of Topic and Vehicle appear then not to be single unified domains underlying single lexical items, but rather more amorphous groupings of all types and levels of information and meanings that may be activated on encountering the Topic and Vehicle. Furthermore, in real-time processing these 'domains' will be constrained and influenced by the discourse context and what participants bring to the discourse. The richness and variation in this view of domains does not make for simple theory construction or empirical procedures. However, if metaphor processing by real people, in real situations is to be a central focus of research, both need to be tackled. Much empirical work is still needed to determine how mental representations are accessed in metaphor processing, and the accessing demands and outcomes of different kinds of metaphorical language.

Q2   What degree/kind of difference is needed between the Topic and Vehicle for metaphor identification?

The unexpected introduction of a contrasting *something else* into on-going talk or text may signal the occurrence of metaphor to participants and/or to the analyst. The nature of that contrast between Topic and Vehicle has been used in the literature as an identifying feature of metaphor. It has been variously labelled as a "tension" (e.g. Wheelwright, 1968), a "conceptual incongruity" (e.g. Kittay, 1987), an "anomaly" (e.g. Tourangeau & Sternberg, 1982; Ortony, 1979b) or as "contrary to accepted practice" (Matic & Wales, 1982: 246). Terms such as anomaly and incongruity, that label a presumed violation of receiver expectations, are clearly going to be very difficult to operationalise for much applied research. In real-time discourse processing, anomaly or incongruity is a graded feature of activated concepts underlying lexical items that will depend on the immediately previous discourse, participants' background knowledge, and their shared knowledge. For example, in my school data, a teacher says, **Alex is a packed lunch now**. Considered out of context, this has the form and cross-domain anomaly required of a metaphor, but once the discourse conventions of the classroom are taken into account, the anomaly disappears and it may be better identified not as metaphor, but rather as a case of ellipsis or metonymy. Anomalies that can be shown to have arisen from such ellipsis, or from errors, need to be eradicated by the analyst from possible identifications of metaphor (Kittay, 1987; Gibbs, in Chapter 2, takes a similar view). However, in many cases, categorising something as ellipsis remains a matter of judgement; the researcher or analyst must be explicit about the grounds on which such judgements are made, so that others may contest the claims or try to replicate the study.

Establishing Topic–Vehicle incongruity relative to a particular discourse context can make use of the Frame–Focus distinction introduced by Black (1962), where the Focus is a stretch of language that is identified as anomalous with respect to the surrounding 'Frame' of the metaphorical sentence (see also Steen, in Chapter 5). For Black, the Frame was a sentence (though with the Focus removed): Kittay (1987) generalised this to a "minimal frame" which can be a phrase, a sentence or a longer unit. For non-explicit Topics, a notion of Frame is needed which is broader than 'surrounding verbal context' against which the Vehicle (or Focus) appears anomalous; Kittay accordingly proposed the idea of a "default frame" which is constructed by participants from the discourse up to this point and represents their discourse expectations. The Focus-Frame is a 'soft' analytic tool, in that Frame boundaries may be fuzzy in the analysis of real discourse. It may however, for this reason, be more effective in the analysis of language in use than a requirement for a clear distinction between Topic and Vehicle domains.

The degree of difference between Topic and Vehicle domains required for the existence of metaphor is ultimately a matter for decision by the researcher. Within a particular discourse context, several different Vehicles may be used to refer to the same Topic, each generating a different degree of incongruity. In the following comparisons taken from a discussion about the nature of volcanic lava (the Topic), there are three possible Vehicle items:

1. volcanic lava is like *runny butter*
2. ... or *sticky treacle*
3. Is molten lava like *wax*?   (Author's data)

Whereas 1 and 2 may be held to be juxtaposing 'different domains', and thus to create metaphorical similes, the third case is less clear, and the domains may be judged too close for metaphor. Naturally occurring data will frequently produce situations like this, forcing the researcher to make a series of decisions about metaphoricity as judged by perceived domain difference.

Metaphor theory at Level 1 very often deals with the problem of the degree of difference by working with Topics and Vehicles that are uncontroversially anomalous or incongruous, as in the choice of exemplar metaphors. If research aims require the compilation of a set of metaphors to use with informants, then it is reasonably straightforward to do so, using examples of this type of "active strong metaphor" (Black, 1979: 26). Pilot studies can be carried out on the perceived metaphoricity of initial sets; for an example of a study that does this with idioms, see Harris, Lahey and Marsalek (1980). If, however, a study requires the identification of metaphors in text, and hence to employ Level 2 frameworks, the researcher will need to work through the issue of completeness and ask whether what is to be identified is *every metaphor in the text exhaustively*, or *just certain key metaphors that link into particular concerns*. In Chapter 6, I deal with issues connected with the first scenario; the papers by Gwyn, Block, and Cortazzi and Jin work with the second. Both types of research are important; the first type can produce overall pictures of metaphor use, which the second type of study can then exploit as part of the process of ensuring representativeness and validity. What must be remembered in either case, is the need once again to be explicit in stating the identificational criteria applied to the data, so that the research is replicable and, for Popperians, falsifiable.

A relatively recent Level 1 approach to the nature of Topic and Vehicle difference has come from the psychologists Glucksberg and Keysar (1990, 1993), who propose that metaphor be seen as a class-inclusion statement, with the Vehicle term a prototypical example of a category acting the role of superordinate. In their example **My job is a jail**, the Topic term **job** refers to a specific job, but the Vehicle term **jail** refers to a category. Steen raises Level 2 objections to this theoretical view, by pointing out that, in less familiar metaphors, the category that underlies the Vehicle term may not be mentally represented, but may be constructed in processing through similarity and analogy (Steen, 1994: 15). While the category-inclusion view of metaphor adds a valuable new way of thinking of Topic and Vehicle terms, it may well turn out to be somewhat limited in applicability. For example, in terms of word class, it has only so far been applied to nominal metaphors of the A IS B format, in which A and B seem to be at parallel levels of generality, somewhat above the basic level (Lakoff, 1987a). Glucksberg and Keysar suggest (1993: 423) that it may work too for predicative metaphors, but data from real talk hints at a more complex picture for which a range of possible types of Topics and Vehicles, at different levels of generality, will occur. An analysis of metaphorical language use in a secondary school drama lesson showed that the teacher used two different Vehicles to refer to the same Topic when she was trying to describe to pupils the organisational structure of a play that included flashback scenes:

the play takes the form of *a circle*
the shape of the play   (Author's data)

Both **a circle** and **the shape** can be seen, in line with Glucksberg and Keysar, as superordinate categories. However, it would also be possible to classify **a circle** as a type of **shape,** and thus at a lower level in a general-to-specific hierarchy. Interviews with five pupils (aged 13/14) revealed that the Vehicles were not equivalently super-ordinate at a conceptual-processing level either. While the pupils could explain the first metaphor to the interviewer, they could not produce an explanation of the second. A class-inclusion analysis is insufficiently discriminating of types of metaphor. It may be that, by building theory from a small set of selected metaphors of a certain type, 'class-inclusion', like many other Level 1 attempts at theory construction, has also firmly cemented in place its own limits.

In some cases, the Topic–Vehicle domain difference is established theoretically, at an initial stage of the design. However, this is not always an appropriate solution, and a number of techniques have been developed over the years to test the significance of the domain difference empirically (see Tourangeau & Sternberg, 1981, 1982; Wales & Coffey, 1986).

Q3 How is the Topic 'seen in terms of' the Vehicle?

In this third section, I expand upon the notion that the choice of Vehicle term from a domain distinct from the Topic acts to bring something extra to an understanding of the Topic, and perhaps of the Vehicle too, in the discourse. This process of analogical reasoning or 'seeing in terms of' appears to be a basic human skill or ability (Vosniadou & Ortony, 1983; Cohen & Stewart, 1994) that is evidenced in infancy when babies can be shown to respond similarly to increases in the intensity of light and increases in the pitch of sounds played to them. In an empirical study that explored how people could make sense of anomalous word pairs, Matic and Wales (1982) found that subjects experienced no problems making sense of constructed anomalous collocations. Evidence from children's com-prehension of metaphor also demonstrates that the cognitive mechan-isms for making sense of metaphor operate from early childhood, and that problems are more likely to derive from lack of familiarity with, or partial knowledge of, Topic and Vehicle terms (Vosniadou, 1987). This kind of 'seeing in terms of' is the "metaphoric processing" contrasted by Gibbs (in Chapter 2) with "metaphor processing", that is to say the processing of any stretches of language identified as metaphor – a Level 2 distinction indicated by Steen (1994). In processing linguistic metaphor, discourse participants may or may not employ special processing mechanisms to make sense; they may activate previously stored meanings for familiar metaphors, or they may process the linguistic metaphor literally. Metaphoric processing, on the other hand, always involves active processing across incongruent domains through 'analogical reasoning', which is seen (e.g. Vosniadou & Ortony Eds., 1989) as the basic mental process underlying metaphor and analogy, and which involves the transfer of relations (not just features) from Vehicle to Topic (Gentner, 1989).

Both metaphor processing and metaphoric processing are Level 2 concerns, whereas at Level 1 we are concerned to produce a theoretically adequate explanation of metaphor interpretation or production. It is quite possible to produce an adequate Level 1 theory of processing which does not accord with processing evidence, such as the lack of evidence of extra processing effort or time required for metaphor processing (Gibbs, 1994). As we saw in the previous section, Level 1 theories may limit the categories of metaphor they attempt to deal with; Black's interaction theory (1979) only covers strong active metaphors, that are assumed to be processed metaphorically. Lakoff and Johnson (1980), in working with conceptual metaphor, are looking at language that is potentially metaphorical, in that it *could* be processed metaphorically, although very often it may not be. Notions of 'dead metaphor' and degrees of metaphor death are addressing, at Level 1, the Level 2 phenomenon of metaphor/metaphoric processing. To label a particular metaphor as 'dead' is in effect to assign to it a very low probability of being given 'active analogical processing' by members of particular discourse communities.

The Aristotelian view of understanding metaphor is a process of finding the shared 'ground' between Topic and Vehicle: similarities within differences. The simplest version of this has metaphor as working through implicit comparison of the two ideas, with every metaphor a reduced simile that can be expanded back into the literal. Black attacked this view as being based on – now suspect – notions of similarity (Black, 1962; Rips, 1989). Later theories of metaphor interpretation have used the idea of matching or comparison of attributes, properties, predicates or features of Topic and Vehicle domains, and a connectionist view is little more than an extension of this, in which the network nodes represent more micro-level features (Chandler, 1991). Levin (1977) developed a theoretical view in which metaphor was seen as operating through processes of feature addition or deletion. Ortony (1979c) introduced the idea of "differential salience" of features to account for the asymmetry of transfer of features from Vehicle to Topic, although we are still left with the problem of explaining why some features are perceived as more salient than others. The reader is referred to Kittay (1987) for a thorough critique of atomistic theories of metaphor interpretation.

As I noted earlier, similarity, as the key mechanism in classifying and creating categories, has been displaced by theory- or explanation-based views in recent work in cognitive psychology (Ross & Spalding, 1994; Rips, 1989), and this is paralleled in views of metaphor interpretation that highlight the transfer of relations between domains in processes of analogical structure mapping (Steen, 1994; Gentner, 1989); 'relations' within domains are precisely what a theory-based view of domains or concepts adds to features or attributes. Feature similarity can then be seen as a heuristic for making sense across incongruent domains, as it is for classification (Rips, 1989), or as an emergent feature of relational mapping (Vosniadou, 1989). It can be argued then that adequate Level 1 theory about the interpretation of metaphor will need to operate, not just with features or attributes in domains, but also with the relations or explanatory links between them. It will also need to account for how such links may be 'transferred' from Vehicle to Topic.

In applied linguistic research, centrally concerned with language in use, the processing of metaphorical language takes place in the context of the discourse, and, I have suggested, this must be taken account of from the very foundations of theory construction and development of analytic frameworks. Because much metaphor theory is not explicitly related to specific discourse contexts, it may *appear* to work with context-free language in explaining comprehension or production. In fact, however, context is still (and always) present; it is merely assumed as common shared knowledge and therefore not in need of explicit theoretical attention. What I am arguing for in this chapter is the centrality of the contextual nature of language in use; the human and discourse context of language use is inherent in the joint construction of discourse goals and in the use of metaphor to achieve those goals. Processing metaphorical language takes place in context and draws on the discourse expectations of participants. It follows that the theoretical frameworks used to operationalise metaphor must do so too.

At Level 1, relevance theory seems to offer a theory that takes into account contextual effects in which metaphor can be seen as one type of "loose talk" (Wilson & Sperber, 1988; Sperber & Wilson, 1986). In their 1988 article, Wilson and Sperber go so far as to suggest that loose talk is probably basic to communication; however, the label still suggests that it is a deviant form of some other "tight" talk. Gibbs (1994: 231–232) criticises a relevance theory approach for its lack of fit with Level 2 evidence, when he points out that it implies extra cognitive effort from listeners, for which there is in many cases no evidence.

In a connectionist parallel to relevance theory, Holyoak and Thagard (1989) found that the design of a computer program to 'interpret' analogy needed to incorporate a condition of "pragmatic centrality" on activated interpretations, to inhibit those that were inappropriate to context. Human processing, though, deals unproblematically with open-endedness; discourse problems do *not* generally arise as a result of loose talk and the degree of looseness appears to be chosen to match discourse expectations and needs. Ambiguity is deliberately exploited in humour, and employed subtly, and sometimes deliberately, in the pursuance of communicative goals (Schegloff, 1984). Discourse context does not provide an extra constraint to be applied at some point in processing metaphor, but works to determine the nature of language, of processing and of activated information.

Cognitive views of metaphor as inherent to conceptual structure attempt to explain processing evidence at a theoretical level in a slightly different way. If our mental representations are metaphorically structured, then activation in processing would be automatic (Lakoff & Johnson, 1980). Explaining processing in this way is limited – it can only account for some types of metaphorical language. An adequate theory would need to account in addition for the corpus evidence now starting to emerge of partial and overlapping systems of metaphor use in language (Deignan, in Chapter 9; Gibbs, 1994). Quinn further suggests that conceptual metaphor has a cultural basis, rather than a purely cognitive basis, and that people acquire metaphors that reflect the thinking of their socio-cultural group(s) (Quinn, 1991; Quinn & Holland Eds., 1987; see also Cortazzi & Jin in Chapter 8). There would seem to be room for both approaches to conceptual metaphor: some may well be experientially based (Johnson, 1987), while other systematic uses of metaphorical language may be built up through social interaction and influence. Both retain the possibility of deliberate and non-conventional use of metaphor to achieve particular discourse or behavioural goals.

As with the activation of mental representations, it would seem that we are still far from understanding the complexity of the human brain at work in making sense of analogies by finding connections between concepts, and theories of metaphor interpretation and comprehension are our rather poor and partial attempts to capture some aspects of the little we do know. What we can say is that models of metaphor processing need a level of complexity that matches the type of metaphor under consideration. Topics and Vehicles may be such that similarities are pre-existing, either because the metaphorical link is very simple, or because the Topic is mentally structured and stored in terms of the Vehicle (Gibbs, 1994). In simple cases, such as **volcanic lava is like runny butter** (Author's data), the simple models of Substitution or Implicit Comparison may suffice to account for the interpretation of metaphor (Black, 1962). If conceptual metaphor is assumed to be involved, then the theoretical work of Lakoff and Gibbs will be appropriately invoked. If links between Topic and Vehicle have to be constructed afresh in interpretation, because of a high degree of incongruity, then a more complex model is needed.

Operationalising metaphor: conclusions

In this chapter, I have tried to suggest that applied linguistic researchers of metaphor need to bear in mind the following:

THE NEED FOR SUBTLETY IN CONSTRUCTING AND USING METAPHOR THEORY

- Differentiated theory is required to describe and explain different aspects of metaphorical language: different language forms, different degrees of familiarity, different levels of generality.
- Differentiated theory is required to describe and explain different aspects of metaphor processing: different temporal points of processing (a point taken up further by Gibbs in Chapter 2); difference in Topic–Vehicle contrasts.

THE NEED FOR CLARITY IN LEVELS AND TYPES OF ANALYSIS AND REPRESENTATION

- It is important to be clear as to whether operationalising 'metaphor' is being done at the theory level or at the processing level. That is to say, is evidence required of active metaphorical processing, or is the concern to establish an internally consistent framework, without reference to real-time processing?
- At whichever level operationalisation is carried out, analytic frameworks need to satisfy constraints from both higher and lower levels.
- Arbitrary decisions seem to be unavoidable; they should at the very least be explicit.

THE NEED FOR A VIEW OF METAPHOR AS AN ASPECT OF LANGUAGE IN USE, SITUATED WITHIN PARTICULAR DISCOURSE CONTEXTS

- Data sources may include naturally occurring discourse, corpora or native-speaker introspection.

- Operationalisations of metaphor and metaphor processing need to take account of the contexts of use and of discourse participants who have built up experience with metaphorical language as members of various socio-cultural groups.
- Inferences, or claims for representativeness, made across different discourse contexts, or between community norms and individuals, need to be justified and described explicitly.

Metaphor in use is a complex socio-cultural and psycholinguistic phenomenon that requires the application of multiple investigative methods – triangulation from large corpora, empirical studies of reactions, introspection and theory that accommodates gradedness, prototypicality, relativisation to discourse context and social groups. Honeck's "conglomeration of discontinuities" may yet be a sign of progress towards coherent multiplicity.

2 Researching metaphor

Raymond W. Gibbs, Jr

Introduction

Studying metaphor sometimes seems like an overwhelming experience. Contemporary scholars wishing to understand something about
how metaphor is created, understood and applied often find their
heads spinning as they try to get a handle on the voluminous
literature on the topic. If you sit down and try to search any of the
many databases on recent research publications for articles with
metaphor in the title, you will quickly see that there are literally
thousands of such papers. Even as far back as 1979, literary critic
Wayne Booth commented, somewhat tongue in cheek, that the
growing interest in metaphor was so great that by the year 2039,
"there will be more students of metaphor than people" (Booth, 1979:
47). As we approach the millennium, I am beginning to believe that
Booth's prophecy might turn out to be literally true!

In my own experience in the contemporary world of metaphor
research in cognitive science, I often encounter scholars, including
those who study metaphor and those fearful to do so, voicing
concern that there are actually too many different theories of
metaphor. For example, in the field of cognitive psychology alone,
there are a number of contenders for the best metaphor-theory
contest, among them being salience-imbalance theory (Ortony,
1979c; Ortony *et al.*, 1985); domains-interaction theory (Tourangeau
& Sternberg, 1981, 1982); structure-mapping theory (Gentner, 1989;
Gentner & Clements, 1988); class-inclusion theory (Glucksberg &
Keysar, 1990); and conceptual metaphor theory (Lakoff, 1987a;
Lakoff & Johnson, 1980; Gibbs, 1994). Outside of psychology, there
are several other theories that are currently studied and debated,
including speech act theory (Searle, 1979); no-meaning theory
(Davidson, 1979); semantic-field theory (Kittay, 1987); similarity-
creating theory (Indurkhaya, 1992); and relevance theory (Sperber &
Wilson, 1985/86). Clearly, there are plenty of ideas on how best to

explain metaphor. The diversity of views on metaphor and the widely different methods used to study metaphor use and understanding can sometimes intimidate scholars, so I have often been told, from taking the plunge into the murky waters of metaphor research.

Throughout my years studying metaphoric thought and language, I have often been asked by students and fellow metaphor enthusiasts how best to do metaphor research. My aim in this chapter is to provide a set of distinctions/guidelines that scholars should be cognisant of as they undertake to research and apply metaphor. These guidelines include:

- Distinguish different kinds of metaphor in language.
- Distinguish metaphor from metonymy.
- Distinguish between the processes and products of metaphor.
- Distinguish metaphor processing from metaphoric processing.
- Distinguish how metaphor in language and thought interact.
- Recognise the embodied motivation for metaphor in thought and language.

I am afraid to say that these distinctions/guidelines are not often followed by even the most experienced metaphor scholars, so my hope is that, as we approach the millennium and maybe find everyone doing metaphor research, the concerns raised here will be useful in mapping out a comprehensive view of metaphor in all of its contexts of use in language and thought.

Six guidelines for research

Distinguish different kinds of metaphor in language

My first guideline is to urge metaphor researchers to recognise that metaphor is extremely diverse and to be careful to distinguish between different forms of metaphor in language. Too often metaphor scholars focus on single examples and either miss making important generalisations or mistakenly assume that selected examples of metaphor accurately reflect all aspects of metaphoric language. The study of idiomaticity, for example, failed to acknowledge the metaphorical roots of many idioms because scholars tended to examine only a few of these conventional phrases, such as **kick the bucket**. As researchers began to examine idioms more broadly, and sought greater generalisations in their linguistic analyses, they found that many idioms were indeed partly analysable and motivated by enduring conceptual metaphors (Gibbs, 1994; Lakoff, 1987a). Furthermore, most studies of classic metaphoric language in psychology, linguistics and philosophy have focused on *A is like B* or *A is B* statements, such as the famous line **My luve is like a red, red rose** from a poem by Robert Burns, or, what is perhaps the most analysed metaphor in history, when Romeo says at one point in Shakespeare's *Romeo and Juliet*: **But soft! What light through yonder window breaks? It is the East, and Juliet is the sun.**

But metaphor is much more than simple *A is like B* or *A is B* statements. Researchers need to be aware of the diversity of metaphoric forms and recognise that a particular theoretical account for one aspect of metaphor may not apply to other forms of metaphorical language. Let us briefly consider a few of the ways that metaphor is expressed in English. First, there are many verbal expressions that describe complex relations among several terms. Thus, a large number of proverbial expressions, sometimes called *xyz* metaphors, convey meanings through the complex interactions of their terms (Turner, 1991):

The love of money is the root of all evil.
Children are the riches of poor men.
Religion is the opiate of the masses.
Language is the mirror of the mind.
Wit is the salt of conversation.
Custom is the guide of the ignorant.

xyz metaphors like these involve complex mappings in which, as Turner (1991) argues, readers must understand the conjunction between *x* and *z*, which is interpreted in terms of a conceptual domain containing *y*. More specifically, readers must find some *w* in their conceptual knowledge that stands in a relation to y, which can be referred to conventionally by the phrase *y of w*, and must then map the relation of *y* and *w* onto the conjunction of *x* and *z* (Turner, 1991: 200).

Consider the metaphor **Children are the riches of poor men.** Readers must interpret the relationship between **children** and **poor men** metaphorically in terms of the relationship between **riches** and **rich men**. The set of mappings here is clearly more complex, and more difficult to describe simply, than are the mappings of simple *A is like B* expressions, the type of verbal metaphors most often analysed. Several psychological studies provide evidence that ordinary readers can make easy sense of these phrases, and thus appear to make the correct mappings, even if they are not always able to verbally explain all aspects of these meanings (Gibbs & Daughters, *in preparation*). Other than Turner's (1991) explication of *xyz* metaphors, no current theory even addresses how these expressions are understood. Yet any comprehensive theory of metaphor must be capable of explaining how *xyz* metaphors are created and understood.

Consider now the opening lines of a poem by Archibald MacLeish entitled *Ars Poetica*:

> A poem should be palpable and mute
> As a globed fruit,
>
> Dumb
> As old medallions to the thumb,
>
> Silent as the sleeve-worn stone
> Of casement ledges where the moss has grown –
>
> A poem should be wordless
> As the flight of birds.

In these few lines, MacLeish comments on the possibility that poems may be metaphorically understood in a variety of ways, such as his vision of poetry as part of nature, or that poems convey meaning by spatial language, or that poems talk about themselves while presenting descriptions of the external world. We must compute a variety of complex mappings to best make sense of the poetic interpretations for even these few lines of MacLeish's poem. The mappings here are diverse and extend well beyond the set of mappings that arise for any single *A is like B* metaphor. Of particular interest here is that each additional mapping may contradict, or clash, with meanings inferred earlier. Thus, although we clearly infer that poems must be *mute, silent* and *wordless*, the ways these mappings are elaborated upon are quite different and rely on very different domains of experience (e.g. **a globed fruit, sleeve-worn stone** and **the flight of birds**). How each of these mappings combine to express a meaning or meanings for the poem as a whole (and I have only given the first few lines of this poem) remains a distinct challenge for students of poetic metaphor.

Another frequently encountered metaphor in literary texts involves not the mapping of concepts from one domain onto another, but the mapping of images, called *image metaphors*. Image metaphors reflect the mapping of mental images from one source of knowledge onto the mental images from another. Poets often write for the express purpose of creating disturbing new images, ones that result from the mappings of image structures from widely disparate knowledge domains. Consider the opening lines from the surrealist poet André Breton's *Free Union* (Breton 1931/1974):[1]

---

[1] The poem as printed here is a translation from the French original. The translation process inevitably affects the nature of the metaphor, sometimes in quite drastic ways.

My wife whose hair is brush fire
Whose thoughts are summer lightning
Whose waist is an hourglass
Whose waist is the waist of an otter caught in the teeth of a tiger
Whose mouth is a bright cockade with the fragrance of a star of the first
    magnitude
Whose teeth leave prints like the tracks of white mice over snow
Whose tongue is made out of amber and polished glass
Whose tongue is a stabbed wafer
The tongue of a doll with eyes that open and shut
Whose tongue is incredible stone
My wife whose eyelashes are strokes in the handwriting of a child
Whose eyebrows are nests of swallows

These novel image mappings, about hair, thoughts, mouths and teeth, open up new possibilities for further explorations of the mappings between different knowledge domains. The power of poetic metaphor comes from the poet's ability to create many such novel, one-shot kind of mappings between different mental images. Not surprisingly, the account of how people comprehend image metaphors will differ significantly from that involved in interpreting cross-domain mapping metaphors (Lakoff & Turner, 1989). Experimental research has shown that ordinary readers of Breton's poem clearly acknowledge that they draw different mappings to understand, and aesthetically appreciate, the image metaphors here than when they read verbal metaphors that express meaning cutting across different knowledge domains (Gibbs & Bogdonovich, *submitted for publication*).

Most generally, the empirical study of how people interpret poetry in which various complex mappings are explored for a single topic (e.g. the nature of poetry), or even several related abstract topics, is only in its infancy (see Kreuz & MacNealy, 1996). Current theories of metaphor might, in different ways, have something to say about how poetry is created and understood, but no comprehensive attempts to do this have been forthcoming (but see Lakoff & Turner, 1989; Turner, 1991, 1996). We clearly need more empirical and theoretical work on metaphor in poetry.

Single metaphorical comparisons are elaborated in complex ways not only in poetry, but in expository prose as well. Consider this paragraph from an essay by H. Kallen (1915), entitled *Democracy versus the Melting Pot*, in which Kallen used the striking metaphor of an orchestra to define his ideal for American civilisation.

However, for the purposes of this paper this is not an issue; the discussion relates to the text in its English translation.

As in an orchestra, every type of instrument has its specific timbre and tonality, founded in its substance and form; as every type has its appropriate theme and melody in the whole symphony, so in society each ethnic group is the natural instrument, its spirit and culture are its theme and melody, and the harmony and dissonances and discords of them all make the symphony of civilization, with this difference: a musical symphony is written before it is played; in the symphony of civilization the playing is the writing, so there is nothing so fixed and inevitable about its progressions as in music, so that within the limits set by nature they may vary at will, and the range and variety may become wider and richer and more beautiful.

Once again, the number of complex entailments that arise from the mapping of an orchestra performing onto the concept of society requires a fairly sophisticated view of metaphor: one that explicitly attempts to elucidate some of the complex domains of knowledge in both the source and target domains. As was the case for under-standing poetry, little empirical work has been done on compre-hending extended metaphorical mappings in literature (see Steen, 1994). This also represents another distinct challenge for future metaphor researchers.

Metaphor, of course, is not just seen in poetry and great writing, but infiltrates many aspects of everyday speech. Consider some of the conventional ways that we talk about love and our love relationships in everyday situations:

We're at a crossroads.
We'll have to go our separate ways.
We're just spinning our wheels.
Our marriage is on the rocks.
We're going nowhere.
We can't turn back now.
It's been a long bumpy road.
We've gotten off the track.
The relationship is a dead-end street.

Until the emergence of cognitive linguistics in the last 15 years (Lakoff & Johnson, 1980; Johnson, 1987; Sweetser, 1990; Turner, 1991), scholars never recognised the systematic ways people talked about love, to take just one example, in a wide variety of languages, nor did scholars consider the idea that such talk might reflect important generalisations about people's metaphorical conceptuali-sations of love. Individual linguistic expressions, such as **We can't turn back now** and **We're spinning our wheels**, were previously perceived to reflect entirely different, and mostly dead, metaphors.

Yet these expressions do not exist individually as random clichés, but reflect different aspects of our ordinary metaphorical conception of love as a kind of physical journey. Each expression listed above reflects a particular entailment of the mapping of journeys onto love, a metaphorical mapping in which our knowledge of a concrete domain of experience (i.e. journeys) helps us better structure our understanding of a more abstract concept (i.e. love). Conceptual metaphors, such as LOVE IS A JOURNEY or LIFE IS A JOURNEY, are evident throughout ordinary language. Very few extant theories of metaphor attempt to explore the metaphorical roots of conventional, including idiomatic, language, or seek links between conventional language and more creative, poetic uses of metaphor. Scholars who advocate the conceptual metaphor view have considered these issues in greatest depth (Lakoff, 1987a; Lakoff & Johnson, 1980; Lakoff & Turner, 1989; Johnson, 1987), yet the challenge remains for other metaphor scholars to seriously explore metaphor in both its mundane and poetic forms.

Finally, metaphor also plays a major role in our understanding of individual words, especially in making sense of how a single word can express a multitude of related meanings (i.e. polysemy). Consider the word **stand** in the following statements:

We *stand* to sing the national anthem.
Ray *stands* 6'5" tall.
The clock *stands* on the mantel.
I can't *stand* the job I have.
The part *stands* for the whole.
The law still *stands*.

Our interpretation of the first three expressions relies on our physical understanding of the concept of **standing**, while the second group of statements metaphorically elaborates on different aspects of the physical sense of **stand**. We are not ordinarily aware that the non-physical senses of **stand** are motivated by metaphor. Yet psycholinguistic studies have shown that people have tacit knowledge of the metaphorical connections between the physical and non-physical senses of polysemous words, such as **stand** (Gibbs *et al.*, 1995). That is, people make sense of different uses of **stand** because of their tacit understanding of several image schemas that arise partly from the ordinary bodily experience of standing. People perceive different senses of **stand** as similar in meaning, partly on the basis of the underlying image schema profile for each use of the word in context. This work demonstrates that the meanings of the polysemous word **stand** are not arbitrary for native speakers, but are motivated by people's recurring bodily experiences in the real world. It appears, then, that metaphorical processes play an essential role in motivating why it just makes sense to use certain polysemous words like **stand** in the many ways we do (see also Lakoff, 1987a; Sweetser, 1990). Note also how the ideas of something standing for another thing is a key characteristic of metonymy.

I have focused in this section on only a few of the ways that metaphor exists in language. My belief is that no single theory of metaphor presently available will account for all of the different kinds of metaphor, nor perhaps will any one theory be able to do so in the future. The complexity of metaphor in language may require several types of theories to explain how people think of and interpret such language (see sections that follow). But scholars too often propose theories of metaphor as if only a single account is needed to explain all the ways that metaphor both exists in the language and is applied in a variety of contexts. My recommendation is that scholars must be careful to acknowledge the limits of their theories, and to recognise that their accounts of metaphor most often are limited to particular kinds of metaphor.

Distinguish metaphor from metonymy

My second guideline is to recognise that metaphor must be distinguished from metonymy. In their eagerness to see metaphor in many areas of language and thought, scholars sometimes fail to distinguish between these different tropes. There are key differences between metaphor and metonymy, despite the fact that both express mappings between things. In metaphor, there are two conceptual domains, and one is understood in terms of another, usually very different, knowledge domain. Metonymy involves only one conceptual domain, in that the mapping or connection between two things is within the same domain (Croft, 1993; Gibbs, 1994). A convenient way of distinguishing the two kinds of figurative trope is to apply the '*is like*' test. Figurative statements of the X *is like* Y form are most meaningful when X and Y represent terms from different conceptual domains. If a non-literal comparison between two things is meaningful when seen in a X *is like* Y statement, then it is metaphorical; otherwise it is metonymic. For example, it makes better sense to say that **The boxer is like a creampuff** (metaphor) than to say **The third baseman is like a glove** (metonymy).

My recommendation that scholars carefully distinguish between metaphor and metonymy does not mean that these two tropes never appear together. One study of the interaction of metaphor and metonymy in expressions for linguistic actions observed both instances of metaphor arising from metonymy and metonymy within metaphor (Goossens, 1990). Consider the phrase **shoot your mouth off** ('to talk foolishly about something that one does not know much about, or should not talk about'). The source domain in this metaphorical mapping is the foolish use of firearms that is mapped onto the target domain of unthoughtful linguistic action. When the word **mouth** is integrated into a scene relating to the use of firearms, it must be reinterpreted as having the properties of the gun alluded to in the phrase **shoot your mouth off**. In the target domain, however, there is a first level of interpretation which amounts to something like 'to use your mouth foolishly' in which **mouth** metonymically stands for the speech faculty. This interaction of metonymy with metaphor motivates why **Don't shoot your mouth off** means 'Don't say anything rash'. Analyses like these, of the interaction of metaphor and metonymy in expressions for linguistic action, illustrate how tropes are frequently combined to give rise to ordinary linguistic expressions.

I urge metaphor researchers to be careful not to overextend the identification of metaphor to metonymy (while also noting that many clichéd, seemingly literal forms have metaphoric bases). Of course, the fact that a linguistic expression is not metaphorical does not imply that it is literal (see Gibbs *et al.*, 1993; Lakoff, 1986, for data and discussion on the problem of specifying literal meaning). A non-metaphorical expression may easily be metonymic, ironic, oxy-moronic, and so forth, or combine with metaphor in various inter-esting ways.

Distinguish between the processes and products of metaphor

A major problem with current theories of metaphor is that many researchers fail to distinguish between how metaphor is processed and the meanings that are produced once a metaphor has been understood. Consider Romeo's famous statement **Juliet is the sun** in Shakespeare's *Romeo and Juliet*. Each of us can read this statement and reflect upon several of its possible metaphorical interpretations. When we think about the process of how we interpret this metaphor, we are mostly consciously pondering the products, or the results, of various cognitive processes that occur very quickly, mostly uncon-sciously, as we comprehend this verbal metaphor. But the *processes* of metaphor understanding are different from the *products* that we consciously think about when we read or hear metaphors. We need to be quite careful to distinguish between the processes and products of metaphor understanding (Gibbs, 1993, 1994).

Philosophers, linguists and literary theorists primarily focus on metaphor understanding as a product and try to infer something about the processes of metaphor comprehension. Psychologists or psycholinguists, on the other hand, primarily study comprehension processes with an eye towards explicating something about the products of metaphor interpretation and recognition (i.e. what metaphors mean). This difference in theoretical focus, in my view, arises from the different methodologies available to scholars in related academic disciplines. Experimental psychologists/psycholinguists use a variety of scientific techniques to tap into on-going, very fast, mostly unconscious, cognitive and linguistic processes. Linguists and philosophers rely on their trained intuitions about linguistic structure and behaviour. Too often, though, scholars in different disciplines mistakenly try to infer something about metaphor processes from an examination of metaphor products and *vice versa*. Scholars in all fields talk about *metaphor understanding* as if it were a single activity, rather than a process that occurs in real-time along a variety of temporal dimensions, starting in the first milliseconds of unconscious processing and extending up to long-term, reflective analysis.

A theory of metaphor processes (i.e. how we produce and comprehend metaphors) is, however, quite different from a theory of what meanings we consciously infer once metaphors have been understood. One reason why scholars have traditionally viewed metaphors as being deviant, ornamental language, and more difficult to understand than literal language, is because speakers can, at times, consciously identify some utterances as literal and others as figurative. To say that people employ distinct cognitive mechanisms to understand a metaphor such as **Juliet is the sun** because we can identify the verbal expression as metaphorical, makes an unwarranted inference about a process of understanding from an examination of a product of understanding. Similarly, to say that some metaphors are more apt or aesthetically pleasing than others does not necessarily indicate that people understand 'good' metaphors differently from 'bad' ones.

An important motivation for the plurality of theories of metaphor is that metaphor scholars wish to explain both *processes* and *products*. Nonetheless, accounting for both the processes and products of metaphor understanding requires different kinds of methodological analyses and theoretical descriptions. Investigating how people immediately make sense of metaphors demands methodologies that can tap into the unconscious set of mental events that often occur in just a few seconds. On the other hand, determining what psychological events lead a reader or listener to appreciate the poetic quality of metaphor requires a very different set of methodologies to look at an individual's consciously determined aesthetic values. We clearly must appreciate the specific time-course that underlies the experience of metaphor understanding (Gibbs, 1993). One way of doing this is to recognise that the temporal continuum of linguistic understanding may roughly be divided into moments corresponding to linguistic comprehension, recognition, interpretation and appreciation. Consider each of these in turn.

Comprehension refers to the immediate, moment-by-moment process of creating meanings for utterances. These moment-by-moment processes are mostly unconscious and involve the analysis of different linguistic information (e.g. phonology, lexical access, syntax) which, in combination with context and real-world knowledge, allow listeners/readers to figure out what, say, a metaphor means or what a speaker/author intends by his or her reading of a metaphorical expression. Contemporary psycholinguistic research suggests that comprehension processes operate very quickly within the time span of a few hundred milliseconds up to a few seconds at most (Gibbs, 1994; Hoffman & Kemper, 1987).

Recognition refers to the conscious identification of the products of comprehension as types. For example, the meaning understood by a reader of a particular utterance may be consciously recognised as being metaphorical (e.g. the meanings we infer from reading **Juliet is the sun**). Even though many literary theorists and philosophers assume that such a recognition (e.g. that some utterance is metaphorical, as opposed to literal or ironic) is a requirement for understanding what an utterance or text means, it is by no means clear that recognition is an obligatory stage in people's understanding of what utterances mean, or of what speakers/authors intend. Listeners, for instance, probably do not have any awareness or conscious recognition that different utterances in conversation are ironic, idiomatic, hyperbolic, literal and so on. Instead, they focus primarily, unreflectively, on understanding what speakers or writers intend to communicate by their production of metaphor (Gibbs, 1993).

Interpretation refers to analysis of the early products of comprehension as tokens. One can consciously create an understanding for a particular type of text or utterance as having a particular content or meaning. For instance, a literary critic might view some text or utterance as revealing a metaphorical or an allegorical theme (a matter of recognition) and then attempt to specify the exact content of this theme. Interpretation processes operate at a later point in time than comprehension processes, and they usually require conscious reflection about what a text or speaker means.

Finally, *appreciation* refers to some aesthetic judgement given to a product either as a type or token. This too is not an obligatory part of understanding of linguistic meaning, since listeners/readers can easily comprehend utterances or texts without automatically making an aesthetic judgement about what has been understood. Psychological evidence shows that metaphor comprehension and appreciation refer to distinct types of mental process (Gerrig & Healey, 1983).

In addition to these different aspects of the time-course of metaphor understanding, scholars must also explain something about the processes and products involved when people (both laypersons and critics) re-read and translate metaphors. It is surprising that so little work has been devoted to these key aspects of how people often encounter and apply metaphor. If anything, literary critics, as well as many linguists and philosophers, tend to assume that the processes used when re-reading a metaphor refer to underlying cognitive operations when metaphors are first comprehended (Gibbs, 1992; Gerrig, 1993). But these critical analyses of metaphor, including when metaphors are translated, should be best understood in terms of interpretation processes (as described above).

My general point in this section is to suggest two specific guidelines. First, scholars must recognise the diversity of experiences that underlie what it means to understand a metaphor. We should acknowledge that several theories of metaphor might be needed to account for the different temporal dimensions of metaphor understanding. Second, scholars must recognise the limitations of their research methodologies to study metaphor understanding, and not mistakenly attempt to draw inferences about one aspect of metaphor use when employing a method that is only relevant for exploring a different temporal aspect of metaphor understanding.

Distinguish 'metaphoric processing' from 'processing metaphor'

Another important aspect of metaphoric thought and linguistic understanding that deserves further attention is the distinction between **metaphoric processing** as a general mode of understanding that can be applied to any kind of situation or language, and **processing metaphoric language**. The empirical studies on metaphoric discourse have predominately examined how different aspects of verbal metaphors are understood. But there are many instances, especially in reading literature, when a specific metaphoric processing is given to a particular text. Various literary theorists have noted how it is possible to produce a high poetic reading of a poem or text because of a reader's explicit literary way of interpreting it (Lodge, 1977; Steen, 1994; Wellek & Warren, 1949). For instance, there are many poems and classic texts, such as Dante's *Divine Comedy* or Melville's *Moby Dick*, that are best understood and appreciated as having a strong allegorical character once they are interpreted metaphorically. Many children's fairy tales can clearly be metaphorically analysed as referring to domains of experience quite outside the local characters and situations in these stories. Children hearing stories like *Snow White*, *The Three Little Pigs*, *Hansel and Gretel*, and *Rapunzel* appear to make allegorical connections between the characters and events in these tales and their own lives. In most cases, our first readings of these texts do not immediately lead us to infer the explicit allegorical nature of these texts. But our bias to process events metaphorically helps lead us over time to recognise the allegories often explicitly intended by authors for us to understand. This relation between metaphoric processing and the interpretation of allegory is an exciting topic for future study in researching and applying metaphor.

Metaphoric processing, as opposed to processing metaphoric language, may be distinguished as an intentionally selected strategy of reading (Steen, 1994). When readers adopt such strategies, the processing that occurs is metaphoric, even though there is no special linguistic or textual material that is either metaphoric or motivated by metaphoric modes of thought. In this way, metaphor might legitimately be viewed as one type of cognitive strategy that colours people's imaginative understanding of texts and real-world situations. Of course, it is quite possible that people, at least in some situations, might immediately, and non-strategically, begin to process a text or situation metaphorically. What triggers this type of processing in the absence of explicit verbal metaphors is somewhat unclear. Yet, just as people might quickly conceptualise some real-world experience (e.g. falling in love) in metaphorical ways to better understand that experience, people might employ metaphoric processing as an indispensable part of making sense of many ordinary events in their lives (Gwyn, this book). Thus, metaphoric processing might not just be a special literary strategy employed by readers when interpreting texts.

In any event, we must be careful to distinguish metaphoric processing from processing metaphoric language and turn some of our attention to what metaphoric processing strategies reveal about the ordinary poetic character of human cognition. I believe that the study of metaphoric processing is one of the important challenges for the future in terms of how metaphor is applied in ordinary, literary and scientific contexts.

Distinguish how metaphor in language and thought interact

Consider, again, some of the verbal expressions English speakers often employ in talking about love:

We're at a crossroads.
We'll have to go our separate ways.
We're just spinning our wheels.
Our marriage is on the rocks.
We're going nowhere.
We can't turn back now.
It's been a long bumpy road.
We've gotten off the track.
The relationship is a dead-end street.

Cognitive linguists have argued that the systematicity of conventional expressions like these provides an important source of evidence for the idea that people think metaphorically (Lakoff & Johnson, 1980). That is, people metaphorically conceptualise their love experiences in terms of their concrete knowledge of physical journeys and consequently speak metaphorically about aspects of the source-to-target domain mapping. I think it is fair to say that these claims are, perhaps, the main reason why metaphor has exploded as a topic of interest in the humanities and social sciences over the past 15 years.

Yet there exists a great deal of scepticism, especially in cognitive psychology, about whether metaphor is part of human cognition and not just one, mostly ornamental, aspect of language (a good recent example is found in Murphy, 1996). How can we determine to what extent the language people speak reflects something about the ways they possibly think metaphorically? To answer this question, I think it is quite important to consider several possible hypotheses on the interaction of metaphoric thought and language (Gibbs, 1994). My recommendation here is that metaphor scholars be careful in considering each of these in their attempt to study the possible links between metaphor in language and metaphor in thought.

HYPOTHESIS 1
Metaphoric thought might play some role in changing the meanings of words and expressions over time, but does not motivate contemporary speakers' use and understanding of language.

HYPOTHESIS 2
Metaphoric thought might motivate the linguistic meanings that have currency within linguistic communities, or may have some role in an idealised speaker/hearer's understanding of language. But metaphoric thought does not actually play any part in individual speakers' ability to make sense of, or process, language.

HYPOTHESIS 3
Metaphoric thought might motivate individual speakers' use and understanding of why various words and expressions mean what they do, but does not play any role in people's ordinary on-line production or comprehension of everyday language.

HYPOTHESIS 4
Metaphoric thought might function automatically and interactively in people's on-line use and understanding of linguistic meaning.

These hypotheses are not mutually exclusive of one another, but reflect a hierarchy of possibilities about the interaction between metaphoric patterns of thought and different aspects of language use and understanding. Several kinds of empirical evidence from cognitive linguistics and psycholinguistics support some of these ideas. Linguistic studies on the role of metaphor in semantic change support hypothesis (1) (Sweetser, 1990), while other research on the systematicity of different linguistic expressions demonstrates a tight link between conceptual metaphors and idealised speakers' understanding of various verbal expressions as suggested by hypotheses (2) and (3) (Lakoff, 1987a; Lakoff & Johnson, 1980). Many psycholinguistic experiments support the claim in hypothesis (3) that metaphoric thought motivates why many words and expressions mean what they do to contemporary speakers, and also influences people's learning of different linguistic meanings (Gibbs, 1994). Finally, very recent work from experimental psycholinguistics suggests that hypothesis (4) might be true to some extent (Gibbs *et al.*, *submitted for publication*).

One reason why it is imperative, in my view, to distinguish between the different possibilities on how metaphoric language and thought interact is because many psychologists, linguists, philosophers and educators play fast and loose between these different possibilities, when they claim that metaphoric cognition either does or does not play a role in language use and understanding. For instance, some cognitive linguists have claimed, based on the systematic analysis of linguistic expressions, that "Our ordinary conceptual system, in terms of which we both think and act, is fundamentally metaphoric in nature" (Lakoff & Johnson, 1980: 3) and that "metaphor must be regarded as irreducible, primary cognitive functions by which we create and extend structure in our experience and understanding" (Johnson, 1987: 192). But the analysis of linguistic expressions by itself does not imply that all concepts are metaphorical (a claim falsely attributed to Lakoff and Johnson, 1980), or even that any particular concept is comprehended via metaphor to some degree. The hypotheses listed above provide a rough way to think more analytically about how metaphor in language might be influenced by metaphor in thought. Metaphor scholars, from all academic disciplines, must be careful to make appropriate theoretical claims given the limits of the methods they employ in studying metaphor.

Moreover, it is quite possible that the detailed study of any single concept or specific list of linguistic expressions may reveal that metaphor helps structure some aspects of how a concept is mentally represented. Of course, given the compelling linguistic evidence on the rich, metaphoric nature of many abstract concepts, cognitive psychologists face the challenge of constructing empirically adequate, non-metaphorical models of abstract concepts. These alternative, non-metaphorical models of abstract concepts must be capable of explaining how such concepts are directly represented, as well as how people draw systematic inferences about these concepts when talking about them in everyday language. Linguists, educators, philosophers and others should also, as part of their ordinary study of metaphor, always try to find alternative ways of explaining the linguistic data at hand before assuming that a metaphorical account is the best way to go.

The embodied motivation for metaphor in thought and language

My aim with these guidelines is to emphasise that metaphor scholars should recognise some of the complex motivations for why (a) people think metaphorically and (b) use metaphors so frequently in language, problem-solving, remembering, creativity and so forth. But where do metaphors come from? Why is it that certain conceptual metaphors, but not others, are used by people in speaking about abstract concepts? The traditional view of metaphor is that people employ metaphor for strictly communicative purposes (e.g. compactness, vividness) (Ortony, 1975). Many scholars now recognise that metaphor is essential for how people communicate about abstract, difficult-to-talk-about ideas, and about aspects of ordinary experience. In this way, metaphor is indeed necessary and not just nice or ornamental (Ortony, 1975).

Yet a great deal of linguistic evidence suggests that much metaphorical thinking arises from our embodied experiences in the world (Johnson, 1987; Lakoff, 1987a, 1990). For example, central to people's understanding of the conceptual metaphor ANGER IS HEATED FLUID IN A CONTAINER is the embodied experience of containment. People have strong kinesthetic experiences of bodily containment, ranging from situations in which their bodies are in and out of containers (such as bathtubs, beds, rooms or houses), to experiences of their bodies as containers which substances enter and exit. An important part of bodily containment is the experience of bodies being filled with liquids, including stomach fluids, blood and sweat. Under stress, people experience the feeling of their bodily fluids becoming heated. These various, recurring bodily experiences give rise to the development of an experiential *gestalt*, called an image schema, for CONTAINMENT (Johnson, 1987).

Image schemas emerge throughout sensorimotor activity, as people manipulate objects, orient themselves spatially and temporally, or direct their perceptual focus for various purposes. Image schemas cover a wide range of experiential structures that are pervasive in experience, have internal structure, and can be metaphorically elaborated to provide for our understanding of more abstract domains (Gibb & Colston, 1995; Johnson, 1987; Lakoff, 1987a). The CONTAINMENT schema, to continue with this example, is metaphorically elaborated in a large number of abstract domains of experience (e.g. concepts about emotions, the mind, linguistic meaning, moral obligations, social institutions). Moreover, this schema helps motivate some of the complex ways that people structure single abstract concepts. For instance, the conceptual metaphor ANGER IS HEATED FLUID IN A CONTAINER takes the image schema for CONTAINMENT as part of its source domain and maps this image-schematic structure onto anger, which gives rise to a number of interesting entailments. Thus, people know that when the intensity of anger increases, the fluid in the container rises (e.g. **His pent-up anger welled up inside of him**), people know that intense heat produces steam and this creates pressure in the container (e.g. **Bill is getting hot under the collar, Jim's just blowing off steam**, and **He was bursting with anger**), and people know that when the pressure of the container becomes too high, the container explodes (e.g. **She blew up at me**). It is extremely difficult to explain the richness of these metaphorical inferences without appealing to people's embodied experiences of heated fluid in containers that are then metaphorically projected to help individuals make sense of their anger experiences.

In a similar way, consider why the concept of happiness is understood in terms of being 'spatially up', and not in terms of being 'down'. The important cognitive linguistic work on embodiment in metaphor provides a good answer to this question. The conceptual metaphors HAPPY IS UP and SAD IS DOWN are illustrated by the following linguistic expressions: **I'm feeling up, That boosted my** spirits, My spirits rose, You're in high spirits, Thinking about her always gives me a lift, I'm feeling down, I'm depressed, He's really low these days, I fell into a depression and My spirits sank. These expressions reflect the recurring bodily experiences that drooping posture typically goes along with sadness, depression and ill-health, while erect postures are associated with positive emotional states, good health and higher states of consciousness.

Finally, children's kinesthetic, embodied experiences as containers provide exactly the kind of foundation they need to understand many conventional metaphors. For instance, researchers need not assume that children must have sophisticated theories about physics for them to have a metaphorical concept for anger (Gibbs & Colston, 1995; Mandler, 1992). This does not mean that children only learn metaphorical expressions because of their own embodied experiences. Children are likely to learn something about metaphorical thought from their exposure to conventional language that is, at least partly, motivated by metaphor (e.g. the concept of TIME IS MONEY in **We are saving time, wasting time, investing time, borrowing time** and so on).

The embodied motivation for metaphor provides a natural, non-arbitrary reason for why people regularly construct the asymmetrical metaphorical mappings they do, to better understand many abstract concepts. People do not necessarily learn to form metaphorical representations only from their embodied experiences, because their experience with the language itself will help them to tacitly infer, via generalisation, many metaphorical concepts. But it is clear that there are important links between people's recurring bodily experiences, their metaphorical projections of these image schemas to better structure many abstract concepts, and the language used to talk about these concepts. An important future challenge for metaphor researchers will be to provide detailed, experimental tests of the idea that image schemas partly motivate people's understanding of abstract, metaphorical concepts. The bottom line, though, is that metaphor scholars must explicitly recognise how the source of many metaphors in thought and language resides in pervasive patterns of bodily experience.

Conclusion

Doing research on metaphor requires scholars to think carefully about the limitations of their linguistic materials and the methodologies they use, before drawing any theoretical claims about the nature of metaphor, or about how metaphor is applied in different linguistic, cognitive and social contexts. I have suggested several guidelines that will, hopefully, enable both novice and experienced metaphor researchers to travel more effectively through the labyrinth of metaphor as it appears in language and thought. Keeping these guidelines in mind should help scholars formulate their specific research programmes in researching and applying metaphor, and critically evaluate the findings and theoretical claims of other metaphor scholars. Metaphor is undoubtedly one of the most complicated topics in the intertwined domain of language and thought. Yet the rewards of studying and applying metaphor are enormous. I urge all to take the plunge (not haphazardly, but carefully) and, as we now frequently hear in the media 'Just do it!' As a great enthusiast of all things metaphoric, I am delighted with the surge of interdisciplinary interest in learning more about how metaphor influences learning, thinking and linguistic behaviour. The chapters in the present volume are wonderful testimony to some of the terrific work that is now being done on researching and applying metaphor.

3 Validating metaphor research projects

Graham Low

Introduction

The extent to which applied linguistic researchers attempt to describe or control the validity of what they are doing appears to vary markedly. What is standard practice in psychology and sociology is not, at least in my experience, quite so standard when it comes to areas like language education, or even straight linguistic description. Essentially, *any* research report needs to include overt discussion of the extent to which the reader can be confident about the nature of the data which has been selected or omitted from the study, about the techniques of analysis and categorisation used, and about the extent to which the data support the conclusions proposed. It must, however, be admitted that, when it comes to applied language research, this is not always quite as simple a demand as it may at first sight appear.

The object of Chapter 3 is accordingly to examine some of these 'not quite so simple' aspects of validity, with respect to metaphor research projects and their method, data and conclusions. Validity will be taken in the very broad sense referred to above, of giving confidence to an observer that the data and the researcher's actions are appropriate to the task in hand. This is akin to the notion of validity developed in Messick (1980: 1014; see also Low, 1996b). The hope is that the paper will act as a bridge between the first two chapters of the book, which take a panoramic view, and the later chapters, the majority of which describe actual empirical studies.

Thinking about metaphor identification procedures

If one is working with naturalistic data, it will be necessary to create an appropriate metaphor identification procedure. Detailed discussions of the identification procedures developed for particular projects can be found in Chapters 6 (Cameron) and 7 (Block). In this section, I would like to take a broader perspective and examine some of the practical implications of the point made in Chapter 1, that the nature of the identification procedure adopted needs to fit the aims of the research. To this end, I shall focus on two deceptively simple, practical questions: *Who is going to do the identifying?* and *What will the identification task involve?*

Can't the researcher decide unilaterally what is 'metaphorical'?

The idea that the researcher examines the text and unilaterally decides what is and is not metaphorical is perhaps the commonest approach to identification (e.g. Sayce, 1953; Brooke-Rose, 1958; Drew & Holt, 1988). It is essentially the procedure used by Cortazzi and Jin (in Chapter 8) with respect to their interviews with practising teachers, by Deignan (in Chapter 9) in her corpus analyses – she calls it "informed intuition" – and by Gwyn (in Chapter 10) in his examination of language and serious illness.

There are perhaps two main advantages to unilateral identification, in addition to the relative ease and speed with which the procedure can be carried out. Firstly, the researcher can set up identification criteria specific to the research project – which people other than the researcher might find hard to employ. Secondly, it is possible to be highly responsive to the text being studied and to bring a wide range of experience from areas such as linguistics and literature to bear concurrently on identification decisions.

There can, however, be serious dangers with unilateral identification. For example, there is always going to be a measure of subjectivity or randomness in identifying expressions which are not actually referred to, or demarcated by the speaker(s), as metaphoric. While there are certainly occasions where metaphor *is* demarcated in texts – a group of children talk about the metaphors they have collected (Cameron, in Chapter 6), or a teacher in Cortazzi and Jin's study (Chapter 8, account 1) clicks his fingers, then says "it seemed to click" – by no means all metaphor is explicitly indicated. Indeed, Cameron's (1997b) exploration of classroom discourse found primary teachers flagging that words were *not* to be taken metaphorically, rather than the other way round.

A second danger involves a recency effect; metaphor researchers are likely to have a heightened sensitivity to metaphors with which they have been working in the recent past. This may lead to consistently *over*-interpreting expressions which are only peripherally relatable, or just about relatable with hindsight (Sayce, 1953: 60), to the metaphor concerned. Alternatively, recent experience with one metaphor may lead to *under*-identifying others.

There is in fact a whole series of problems relating to familiarity in one form or another. Firstly, there is increasing familiarity with specific words. A jargon term, for example, might be perceived as progressively less metaphoric the more it is used within a discourse, and it might become decreasingly tagged. Metaphoric 'death' can, as Goatly (1997) and others have pointed out, be an *intra*-speaker phenomenon, which can occur *within* a single text or interaction. Conversely, frequent repetition of a phrase within a text might serve to *in*crease its salience and to make the speaker or listener increasingly aware of its metaphoric nature. This could then lead to *in*creased commenting on (or demarcating) of the expression concerned. Secondly, there is familiarity with the overall text/transcript. Gibbs (Chapter 2, Guideline 3) notes the need to distinguish between initial (rapid) reactions to metaphor and extended reflection. Gibbs focuses on the distinction between *process* and *product*, but there is also a very practical implication concerning metaphor identification. This is the fact that the more the researcher reads (and reflects on) the text, the more metaphors tend to be identified. In such a situation, the number of readings and the time spent reflecting on the text themselves become important variables. A third relevant type of familiarity concerns the researcher's knowledge of the people and the topic area being studied. Although most researchers probably feel that they can identify large degrees of textual incongruity and/or innovation reasonably easily, it is nevertheless the case that the perception of both 'incongruity' and 'innovation' can depend heavily on one's knowledge of the Topic (or source domain) and one's familiarity with discourse concerning it. Both Sayce (1953: 59) and Steen in Chapter 5 note that recognising an expression as metaphoric can in many cases depend solely on the reader's understanding of the context.

Gwyn's analysis (in Chapter 10) of his interview data relies on his own ability to recognise a shift from one domain to a second "distinct domain of experience", and to identify a subgroup of less "conventional types of metaphor associated with illness". While the results in most cases are unlikely to prove controversial, the identification is, as Gwyn notes (p. 218), occasionally arguable. An interesting example of this concerns Bill, who alters his lifestyle after a four-way bypass operation, and starts to walk regularly. Gwyn suggests that walking and illness are distinctly different domains, and that Bill walks as a way of helping him overcome the illness. Bill's 'walking' is accordingly classified as metaphoric and as valid data for the study, but it is possible that other researchers might have categorised it differently.

Despite the popularity of unilateral identification, other approaches are possible. In the following subsections, I would like briefly to indicate what some of the alternatives might be. It is, however, important to recognise that, whatever the faults of unilateral identification, the alternatives are not problem-free either.

Can't the speakers report afterwards what was metaphoric?

Steen (1994) and Cameron (in Chapter 6) propose that Think–Aloud protocols can be used in metaphor identification (though Steen voices some reservations in Chapter 5). Thus concurrent Think–Aloud techniques might be used to induce people to talk while they carry out some task, or immediately retrospective Think–Aloud protocols might be used afterwards, as a debriefing session where people report on what they said earlier.

Alternatively, the participants in an interaction could be asked to review the tape/transcript at a later date and mark all examples of metaphors they themselves used, and/or felt the other person(s) used. A comparison of the result with analyses of the tape previously – and it must be previously to avoid bias – carried out by the researcher can yield extremely interesting data. However, it has to be recognised that this form of retrospective verbal report suffers from all the problems of reactivity, memory and selective reinterpretation which have been discussed at length in the research literature in connection with Think–Aloud protocols (e.g. McGhee, 1985; Russo *et al.*, 1989; Stratman & Hamp-Lyons, 1994). There can be serious problems if subjects create reports of their activities which are either tailored to what the researcher wants to find, or which put themselves in a more favourable light.

Can't the researcher simply ask the speakers what they meant?

Post-hoc techniques designed to minimise researcher bias will not necessarily work where metaphor is at issue. For example, the use of what Grotjahn (1991) and others have called *consensus data*, where provisional interpretations are repeatedly suggested to informants until they agree that this is what they probably thought, will not work satisfactorily in cases where the speaker did not actually have a specific meaning in mind – as might well be the case with metaphoric expressions. Again, in situations where the speaker was intentionally trying to be vague or to avoid taking responsibility, the consensus-data technique would clearly be unlikely to produce helpful results.

The researcher might accordingly feel the need to question more aggressively, but if the informant considered that the questioning had become an unwelcome interrogation, some form of evasive action might well be taken (see Low, 1991).

Post hoc questioning also has the inevitable effect of increasing information density, and the need to ask the informant to make decisions about numerous pieces of very similar linguistic data may well result in a rapid mental overload. In fact, the problem of 'multiple decisions' relates to considerably more than *post hoc* debriefing. Any study which attempts to discover how individuals structure conceptual metaphor complexes (such as anger or communication), or which examines the stylistic choices which individuals consider to be available to them at specific points in texts or tasks, will need to find a technique that maximises the number of decisions but minimises overload. One solution that is often recommended is that of a *pile sort* (see Brown, 1986; Weller & Romney, 1988). This generally involves rating a set of opinion cards by arranging them physically in piles on a table; in Chapter 11, I use a pile sort with a two-stage classification task to examine reactions to personification expressions such as **This essay believes** in academic essays. While the task worked relatively well with university staff, it is of some interest that a later attempt to extend the exercise to ESL graduate students in the same departments (reported informally in Risiott, 1997) was much less successful. It led in one or two cases to what one might call a 'delayed halo' effect. Students reported after five or six weeks that the pile sort had made them use more personification and that the examples on the cards *had* to be acceptable English because they had been written down (typical examples were "When I wrote my introduction I remembered **this essay thinks** ... I have now adapted my views", or "Can you really say that in English? I thought not, obviously I was wrong").

Should the speaker(s) be totally excluded from the identification?

Adult speakers and writers may well be unable to decide retrospectively whether they used a term for intentional effect. Moreover, they may not highlight this inability even if a *concurrent* Think–Aloud protocol is used. The chances of a young child being able to discuss the question would seem on the surface to be even lower, as there is considerable research evidence that metalinguistic skills are acquired more slowly than many core linguistic skills (see Pollio & Pollio, 1974; Winner, 1988, Chapter 3). A strict conversation analyst would argue that retrospective reports and *post-hoc* debriefings should not be used anyway, since these result in mentalistic accounts, with a high degree of uncertainty. Only features that "are expressed in and through the sequential organization of interaction" (Heritage, 1996) constitute a valid focus of study. So, unless intentions, plans or expectations are mentioned *during* the interaction, they remain in the participants' heads, unobserved and unobservable; all that can be established with any certainty is people's *orientation* to a topic.

This restricted position would seem to pose insuperable problems where the focus of the research involves teaching and learning. It is extremely hard to see how a researcher can describe or evaluate what goes on in a classroom in any meaningful way, without reference to the teacher's lesson plan, or to the teacher's and the learners' expectations (Seedhouse, 1996). Only some form of pre-lesson plan, and/or *post-hoc* debriefing by the researcher, can hope to indicate the link between the language used, the reasons for its use and whether it was ultimately worth using it.

Is a third party preferable to either the researcher or the speaker?

In order to reduce bias, it is fairly common for researchers to present a transcript not to the participants, but to a series of uninvolved third parties and ask them, "Can you isolate the metaphors used by the speakers in this text?" There are, however, essentially three problems with the use of third parties.

The first problem is that different people may use different definitions of metaphor, unless they are given one by the researcher. On the other hand, if the researcher *does* provide a definition, the nature of the task changes and the problem for the researcher becomes one of maximising the reliability of applying his or her predetermined ideas.

A second difficulty is that third parties may want to gloss their decisions using a wide range of terminology. Informant-generated key terms can be hard to interpret or compare, but if the researcher limits possible glosses to five or seven predetermined phrases, the result may well bear little relationship to the way the people concerned actually think.

Another problem with the use of third parties which does not seem to have been raised in the literature, but which could be a serious problem, is that people who have read books on conceptual metaphor may well constitute a set of hypersensitive metaphor recognisers. Such people might well identify a larger set of items as metaphoric than do other 'identifiers'. Indeed, as language teachers increasingly begin to use the semantic networks proposed by, for example, Lakoff and Johnson (1980) as part of their teaching programmes (Ahlers, 1997; Niemeier, 1997), groups of learners as well as teachers may become highly sensitised identifiers and possibly users of metaphor.

The data in Figure 1 (below) constitutes an example of third-party identification. It comes from part of an exercise by Cameron (1997b). Twenty-five people, comprising seven native speakers and 18 non-native speakers, were asked to underline any metaphors in short extracts from a children's science book, *The Ozone Layer* (Bright, 1991). The figures for the native and non-native speakers were virtually identical in all cases, so only the overall percentages are given here.

The results support the comment made by Cameron in Chapter 1 that in some contexts "verb metaphors [are] more common than nominal metaphors". Beyond the question of relative frequency, perhaps the most obvious characteristic of the above results is that everyone recognised **blanket** as a metaphor, but no-one picked out the particles, the phrasal verbs, or the verb **make**. This would seem to

INTRODUCTION	RECOGNITION RATE (%)	
It may seem strange that the liquid used to cool the air in a fridge could be harmful to life on Earth. However, when old fridges are destroyed, harmful gases can **escape** into the atmosphere. The atmosphere is the **blanket** of gases that surrounds the Earth. It is **made up** of several layers. One of these layers contains ozone, a gas which **protects** us from the sun's harmful ultraviolet light.	escape	20
	blanket	100
	made up	0
	protects	16
DANGERS AND BENEFITS		
The Sun and the atmosphere **make** life on Earth **possible**. The Earth is **kept warm** by the Sun's heat, and the atmosphere **traps** some of this heat so that it doesn't **escape** into space. But not all the energy **made by the Sun** is safe. Dangerous forms of radiation called ultraviolet, or UV, light are also **given out**, and these can be harmful to life.	make possible	0
	kept warm	20
	traps	84
	escape	64
	made by the Sun	0
	given out	0

Figure 1   Metaphor identification rates (from Cameron 1997b)

NB. Original formatting of texts 1 and 2 retained.

indicate a clear convergence of personal constructs about the nature of metaphor, and to support Langacker's (1986) contention (contra Lakoff & Johnson, 1980) that many phrasal verbs are fully grammaticalised and *not* meaningful metaphor.

If we look at **escape**, rather than just **blanket**, a slightly more complex picture emerges; where **escape** followed a word already perceived as metaphoric (**traps**, and possibly **kept warm**, in Text 2), the identification rate rose from 20 per cent to 64 per cent. If the explanation is simply that metaphor clusters act as consciousness-raising devices, then why did so few subjects underline **protect** in Text 1, which followed **blanket**? The only solution that I can find is that, in Text 2, **kept warm**, **trap** and **escape** came together visually in a vertical column, whereas in Text 1, **blanket** and **protect** were two lines apart and at opposite edges of the text. It looks therefore as though both *local linguistic context* and *local visual context* played a significant part in people's identification of metaphor.

In brief, the results illustrate both the benefits and the problems of third-party identification. On the negative side, there was certainly variation between the 25 subjects, making it hard to know whether to include **protects** and **escapes** in any subsequent data analysis. On the positive side, the variation did seem to be patterned and the patterning suggested that metaphor identification can be heavily context-dependent. The possible role of local visual context in this connection is particularly important, as layout is a basic feature of all written stimulus materials. The clear suggestion is that layout is a factor of discourse context which the metaphor researcher needs to take into account and, if elicited data is to be used, control.

The moral of this section is that reliance on the researcher alone for views about what is metaphoric can be dangerous, and that both the metaphor users involved and third parties can prove to be valuable supplementary or alternative identifiers. Indeed, complex identification procedures involving triangulation between the different groups are possible. However, the information provided by the users or by third parties needs to be treated with considerable caution and must be shown to be relevant to the research task.

Thinking about representativeness of metaphors

Where research involves the creation in advance of a set of metaphoric expressions which will be presented to experimental subjects, or else analysed directly by the researcher, the major problems are likely to revolve around aspects of context and the representativeness or 'naturalness' of the dataset.

A good illustration of the 'naturalness' problem comes in an otherwise excellent study by Tourangeau and Sternberg (1981). The paper reported an investigation into what made metaphors apt. Subjects rated lists of 64 sentential metaphors all of the same form (e.g. **The owl is the horse among birds**). In a follow-up experiment subjects were asked to select the best item from a closed list to fit, e.g. **A crab is a _____ among sea creatures**. The problem is that this form of sentence is one that is unlikely to occur regularly, as the authors admitted on the final page (p. 53), either in conversation or in literature. It may perhaps be used occasionally, in archaic sounding formulae such a **You are a prince among men**, but even here the intent is likely to be ironic. The notion of aptness itself is also problematic since in this particular case no context or genre was provided, nor any indication of intended rhetorical (or cognitive) effect within the text. What is apt for, say, a Sylvia Plath poem is not likely to be apt in a realistic television police drama or the introduction to a government accident report. Tourangeau and Sternberg (1981) consistently assumed that aptness is in some way an inherent characteristic of a metaphor. The combined result of both the 'naturalness' and the 'aptness' problems is that the reader is left to decide on the value of the absolute aptness of a form that appears unlikely to occur.

Todd and Clarke, in Chapter 12, conclude that one way to overcome the 'naturalness problem' is to base manipulated data on recordings of actual conversations, and they use this approach to create a series of short parallel texts, as part of their False Transcript Method. In Chapter 11, I attempt to reduce the 'aptness problem' in two related ways. One is by specifying the genre concerned and the type of writer as well as the function and location in the text of the manipulated data (namely, 'taking-a-position statements' in introductions to university essays by students for whom English is a foreign language). The second is by preceding the activity involving 'manipulated' data with a naturalistic phase, where subjects react to genuine essay introductions which contain position statements of the sort to be used later.

A rather different problem relating to representativeness concerns the frequency with which different types of figurative expression are actually used. If one is, for example, comparing metaphors and similes, one might imagine that one could simply collect a group of one or the other and add or delete the **like** (Glucksberg & McGlone, 1992, for example, described metaphors and similes as being for most intents and purposes interchangeable). Such a view is, however, not tenable for at least two reasons. Firstly, a large proportion of metaphoric utterances in naturally occurring discourse do *not* actually mention the Topic or the Vehicle, and are simply reflexes of an underlying metaphoric 'proposition' that needs to be inferred (see Steen, in Chapter 5). This contrasts starkly with similes, which, unless truncated for rhetorical purposes, need by definition to contain both terms. Secondly, some genres appear to show marked preferences for particular figures of speech; for example, a short examination of editorials and book reviews in academic journals (Low, 1997) revealed hundreds of metaphoric expressions, which were at times interrelated in extraordinarily complex ways, but not a single simile. The moral is that extreme care needs to be taken not to match a representative set of similes with a highly *un*representative set of metaphors.

Establishing the representativeness of linguistic data is almost never going to be easy, since the exact boundaries of the domain from which one is sampling can rarely (if ever) be established – indeed, isolating and bounding domains constitutes a serious practical problem where linguistic data that is not in small closed sets (e.g. pronouns) is involved.

One solution is to severely constrain the notion of 'domain'; Croft (1993) for example restricts the domain of a metaphoric term to the expressions presupposed by it. While helpful in many respects, Croft's solution does not address the higher-level question of how to determine bounded sets of metaphoric expressions to which conventional sampling techniques may be applied. An alternative solution is explored by Deignan in Chapter 9, which is to employ a large corpus of texts. This can permit an estimate to be made before carrying out an experimental study, with manipulated utterances, of the relative frequency of, say, similes and metaphors, not just in specific types of discourse, but as Steen points out in Chapter 5, in specific positions in the discourse – such as the high-saliency locations at the start and end of paragraphs. It is, however, important to recognise that this sort of estimate does not guarantee that the composition of the database/corpus is appropriate to the people or the task being investigated. Deignan notes that the way data is accessed in many larger corpora backgrounds the composition of the database with the result that it is, in practice, all too easy to assume that the data must be universally representative.[1]

---

[1] Mainly for reasons of brevity, I have limited the discussion in this section to the selection by the researcher of expressions which s/he categorises in advance as metaphoric. It is important to note that a number of controlled studies approach things rather differently, and use reactions to text which are generated by the subjects (rather than the researcher) as indirect evidence for or against metaphoric processing.

Thinking about extending 'conventional' approaches to validity

Research into using or applying language will almost inevitably cross traditional discipline boundaries, and it is an unfortunate fact, for metaphor research at least, that many validation procedures have been evolved specifically with 'quantitative' or 'qualitative' research traditions in mind. Hence notions such as concurrent and construct validity tend to be treated numerically, as part of statistical models, whereas notions such as triangulation, truth value and neutrality are generally treated verbally, or at any rate qualitatively. My suggestion here is that, as a matter of habit, one tries to think beyond the research tradition in which one is working and consider whether 'other' approaches to validity can be employed, beyond the conventional standard ones.

My first example comes from Conversation Analysis: a supremely 'qualitative' tradition. In their classic 1974 paper on turn-taking, Sacks *et al.* justify their general model/set of rules on the grounds that the phenomena concerned are "grossly observable" (1974: 724), or simply that they "recur". Drew and Holt (1995), describing people's use of idiom and metaphor to terminate topics in conversation, go one step beyond this and indicate the size of their database, but the justifications for the actual generalisations remain similar: "the pattern is ... strikingly apparent" (p. 119) or "recurrent" (p. 120). The 'quantitative' question of precisely *how* recurrent something needs to be before one can make generalisations about the speech community at large is crucial, yet is rarely discussed in much detail in Conversation Analysis accounts.

A nice example of the opposite situation, where a quantitative analysis could be validated by using qualitative notions, occurs in Chapter 12. Todd and Clarke employ an experimental paradigm (the False Transcript Method) to explore whether reactions to metaphor differ from reactions to the corresponding simile and to an equivalent literal version. In one experiment, subjects were asked to rate the apparent age and intelligence of a child who utters certain expressions. A conventional Analysis of Variance (ANOVA) was undertaken to establish whether there was significant variation in the set of three mean reactions. The validity of the ANOVA depends in part on whether the three sets of reactions are genuinely parallel and comparable, and Todd and Clarke duly asked a number of third parties to evaluate comparability. What I would like to do here is to explore their suggestion (p. 263) about the possible role of discourse function and propose that the mixing of quantitative data and qualitative discourse analysis is not only possible, but that the combination of the two can lead to a very rich and productive approach to validation (see also Robson, 1993). My argument starts from what I hope is the uncontroversial assumption that parallel texts will only be comparable if the linguistic expressions concerned play roughly similar textual functions and lead to roughly similar implicatures about the speaker, the listener and the situation in which the interaction is taking place. Such information can be obtained by undertaking some form of discourse analysis, which will almost inevitably be largely qualitative. To this end, I would like briefly to examine two of the texts used by Todd and Clarke from a discourse point of view:

PASSAGE 8

1	Mother:	No don't pull his tail he won't like that
2	Henry:	Want to stroke him!
3	Mother:	Yes you can stroke him ... there he likes that, listen!
4	**Henry:**	**He's an engine** *(metaphor version)*
		He's like an engine *(simile version)*
		He's purring *(literal version)*
5	Mother:	Yes he's purring because he's a happy cat
6	Henry:	(Makes purring noise)

The fact that the child actually makes a purring noise later in the transcript (in line 6) helps to justify the selection of **purring** (in line 4) for the literal version, and the agreement (**Yes**) by the mother serves to retain similar patterns of cohesion and coherence across all three texts. On the other hand, the discourse task implied by the mother's utterance in line 5 shows a measure of difference; in the literal version, the mother is simply adding an explanation to a known fact (the purring), whereas in the metaphor and simile versions, she is actively bringing the conversation back from the **engine** to where she left it (**listen!**), as well as explaining. The difference, however, relates more to the mother than to the child and might not lead us to expect to find differential reactions to the child's language.

PASSAGE 4

1	Mother:	Look at the cat in the garden
2	Paul:	Where? ... Oh yeah
3	Mother:	He's hunting
4	**Paul:**	**A tiger** *(metaphor)*
		Like a tiger *(simile)*
		Cat! *(literal version)*
5	Mother:	He wants to catch the bird
6	Paul:	Oh!
7	Mother:	Oh it's flown away.

Passage 4 is slightly different. There is again little to differentiate the metaphor and simile versions, but **Cat!** in line 4 does alter the literal version. This time the change appears to relate more to the child than the mother. Following **hunting** with **A tiger** serves to create a semantic link, whereby the child comprehends hunting and intellectually moves a step further. **Cat!** makes no obvious link with hunting and might suggest that the child has not been listening, and/or is simply repeating something spoken earlier. Paul's apparent failure to recognise the conversational need to create cohesion and coherence across participants, as well as across turns, might well be interpreted as saying something about his age or level of development. Reactions to age and intelligence might accordingly be based as much on discourse structure as on differences between metaphoric and literal phrases. Thus a consideration of textual cohesion and coherence might lead us to hypothesise different patterns of reactions by adult subjects to Passages 4 and 8.

The importance of checking on the cohesion and coherence of experimental texts extends to a text-type not represented in the present book, but commonly used in metaphor research: the short story, written by the researcher, which has a target utterance embedded in it (e.g. Janus & Bever, 1985), or tagged on as a final 'punchline' (e.g. the studies in Gibbs, 1982; Giora & Fein, 1996). The above discussion suggests that story writers should check (and report) at least three things:

- that each story has the stylistic, age-related and structural features associated with stories, verbal reports or stories-in-conversation (as appropriate);
- that any extra processing (by the readers) of the target utterance is not the result of the researcher's having removed expected discourse links, or added unexpected ones;
- that interpretation and processing of the target utterance (by the reader) is not influenced by the researcher's having placed key explanatory lexis near the target in one version of the story, but several lines earlier in the other.

Thinking about multiple influences on metaphor users

One aspect of validity not yet touched upon concerns the way the researcher conceptualises the target group and the nature of the influences acting on (and between) its members. If one is researching metaphors within a specific group of people, the research focus is inevitably going to lie with that group; the difficulty is that social groupings are rarely hermetically sealed, and it may well be that metaphors used by other groups influence those used by the group being studied, and *vice versa*. This notion of interrelated groups is somewhat akin to the notion of networks in sociolinguistics. It can become particularly important if one is researching the use (or effects) of metaphor within a hierarchical institution such as a school or prison, since social grouping becomes bound up with higher and lower 'levels' of expertise, power or status. In a hierarchical context, not only can the pattern of metaphor use vary within and between levels, but metaphors from one level can have variable impacts, conceptually and/or emotionally, at other levels up or down the system. In addition, influences from specific groups outside the system can have variable impacts on groups/levels inside it. The overall result can prove to be highly complex, but research designs which focus on one group or level need to take some account of metaphors originating from other sources within the system and outside it.

The notion that hierarchical social systems can combine *differential metaphor use* and *metaphor transmission up or down the system as groups/levels interact with each other* can be illustrated by considering the situation faced by a researcher interested in looking at metaphor use by science teachers in secondary schools. At the most academic level are the metaphors coined by the 'professionals', who determine the canon: the scientific metaphors used in research publications, then in graduate and later undergraduate examinations (e.g. ATOMS HAVE NEGATIVE CHARGE CLOUDS; ELECTRONS ARE ARRANGED IN SHELLS). These metaphors tend to filter down into school curricula when they have been fixed, but at the initial stages, individual researchers often play quite devious power games to make certain that their own metaphors 'win' (Knudsen, 1996). Gould (1995: 61) also notes the existence of metaphors that seem to remain within relatively expert circles: he cites as an example from evolutionary biology the highly counterproductive metaphor of a **cone of development or increasing diversity** which "resides largely in textbooks and professional publications for scientists".

As university students become teachers, they will be faced with conventional metaphors developed by research psychologists to describe human concept-formation and learning (e.g. THE BRAIN IS A COMPUTER) and metaphors developed by teacher trainers, such as TEACHING IS WARMING UP MENTAL MEALS (Ormell, 1996), THE LEARNER IS A STUFFED GOOSE, or THE TEACHER IS A FULL JUG (Woodward, 1991: 155).

At the next 'level' down, the teachers must help their learners come to terms in a simplified way with the canonical science metaphors, but they may well coin other metaphors for teaching purposes ('ATOMS ARE HAPPY', R. Low, p.c.), which students are asked to background and replace with more orthodox ones when it comes to examinations. Teachers may in addition develop metaphors to describe their own work, which may draw on previously encountered metaphors (deriving from scientists, psychologists or teacher trainers), but which may rely just as much on general cultural life or personal experience.

The fourth level is occupied by the learners. Learners come to a science class with naive (or natural) models of reality and must then make sense of indirectly presented versions of professional metaphors and directly presented metaphors invented by the teacher. What happens is complex. The following seven quotations are from a study by Harrison and Treagust (1996) of 48 Australian secondary children's images of atoms (*after* they had been taught).

1 "Teacher-initiated metaphors, such as 'electron clouds' ...
   appeared to conjure, in the minds of students, quite different
   models from those intended by the teacher."   (p. 510)
2 "Many students do not interpret teacher metaphors and analogies
   in the intended manner. Rather they transfer attributes from the
   teachers' analog to the target [the Topic] in a literal and
   undifferentiated sense."   (p. 511)
3 "They mistake the model for reality." (p. 531) and "are unable to
   reliably identify where the metaphor breaks down".   (p. 511)
4 "All the students ... saw a shell as acting as a form of protection
   and, where examples were used, they were snail shells, beach
   shells, clam shells and egg shells."   (p. 523)
5 "Other students appeared to have confused the nucleus of the
   atom with the nucleus of a cell"; thus it can "grow" and "break up
   so there's more of them".   (p. 522)
6 "Many students ... find the diversity of models used to represent
   specific phenomena both challenging and confusing."   (p. 514)
7 "This study has ... illustrated the negative outcomes that arise
   when students are left to draw their own conclusions about
   analogical models."   (p. 532)

These quotations illustrate in the clearest way possible the need for research designs to examine the integration of metaphors, both within and between levels of the school system.

Cortazzi and Jin in Chapter 8 explore two of the levels, namely 'metaphors created by (in this case, language) teachers to describe teaching and learning' and 'metaphors created by learners'. They discuss a possible example of transmission across levels when they speculate how language teachers have "taken over" the metaphor of 'scaffolding' developed by Wood, Bruner and Ross (1976) to account for first-language acquisition, then by Edwards and Mercer (1987) and others in an educational context as a specific kind of teaching technique for children. Language teachers have, the latter argue, lost sight of the original precise meaning(s) and, on being introduced to the metaphor on in-service training courses, have used it in a modified sense to account for increases in their *own* awareness of the learning process.

Some further evidence of transmission across levels is discussed by Gwyn in Chapter 10, as part of his study of "the discourse of serious illness". Gwyn discusses how warfare metaphors can get transmitted from popular medical literature, where they function descriptively, to patients, who use them as a means of coping and coming to terms with the disease.

The fifth quotation from Harrison and Treagust (above) is also interesting in a different way. It indicates that interaction between what the teacher says and the interpretation(s) that learners place on it can relate to more than just the children's understanding; it can also affect the researcher's metaphor identification process. The transcripts of the interviews with the children gave the impression that several learners had spontaneously coined the metaphor THE ATOM IS A LIVING ORGANISM, but reference to what the teacher(s) had tried to teach suggested that this was in fact not the case; rather, the children concerned were conflating at a literal level two separate propositions: 'an atom has a nucleus' and 'a cell has a nucleus'. The source of the children's confusion was the dual use of **nucleus** as a technical term. An examination of transmission across levels thus led the researchers to make a significant recategorisation of the children's utterances.

Thinking about generalising from language data to thought or behaviour

Generalisations from metaphoric utterances to social behaviour or conceptual/mental organisation should not be assumed to be true; they need to be justified. Cameron raises this issue in Chapter 1, and Gibbs (in Chapter 2) discusses several of the psycholinguistic implications in some detail; what I want to do here is to consider, albeit very briefly, one or two practical suggestions about what questions might be asked or actions pursued in order to justify a generalisation from language to thought or action.

The pressure to overgeneralise seems to be particularly acute where speakers are talking about particular tasks (such as their job) and the researcher wants to use the utterances as the basis for generalising about the ways in which society or the speakers conceptualise them. Just because a learner says "She lost me then", can one conclude that she operates behaviourally in the clear belief that LEARNING IS A JOURNEY? Or because someone says "I turned off during the drills", can it be assumed that they adhere to the belief that LEARNING IS A MECHANICAL OR COMPU-TATIONAL PROCESS (the examples are from Thornbury, 1991)? The answer, as Gibbs points out in Chapter 2, has to be no. Essentially, in order to demonstrate the validity of generalising from language use to 'belief' or 'conceptualisation', what is needed is additional evidence that the 'underlying metaphor model' affects how the speakers actually go about performing their job, or at the very least evidence that it affects how they talk about it when *not* using conventional idiom. At a practical level, five possible questions to ask in this connection might be:

1 Do the speakers develop (i.e. extend, or 'revivify', in the sense of Pettit, 1982) the conventional expressions?
2 Do they do this with other people's metaphors, as well as their own?
3 Do they explicitly state that this is how they conceive of their job?
4 Do they overtly discuss what aspects of the job relate to the Vehicle (i.e. do they discuss the Grounds of the metaphor? see Goatly, 1997: 98)
5 Do they challenge a colleague or student who uses phrases with different semantic/metaphoric overtones?

Block, in Chapter 7, faces this problem when examining how the utterances of second language acquisition researchers can be used as evidence for the ways in which the researchers conceptualise the research process. Block's answer is to employ the 4-stage model developed by Schön, that he called *Framing* and which tries to account for public behaviour in the face of problematic situations. The model allows the analyst at least a partial means of justifying the jump from utterance to conceptualisation. For example, the jump is more justified if the speakers' behaviour fits all four stages and not just one. This applies particularly to the last two stages of the model ('limiting the choices one makes' and 'selling the conceptualisation to others'), as these describe things speakers will actually do if they conceptualise the topic concerned in the hypothesised way. The details of Framing are explained in Chapter 7; the point at issue here is simply that an analytic method was consciously chosen which permits a degree of validation.

Gwyn, in Chapter 10, tackles a version of the same problem when examining how the acutely and chronically sick attempt to cope with their illnesses. In Gwyn's case, however, Stage 4 of Framing would not be applicable, as sufferers rarely try and 'sell' their illnesses. The researcher's options are thus slightly more restricted where there is less public behaviour and the dataset of utterances is more heavily reliant on elicited narratives or Think–Aloud protocols. However, even here, Gwyn manages to find behavioural correlates for several of the metaphors and symbols that occur in conversation.

In sum, then, justifying generalisations from metaphoric language to thought or action is an important aspect of validating applied linguistic studies. Though the task may seem daunting, solutions are in many cases possible, either by asking supplementary questions about the metaphor users and the data, or, as in the studies by Gwyn and Block, by choosing an appropriate analytic framework.

Conclusion

Analysing how people use, react to and think about metaphor in different contexts is not a simple task. It is extraordinarily easy to overlook important factors, to define metaphoric concepts in inappropriate ways, to make unwarranted assumptions about what metaphor users are actually thinking, or generally to introduce some form of bias into a study. In this chapter I have adopted a broad view of validation, which centres on the idea of researchers attempting to make their actions appropriate to the (research) task and justifying the result. Using this broad view of validity, I have examined five areas where validation problems can and do occur, and where solutions are frequently neither simple nor obvious. These are: determining what to categorise as metaphor(ic) in naturalistic studies, creating adequately representative metaphors in reaction studies, crossing disciplinary boundaries, establishing the major metaphoric influences on the target group, and generalising from metaphoric language to thought or action. I have tried to argue in all cases that even though 'doing' validation is hard and the result is almost never problem-free, it is important to try. However, at the same time it is equally important that the need to impose a practical solution on a research problem does not result in over-simplifying the variety and complexity of metaphoric expressions, and hence in an impoverished dataset. The ideas discussed in this chapter represent in many cases a starting point; as more studies of metaphor in use are undertaken, they will hopefully serve to underpin new and imaginative approaches to validation.

PART II

FROM THEORY TO DATA

4   *Getting your sources right*
What Aristotle didn't *say*

James Edwin Mahon

Introduction and overview

As at least one influential writer on metaphor has pointed out – and there are few who would disagree with him – it is still the case that "Any serious study of metaphor is almost obliged to start with the works of Aristotle" (Ortony, 1979a: 3). Most studies of metaphor, however, have scarcely a good word to say about Aristotle. The obligation to discuss him is considered to be something of a chore. Such studies always insist that Aristotle undervalued metaphor and believed it to be merely an ornamental extra in language. They also insist that he was ridiculously elitist with respect to metaphor, believing that one had to be a genius in order to use a metaphor properly. Partly as a result of this prevailing negative appraisal, the scholarship contained in these studies tends to be rather shallow. Since Aristotle's account of metaphor is fundamentally wrong, it seems, there is not much point in going into great detail about his views, or in consulting more than one of the texts in which he discusses metaphor.

Shallow scholarship about rich and important sources of work on metaphor and language use, however, can impoverish and, at its worst, seriously bias empirical research on the topic. Moreover, getting your sources right is not merely a valuable end in itself – it may also lead to the discovery of insights which support the claims of your current research, or even to the development of new areas for your critical investigation. In this essay I want to argue that a more detailed examination of Aristotle's writings on metaphor yields both of these happy results. Aristotle, it turns out, holds a position on the ubiquity of metaphor in conversation and writing which supports current views about the omnipresence of metaphor in everyday discourse and the print media. What he has to say about how people can express themselves in a clearer and more attractive way through the use of metaphors is also extremely relevant to the concerns of contemporary theorists grappling with the problem of language teaching and learning, since it is Aristotle's view that people actually learn and understand things better through metaphors. Furthermore, his account of metaphor includes a distinction between the *coinage* of a metaphor and the *usage* of a metaphor, one which allows for the ubiquity of metaphors in common discourse, without downplaying the aspect of human creativity involved in the creation of new metaphors. This is a distinction which, I think, should be taken on board by future researchers. Finally, I shall remind theorists that Aristotle was the first to argue for an entirely natural origin of true literary genius, and that in this respect his naturalistic aesthetic theory was a revolutionary one, breaking with a long, elitist, anti-naturalistic tradition of theorising about literary genius. Since Aristotle largely identified literary genius with the ability to coin marvellous new metaphors, it follows that Aristotle was the first to argue for an entirely natural origin of metaphor coinage. The fact that he was able to do this without abandoning or downplaying literary talent should be taken into account by those currently engaged in research on language who tend to overlook the plain fact of literary genius in their pursuit of a more egalitarian account of metaphor.

Aristotle on metaphor in the *Poetics*

Aristotle's discussion of metaphor in the *Poetics* is to be found in Chapters 21 and 22. In Chapter 21 Aristotle states that every word "is either current, or strange, or metaphorical, or ornamental, or newly-coined, or lengthened, or contracted, or altered" (21: 1457b; Butcher, in Nahm Ed., 1950: 27[1]). The terms *current* and *strange* refer to the commonness of a word in the writings and conversation of a people; *lengthened, contracted* or *altered* refer to modifications made to words in Greek; and *newly-coined* refers to newly coined *words* (and not to new combinations of words). Although there is no separate explanation given of *ornamental*,[2] it should be noted that the ornamental is differentiated from the metaphorical. The overall importance of including metaphors in this list, however, is that

---

[1] References to Aristotle's *Poetics* are from the translation by M. C. Butcher, in Nahm Ed. (1950). I have elected to use the Butcher translation because it is the one commonly referred to by other critics, and its phrases are now famous.

[2] It is almost certain that we do not have the complete text of the *Poetics*, and also that, as Grube has said, "More clearly than any other work of Aristotle, the *Poetics* can only have been a set of lecture notes with later additions and interpolations by the lecturer himself" (1958: xviii). As a result, there are many lacunae in the text, among them the absence of a passage explaining the term *ornamental*.

Aristotle appears to classify metaphors as lying outside normal language use.

Aristotle defines *metaphor* as "the application of an alien name by transference either from genus to species, or from species to genus, or from species to species, or by analogy, that is, proportion" (21: 1457b; Butcher p. 28). Since 'lying at anchor' is a species of the genus 'lying', one can say **There lies my ship** (genus-to-species metaphor). Since 'ten thousand' is a species of a 'large number', one can say **Verily ten thousand noble deeds hath Odysseus wrought** (species-to-genus metaphor). Since 'to draw away' and 'to cleave' are each a species of the genus 'taking away', one can say **with blade of bronze drew away the life** (species-to-species metaphor). And since old age is to life as evening is to day, one can say that **old age is the evening of life** (analogy metaphor) (21: 1457b; Butcher p. 28). All metaphors, Aristotle believes, fall into at least one of these four categories, although analogy metaphors are the most pleasing.

This account of metaphor is known as the comparison theory of metaphor. Some contemporary writers on metaphor still accept this account;[3] most, however, do not – at least not without many qualifications. However, it is not my intention here to defend the comparison theory of metaphor against all other contenders. As it stands, Aristotle's account is, in general outline, quite close to the common-sensical understanding of metaphor, and it suffices for the purposes of my essay that he is obviously discussing what we would also call metaphor, even if the comparison theory is applicable to only a limited number of cases. It is the chapter of the *Poetics* which follows this one, where Aristotle elaborates on how metaphors are unusual, and discusses the relationship between metaphor and genius, which is considered to be the more controversial part of his account. This is the part of the *Poetics* on which I will focus.

In Chapter 22 Aristotle argues that the best writing style is that which is clear, but which contains a certain amount of unusual words. "By unusual", Aristotle says, "I mean strange (or rare) words, metaphorical, lengthened, – anything, in short, that differs from the normal idiom" (22: 1458a; Butcher p. 28). Just as it is important to avoid a style which is perfectly clear but mean – that is, a style composed entirely of "current or proper" (22: 1458a; Butcher p. 29) words, so too it is important to avoid a style composed entirely of unusual words. A style composed entirely of metaphors, for example, would be a "riddle" (22: 1458a; Butcher p. 29). Thus a certain infusion of unusual words "will raise it above the commonplace and

---

[3] See, for example, Susan Sontag's (1991), *Illness as Metaphor: Aids and Its Metaphors.*

mean, while the use of proper words will make it perspicuous" (22: 1458a; Butcher p. 29). All unusual words, however, Aristotle cautions, must be employed with propriety. It is in this context that he makes his most famous statement about the relationship between metaphor and genius:

> It is a great matter to observe propriety in these several modes of expression
> – compound words, strange (or rare) words, and so forth. But the greatest
> thing by far is to have a command of metaphor. This alone cannot be
> imparted by another; it is the mark of genius – for to make good metaphors
> implies an eye for resemblances.   (*Poetics* 22: 1458b; Butcher p. 31)

This is the extent of the account of metaphor given in the *Poetics*. Despite its relative brevity, it is probably the most influential account of metaphor ever provided.

The controversy over the account centres on at least four claims concerning metaphor which are attributed to Aristotle on the basis of these statements in the *Poetics*. The first is that, according to Aristotle, metaphors lie outside normal language use. They are a deviant or aberrant form of discourse. The second is that metaphors have no cognitive value, and are considered to be merely decorative extras. As Ortony (1979a: 3) says, "As to their use, [Aristotle] believed that it was entirely ornamental. Metaphors, in other words, are not necessary, they are just nice". The third claim is that metaphors do not possess clarity. As Hawkes puts it, writing about Aristotle's account of metaphor:

> It is abundantly clear that, as an entity in itself, metaphor is regarded as a
> decorative addition to language, to be used in specific ways, and at specific
> times and places. It will also be noticed that 'clarity' is presumed to reside in
> 'ordinary' language, which is non-metaphorical: metaphor is a kind of
> dignifying, enlivening ingredient.   (Hawkes, 1984: 8–9)

The fourth claim attributed to Aristotle is that in order to be able to use a metaphor correctly, a person must have genius. I.A. Richards, among many others, attributes this claim to Aristotle, as I will show later on.

I want to argue that Aristotle makes none of these claims. The misunderstanding of his position which has generated this view is largely due to a failure to appreciate the context of the discussion of metaphor in the *Poetics* and to a confusion of the concepts of *coinage* and *usage*, coupled with a general lack of familiarity with what Aristotle has to say about metaphor in the *Rhetoric*.

The *Poetics* is a treatise about Greek literature, principally tragic and epic verse. It is not a treatise about language. In the chapters of the *Poetics* quoted above, Aristotle is discussing the "making", or *coinage*, of metaphors in literature, and not their *use* in everyday discourse. Here Aristotle is only concerned with language insofar as it is used by tragedians and poets in the writing of their works. He believes, firstly, that metaphors coined by tragedians and epic poets are unusual, and outside of the normal idiom, insofar as they are new combinations of words, combinations which have not been made before. Secondly, he believes that the ability to coin new metaphors which are pleasing and informative – the ability, in other words, to coin *good* new metaphors – is the greatest kind of creative ability a tragedian or epic poet can have. This kind of creative ability is a rare skill which cannot be taught. Thirdly, he believes that metaphors convey truths about "resemblances" that actually exist between things in the world. And fourthly, he believes that metaphors can be lucid, and that those of a good writer always are.

Textual support for this interpretation of his statements about metaphor in the *Poetics* can be garnered from his subsequent discussion of metaphor in the *Rhetoric*, to which I will now turn.

Aristotle on metaphor in the *Rhetoric*

Aristotle's discussion of metaphor in the *Rhetoric* is to be found in Book 3. Many of the statements about metaphor made in the *Rhetoric* rely upon the account of metaphor already provided in the *Poetics*. As he says in Chapter 2 of Book 3, "The nature of each of these kinds of words has already, as I said, been discussed in the *Poetics*; so have the different kinds of metaphor, and the extreme importance of metaphor in both prose and verse".[4] While it is true that the account of metaphor given in the *Poetics* is the definitive account, this certainly should not lead us to ignore what is added to this account in the *Rhetoric*, as many critics tend to do.

Aristotle's *Rhetoric* is concerned with everyday discourse and public oratory, as well as with written prose. He places more restrictions on the kinds of words which can be used in these contexts. He divides up the list of unusual words, previously provided in the *Poetics*, into those which ought to be used and those which ought not. While strange, new or compound words ought not to be used in public oratory and written prose, metaphors ought to be. The reason is that they are ubiquitous in normal conversation and writing. As he says again in Chapter 2 of Book 3:

There is very little occasion in prose to use strange words, compounds, or new coinages ... and the reason has already been stated: they make the

---

[4] References to Aristotle's *Rhetoric* are from G. M. A. Grube's (1958) translation.

language more elevated and unusual than is appropriate. Only current words, the proper names of things, and metaphors are to be used in prose, as is indicated by the fact that everybody uses only these. Everybody does use metaphors, the proper names of things, and current words in conversation, so that the language of a good writer must have an element of strangeness, but this must not obtrude, and he should be clear, for lucidity is the peculiar excellence of prose.   (*Rhetoric* 3, 2: 1404b; Grube pp. 69–70)

Here Aristotle refers to his account of metaphor in the *Poetics*, and points out that a metaphor is "lucid, pleasing, and strange, and has all these qualities to a high degree" (*R*3, 2: 1404b; Grube p. 70). He also says that what Grube translates as its "use" (p. 70), but what I would call its *coinage*, cannot be learned from anyone else. After this reiteration of the claim concerning the ultimate unteachability of the creative ability to coin good new metaphors, Aristotle proceeds to give advice on how to derive *better* metaphors. He cautions that metaphors used in prose must be appropriate and not "farfetched" (*R*3, 2: 1405a; Grube p. 71), and he invokes the proportional method of the analogy metaphor (a : b :: c : d) given in the *Poetics* as an aid to coining metaphors:

Think of it this way: as a purple cloak is to youth, so to old age is – what? The same garment is obviously unusable. If you want to flatter your subject, you must derive your metaphor from the nobler things in the same genus; if you want to censure, from the worse.   (*Rhetoric* 3, 2: 1405a; Grube p. 70)

Aristotle also argues that metaphors should be "made from words that are beautiful in sound, in meaning, or by association to the eye or some other sense" (*R*3, 2: 1405b; Grube p. 72). After arguing that all similes are really metaphors ("all similes become metaphors when the explanation is omitted", *R*3, 2: 1407a; Grube p. 76), the next important statement about metaphor is made in Chapter 10, in the course of outlining how to obtain the most felicitous phrases in writing prose. "Three things should be aimed at: metaphor, antithesis, and vividness" (*R*3, 2: 1410b; Grube p. 89), and about metaphors he says that it is from them that we learn the most. We are attracted to metaphors, he says, precisely because we *learn* from them:

We learn above all from metaphors. When Homer compares old age to wheat stubble, he makes us realise and understand that both wheat stubble and old age belong to the genus of things that have lost their vigor ... we are attracted by those things which we understand as soon as they are said or very soon afterwards, even though we had no knowledge of them before, for then there is a learning process or something very like it, but in the case of the obvious or the unintelligible there is no learning at any time.
(*Rhetoric* 3, 10: 1410b; Grube p. 89)

Aristotle next proceeds to give a whole series of examples of metaphors – principally examples of proportional metaphors – taken from the speeches of politicians and generals. In Chapter 11 he states that the best metaphors are ones which achieve the effect of "bringing things vividly before the eyes of the audience", and argues that this effect is "produced by words which refer to things in action" (*R*3, 11: 1411b; Grube pp. 92–93). This is followed by an important claim about the merit of a metaphor depending upon the correspondence of the metaphor to a similarity actually existing between things in the world:

As I said before, metaphor must be by transference from things that are related, but not obviously so, as it is a sign of sound intuition in a philosopher to see similarities between things that are far apart.
(*Rhetoric* 3, 11: 1412a; Grube p. 93)

Most felicitous sayings, Aristotle goes on to conclude, rely on metaphor, and "the best image involves a metaphor" (*R*3, 11: 1413a; Grube p. 96). He also argues that all proverbs are metaphors, and that "Successful hyperboles are also metaphors, as when it was said of a man with a black eye: **You'd take him for a basket of mulberries**, a black eye, too, being purple, and the quantity of mulberries provides the exaggeration" (*R*3, 11: 1413a; Grube p. 96). Finally he reiterates his important claim concerning the correspondence of metaphors to similarities existing between things in the world: "Poets are hissed off the stage if their metaphors are bad, but good metaphors are much applauded, when there is a true correspondence between the terms" (*R*3, 10: 1413a; Grube p. 96).

As I stated earlier, the account of metaphor provided in the *Rhetoric* is often ignored by critics of Aristotle, and this lack of familiarity with the *Rhetoric* has led to the misinterpretation of his overall position on metaphor. For here Aristotle acknowledges that *everybody* uses metaphors in conversation, and he simply encourages orators and writers to work on producing *better* metaphors. Even if true literary genius cannot be taught, it is at least possible for people to practise coining metaphors, and improve their ability to coin them. Aristotle also extends the scope of metaphor to include hyperboles and proverbs, and discusses at greater length the details of what makes a metaphor successful, pleasing and informative. He stresses the cognitive value of these metaphors, claiming that they are lucid and that they convey truths about the world. He also stresses their pedagogical value: metaphors tell us things about the world which we did not understand beforehand, and the "learning process" is extremely enjoyable. People are attracted to metaphors precisely because they learn new things from them, seeing connections where previously they had not seen any. Metaphors bring things vividly "before the eyes" of listeners or readers, and the pleasing mental effort required to understand them makes them memorable.

This summary of the main points of the discussion of metaphor in the *Rhetoric* provides support for my earlier interpretation of certain statements from the *Poetics*, and undermines the criticisms made by Ortony and Hawkes. If everyone uses metaphors in conversation, it can hardly be the case that for Aristotle metaphors *per se* are unusual. It must be the case that the metaphors of the tragic and epic poets are unusual because they are *new* metaphors. Nor can it be said that for Aristotle clarity resides entirely in ordinary language, since good metaphors are credited with being lucid. They are even said to be the best way to teach people things about the world, and they are thus *superior* to literal explanation. Nor can it be said that for him metaphors are entirely ornamental, since good metaphors convey truths about similarities actually existing between things in the world. As Cooper has pointed out:

The fact is, though, that in addition to judging metaphors as witty or flat, stimulating or dull, vivid or pale, edifying or corrupting, people have always felt a strong desire to appraise them in the terminology of truth and falsity. The urge needs to be understood even if the explanation shows it to be misguided. We must investigate, if not fully sympathize with, the tendency illustrated by Aristotle's insistence that metaphors "fairly correspond to the things signified".   (Cooper, 1986: 199)

With this more comprehensive interpretation of Aristotle's position on metaphor in mind, I now want to address in greater detail the claim attributed to him by various critics that in order to be able to use a metaphor correctly a person must have genius.

Richards on Aristotle, metaphor and genius

In his lectures on rhetoric given at Bryn Mawr in 1936, published that year under the title of *The Philosophy of Rhetoric*, I. A. Richards quotes Aristotle's twin claims in the *Poetics* that the greatest thing by far is to have a command of metaphor, and that the ability to make good metaphors is the mark of genius, and says that in these claims he finds "the evil presence of three assumptions which have ever since prevented the study of this 'greatest thing by far' from taking the place it deserves among our studies" (1936: 89).

The first assumption of which Aristotle is guilty is that "'an eye for resemblances' is a gift that some men have but others do not".

Against this Richards argues that "we all live, and speak, only through our eye for resemblances. Without it we should perish early" (1936: 89). The second assumption of which Aristotle is guilty is that "though everything else may be taught, the command of metaphor cannot be taught". Against this Richards argues as follows:

> But, if we consider how we all of us attain what limited measure of a command of metaphor we possess, we shall see that no such contrast is valid. As individuals we gain our command of metaphor just as we learn whatever else makes us distinctively human. It is all imparted to us from others, with and through the language we learn, language which is utterly unable to aid us except through the command of metaphor which it gives.
>
> (Richards, 1936: 90)

The third assumption of which Aristotle is guilty is "that metaphor is something special and exceptional in the use of language, a deviation from its normal mode of working". Against this Richards argues that metaphor is "the omnipresent principle of all [language's] free action" (1936: 90).

I want to argue that Aristotle is not guilty of these three evil assumptions. Firstly, Aristotle is not claiming that a select few geniuses have an eye for resemblances, whereas the rest of us do not. Rather, he is claiming that there are people – the tragedians and epic poets – who have a *better* eye for resemblances than the rest of us, and who have the ability to coin wonderful new metaphors which capture these resemblances. Aristotle could not consistently claim that nobody except a *genius* has an eye for resemblances and at the same time encourage people in the creation of their metaphors to "derive your metaphor from ... things in the same genus", as he does in the example quoted above from the *Rhetoric* concerning the cloak and old age. For an eye for resemblances is surely required in order to perform *that* task.

Secondly, Aristotle is not claiming that our ability to use metaphors is one which we cannot learn from others. That claim alone would contradict almost every exhortation contained in Book 3 of the *Rhetoric*, where he goes to great lengths to give practical advice on how to use metaphors in order to "bring things vividly before the eyes of the audience" in making speeches. Aristotle must believe that our ability to use metaphors can be learned and improved from reading works such as the *Rhetoric*, otherwise he would not write in such a manual-like way.

Finally, as I have already argued above, Aristotle is not claiming that metaphors *per se* are exceptional. He is only claiming that new good metaphors that are coined by the tragedians and epic poets are exceptional. Although he could not, I think, be said to hold the position that metaphor is *omnipresent* in language, he does at least hold the position that the use of metaphors in conversation is as common as the use of current words and the proper names of things. Consequently, I reject Richards' ascription of these three "evil assumptions" to Aristotle.[5]

Metaphor coinage and literary genius

The value of re-interpreting Aristotle as a theorist who seeks to explain what he calls the "extreme importance of metaphor in both prose and verse" is that it allows for a more thorough evaluation of his position on the relationship between metaphor and true literary genius. Aristotle's position is actually similar to that of Shelley's in his *A Defence of Poetry*.[6] It is the position that true literary genius consists in the ability to coin marvellous new metaphors which capture similarities existing between things in the world. Aristotle also believes that this skill, which the tragedians and epic poets possess, is an entirely *natural* skill.

It is important to note here that, in making this claim about the natural origin of metaphor creation in tragedians and epic poets, Aristotle was breaking with a long, anti-naturalistic tradition of aesthetic theory which asserted that poetry was the result of divine inspiration, and that a poet was a kind of madman. This tradition included Plato's *Phaedrus* and *Ion*, in which it is claimed that:

> Just so the Muse. She first makes men inspired, and then through these inspired ones others share in the enthusiasm, and a chain is formed, for the epic poets, all the good ones, have their excellence, not from art, but are inspired, possessed, and thus they utter all these admirable poems.
>
> (*Ion* 533e; Hamilton and Cairns, 1963: 220)

---

[5] I also reject Richards' claim that Shelley's position on metaphor in his *A Defence of Poetry* is opposed to that of Aristotle, because Shelley observed "that 'Language is vitally metaphorical ...'" (Richards, p. 90). Shelley observed no such thing, because this is a misquotation. What Shelley in fact observed was that "*Their* language is vitally metaphorical ..." – the language, that is, of the great poets (Brett-Smith Ed., 1921: 25) [emphasis added]).

In his summary of Richards' *The Philosophy of Rhetoric*, Paul Ricoeur compounds these two misreadings when he says that "contrary to Aristotle's well-known saying that the mastery of metaphor is a gift of genius and cannot be taught, language is 'vitally metaphorical', as Shelley saw very well" (Ricoeur, translated by R. Czerny, 1978: 79–80).

[6] For more on Shelley's position on metaphor, see my 'Truth and metaphor: A defence of Shelley' (Mahon, 1997).

It was revolutionary of Aristotle to assert, as he does in Chapter 17 of the *Poetics*, that "Hence poetry implies either a happy gift of nature or a strain of madness" (P17: 1455a; Butcher p. 22), and to argue that the former kind of poet, who has an innate gift but who retains his critical sense, is the superior poet. As Murray puts it:

> Despite the brevity of the statement and the complexity of the context in which it occurs, Aristotle is clearly contrasting two types of poet, the *manikos-ekstatikos*, that is the inspired poet (in the Platonic sense of the word) and the *euphuēs-euplastos*, one endowed by nature to be adaptable or versatile. This is the first explicit formulation in Greek literature of a distinction between inspiration and natural endowment (to call it 'genius' as many commentators do is probably stretching the term too much) as alternative sources of poetic activity.   (Murray, 1989: 19)

Aristotle was thus the first thinker to argue for an entirely natural origin for true literary genius, and hence, the first to argue that the ability to coin marvellous new metaphors was indeed a wholly natural ability.

Much of the work being done on metaphor in the latter half of the twentieth century is concerned with stressing the ubiquity of metaphor in conversation and in the print media, against earlier theorists (such as the Logical Positivists) who wished to deny the omnipresence of metaphor. This project is an important and necessary one. As I have shown above, it was foreshadowed in Aristotle's own assertion that everybody uses metaphors in conversation. However, researchers pursuing this project tend to downplay the aspect of creativity involved in the coinage of new metaphors by talented writers. For example, in the opening chapter of *The Poetics of Mind*, Gibbs (1994: 7) argues that "What poets primarily do, again, is not create new conceptualizations of experience but talk about the metaphorical entailments of ordinary conceptual mappings in new ways". About a poem by Emily Dickinson – 'I Taste a Liquor Never Brewed' – he says that:

> It is misleading to assert that a creative poet like Dickinson has actually created a new metaphorical mapping between dissimilar domains when she has only made manifest some of the possibilities about love that are suggested by the conceptual metaphor LOVE IS A NUTRIENT.
> (Gibbs, 1994: 7)

The implication of these claims is that authors such as Dickinson do not really coin new metaphors, but merely elaborate upon generic conceptual metaphors which are basic to entire cultures, or even to the human race (e.g. LOVE IS A NUTRIENT, or ANGER IS HEATED FLUID IN A CONTAINER). Such an implication is certainly interesting, and may perhaps be true in some form – Gibbs' work on the naturalistic origin of metaphors is among the most important and fruitful being done on metaphor creation at the moment.[7] This implication, however, does not alter the fact that writers such as Dickinson are indeed more creative in their use of language than the rest of us. Such writers have an ability to coin new metaphors that delight and educate their audiences which is *rare*, and which wins them recognition for having literary genius.

The lessons to be learned from a more detailed examination of Aristotle's writings on metaphor are many, but among the most important is that, while everyone uses and coins metaphors and thus is creative to some extent, it is still the case that some individuals are better at coining good ones than the rest of us, and thus may be said to possess genius, albeit a wholly natural genius. No-one, I think, could seriously dispute this; we *do* look upon those authors who are able to coin marvellous new metaphors as having the 'mark of genius', and we *do* consider their literary talent to be a natural talent.

The contemporary egalitarian project of establishing that we all use and coin metaphors notwithstanding, we may still look upon certain gifted wordsmiths as having a 'command of metaphor' without thereby relegating the rest of us to mere literal usage. The fear that we would be so relegated were we to admit a definition of literary genius along the lines of metaphor coinage is unwarranted, as Aristotle's writings amply demonstrate.

[7] For more on Gibbs' work, see my 1996 review of *The Poetics of Mind*.

5 Metaphor and discourse
Towards a linguistic checklist for metaphor analysis

Gerard Steen

Introduction[1]

Metaphor research is in need of a comprehensive approach to the language of metaphor in order to give full credit to its linguistic variability, if only so that we can get away from the stale format of *A is B* (Steen, 1994: 8–9, 243–244; *cf.* White, 1996; Goatly, 1997). The idea of a linguistic checklist for metaphor was prompted by the linguistic checklist for style presented by Leech and Short (1981; *cf.* Steen, 1997). My practical interest in such a checklist is its applicability in corpus research, which is where I would like to go next. For if one wants to discriminate between types of metaphor embodying specific configurations of metaphor features of all kinds, corpus research is crucial. Corpus work is also imperative if the object of investigation is the difference between literary and non-literary metaphor, such as I have attempted on a modest scale in my previous work (Steen, 1994). Moreover, corpus research can yield realistic materials for rating studies of metaphor, offering an opportunity to establish the desirable connection between analytic metaphor properties produced in linguistic research on the one hand, and informants' judgements of metaphor on the other. This link was left unexplored in my own work, but it is such an obvious and promising direction of research that it is surprising that it has not been followed more often. Such an approach will eventually also facilitate experimental research on metaphor processing in which metaphor properties can be much better controlled than they are today, or were in my "thinking out loud" studies, reported in Steen (1994).

But that is leaping ahead too far. Fundamental issues need to be resolved before any of this programme can be realised. In what follows, I will attempt to organise some of the issues in such a manner

[1] I wish to thank Lynne Cameron, Peter Crisp and Graham Low for their comments on an earlier version of this paper; all remaining inadequacies are my own.

that they can be coherently and consistently approached. The second section will provide the theoretical groundwork for dealing with some of the main problems in ordering the field, and explore one of the domains in a little more depth. The third section will then continue by presenting the actual checklist, which, it should be emphasised, is still under construction. The final section will provide some more meat to the checklist by demonstrating how it can be applied in analysing just a handful of metaphors from a lyric by Bob Dylan.

Theoretical groundwork

Implicit and explicit metaphor

Let me be frank from the beginning. To the functional linguist, who looks at language from the perspective of its use in spoken and written discourse, metaphor should be a matter of underlying propositions, not linguistic expressions. The assumption is inescapable once it is recognised that not all metaphors are expressed as clauses, phrases or words. In particular, there is a group of metaphors which do not observe clause boundaries and have to be recognised and comprehended by constructing inferences between clauses. As inferences are usually accounted for in terms of implied propositions which are additional to the explicit propositions directly derivable from the sentences of a text (e.g. Gernsbacher Ed., 1994; Weaver *et al.*, 1995), metaphor turns into a matter for propositional analysis.

Let me give an example to clarify what I mean:

(1) I walked to the place where the bird of prey hung ready over the crowd.

(1) is an edited version of a sentence from a narrative about the Amsterdam riot police who are fighting a group of demonstrators, while a police helicopter is making circles in the sky, watching the events on the ground. It is hence clear that the relative subclause of (1), **where the bird of prey hung ready over the crowd**, has a grammatical subject, **the bird of prey**, which is to be taken as a non-literal expression for 'the helicopter'. A propositional analysis of the text, creating a so-called "text base" in the form of a list of idea units or propositions (Van Dijk & Kintsch, 1983), would have to incorporate the following item:

(2) Pi (REF BIRD-OF-PREY HELICOPTER)

The predicate REF is a conventional, specially designed predicate to indicate co-reference between terms; it is predicated of the argument BIRD OF PREY, which is said to be co-referential with the previously used term HELICOPTER. I am using the 'i' as an *ad hoc* device to indicate that proposition (2) does not have a linguistic equivalent in the text itself, but is *im*plicit and derived by means of *in*ference. For further details about this particular method of propositional text analysis, see Bovair and Kieras (1985).

The point I am making is this: nowhere in the text do we find a linguistic expression to the effect that **the bird of prey is the helicopter**. Nor, indeed, do we find (3a):

(3a) The helicopter is a bird of prey.

which would be analysed as (3b):

(3b) P (MOD HELICOPTER BIRD-OF-PREY)

where the intensive relation between the HELICOPTER and the BIRD-OF-PREY signalled by the copula **is** is interpreted as one of semantic modification which requires further interpretation in subsequent rounds of conceptual analysis. Yet every analyst will probably agree that **the bird of prey** in (1) is used figuratively, and that a description of the implied metaphor would have to be based on (2). This is what I mean when I say that metaphors are best approached by the functional linguist as a particular class of propositions, rather than as a class of linguistic expressions of some sort.

Propositions consist of predicates applied to arguments or terms designating referents. They have a conceptual rather than a linguistic status. This suggests that we are talking about ideas, not meanings. Propositions can provide a way in to the knowledge structures of the reader about the relevant items in the mental encyclopaedia (*cf.* Aitchison, 1987). Propositions are hence a bridge between language and thought, forming the smallest idea units deriving from the mental decoding or analysis of linguistic expressions, and are capable of feeding into more complex and abstract conceptual structures. As mentioned above, they are located in what is called the "text base", which is one specific kind of mental representation of the text (Van Dijk & Kintsch, 1983; *cf.* Perfetti & Britt, 1995). In that form, propositions can provide a launchpad for the development of metaphorical thought. Once metaphors are considered in this manner, they lead us away from linguistic analysis to some form of conceptual analysis, as exemplified in the work of Miller (1993), Gentner (1983) and Lakoff (1993).

In a propositional analysis, the words of the text are taken as pointers to concepts, which are presumed to be activated and related according to the syntactic, semantic and pragmatic instructions for processing inherent in the consecutive sentences. Such language instructions are not complete and need to be enriched by pragmatic elaborations, as described by, for instance, Relevance Theory (Sperber & Wilson, 1986; Blakemore, 1991). This is also manifest in the fact that we have had to construct an inference for the comprehension of **the bird of prey** in (1); it is the pragmatic assumption that the text is coherent which guides the reader towards the most suitable candidate from the preceding text, or from the mental picture of the situation, for establishing a meaningful connection between an expression and its context. In this way, the referent of the inferred metaphorical proposition, HELICOPTER, becomes the lifeline of the non-literal predicate, BIRD-OF-PREY, which would otherwise receive an incorrect interpretation, say as a real bird, or no interpretation at all.

What I am capturing by this approach is a very simple fact. The figuratively used words in a metaphor are about something, but that something does not have to be expressed in the same clause; indeed, it may not even be expressed at all, as we have seen above. If the referent is not expressed in the same clause, we are dealing with what I will call 'implicit' metaphor; this makes (1) above an *implicit metaphor*. When the literal referent of a metaphor is expressed in the same clause, it is an *explicit metaphor*; this is the case for (3a).

For the implicit metaphor exemplified by (1), the reader has to establish some form of coherence between the two parts of the metaphor located in the two separate clauses, by means of discourse comprehension strategies and inferences. This is of the essence in discourse comprehension, in contrast to clause comprehension, which is based on strategies of parsing. The two kinds of strategies, and their resulting operations and processes, are only typically related to the two levels of text, for parsing is also affected by considerations of text, and inferencing also occurs within the clause. But one consequence of their relation is the fact that implicit metaphor involves an additional round of inferencing between clauses, or between clause and context (see below), in comparison with explicit metaphor. For an experimental study of related issues, see Gibbs (1990).

Three kinds of metaphor analysis in discourse

The apparently marginal case of implicit metaphor is not merely interesting for throwing light on an initial ordering of the field, sending the functional linguist interested in metaphor away from linguistic structure to a consideration of conceptual structure and function in discourse. It also has consequences for the theoretical conception of well-known notions, such as metaphor Topic and

Vehicle (Richards, 1936) and metaphor Focus and Frame (Black, 1979). Moreover, the presumed link with the function of metaphor in (written) discourse and reading helps to motivate a number of terminological decisions which could alleviate the lack of clarity that seems to persist in talk about metaphor. One object of a linguistic checklist is to standardise the terms we use for the wide range of variables that have been discerned in metaphor usage.

What we have concentrated on so far is usually called the Topic of the metaphor, the literal entity in the world of the text about which something is predicated in a figurative manner. This is best illustrated by returning to (3a), where **the helicopter** would be called the metaphor Topic by most analysts. The Vehicle applying to this Topic would be **a bird of prey**, and it is almost co-extensive with the non-literal predicate identified in (3b). In this usage, the Topic is a referent in the situation model, while the Vehicle expresses an attribute of the referent (see also Cameron, in Chapter 1).

However, the notion of *topic* can also be used in another sense than the referential one used above. Topics can also be what one talks about. As a result, topics are related to comments, which can be either literal or non-literal. This particular angle on the function of expressions in discourse is essentially communicative; it involves speakers having particular things in mind that they want to talk or write about to other speakers. This produces a view of metaphor as utterance (spoken or written), rather than as proposition, which involves idea units or thought. I see no reason why the view should not also be applied in metaphor analysis. (Note that I am using 'utterance' in the pragmatic sense here; it refers to the use of a linguistic expression with some propositional content to convey a message.)

The communicative angle on the functions of expressions in discourse, however, is not identical with the referential, conceptual one we have been developing in the above paragraphs. In the conceptual approach, there is another sense of 'aboutness'; metaphors are about, or have, referents, to which non-literal predicates are attached. In the communicative approach, metaphors are about, or have, topics which receive a non-literal comment. The important point about these two kinds of aboutness is that not all referents in a metaphorical proposition are Topics in a metaphorical utterance, even though the metaphor can be said to be 'about' all of the referents in the conceptual sense analysed by a propositional approach.

To illustrate this, we have to resort to another kind of example:

(4a) The river betrayed its proximity
(4b) P (BETRAY RIVER PROXIMITY)

There are two literal referents in (4b), **river** and **proximity**, 'about which' something is predicated in a non-literal, figurative manner, that there is a relation of betrayal between them. This is a conceptual view of metaphor. However, only one of these referents is the topic of the metaphor in the communicative view; **the river** is the topic of the metaphor 'about which' a comment is made in the rest of (4a), that it **betrays its proximity**. To avoid confusion between the two kinds of analysis, it is better to call metaphor referents just that, so that it is possible to add the communicative perspective without difficulty.

I suggest that we adopt a precise and consistent, linguistically motivated terminology and discard the traditional parlance for the moment, in order to discover what further questions are generated by this approach. The conceptual aspect of the Topic–Vehicle pair has been covered by mentioning *literal referents* and *non-literal predicates*. Thus it seems to make sense to say that the communicative side of the distinction can be covered by employing the distinction between *topic* and *comment*. Both linguistic pairs of notions capture different aspects of the Topic–Vehicle distinction, but together they seem to exhaust what Topic and Vehicle were originally designed to do. Their separate functions and linguistic background facilitates their easy alignment with other domains of linguistic metaphor analysis.

There is another set of terms which has to be related to this discussion, which will provide a third perspective on the analysis of metaphor in discourse. I am referring to Black's (1979) contrast between Focus and Frame, which I will now translate into a variant befitting a discourse approach to metaphor. The contrast between the notions of Focus and Frame is clearly semantic, with Focus referring to the odd term in a linguistic expression which draws the attention of the interpreter, while Frame designates the background against which the Focus can be seen to stand out. In other words, in (3a), **bird of prey** would be the Focus and **The helicopter is an X** the Frame; and in (4a), **betrayed** would be the Focus, while **The river X-ed its proximity** would be the Frame. In practice, the Frame is the next grammatical category up in the linguistic structure of the sentence; it is an incomplete clause in both (3) and (4), in which the Focus functions as an Immediate Constituent (IC) of the clause. All of this is standard, uncontroversial metaphor analysis (see for example Leech, 1969).

However, when we return to (1) (**I walked to the place where the bird of prey hung ready over the crowd**), there is an interesting complication. The metaphor Frame is the verbal context of the figuratively used words **the bird of prey**, i.e. (5):

(5) X hung ready over the crowd

But Frame (5) bears no relation to the metaphorical proposition underlying (1), represented as (2):

(2) Pi (REF BIRD-OF-PREY HELICOPTER)

This should be contrasted with the cases of (3) and (4). In (3a) and (4a), the main words of the Frame, **The helicopter is a X** and **The river X-ed its proximity**, are also the main elements of the metaphorical propositions (3b) and (4b): (MOD HELICOPTER BIRD-OF-PREY) and (BETRAY RIVER PROXIMITY). **Helicopter, river** and **proximity** are the literal referents. In (1), though, the main words of the Frame are not directly related to the metaphorical proposition (2), but form the basis of another, ensuing proposition in the textbase:

(6) P (HANG BIRD-OF-PREY)

The metaphor's Frame (5) contains no indication of the metaphor's referent, HELICOPTER, in (2). In other words, implicit metaphors cannot be described using a Focus–Frame approach of the kind specified in the above pages; what they need is a *referent–predicate* approach.

Of course one could attempt to rescue the Focus–Frame pair by extending the notion of 'Frame' beyond the clause to the level of the text. In other words, it might be argued that the previous sentences act as a Frame against which the designation of a literal referent, say **helicopter**, by means of a non-literal expression, say **bird of prey**, stands out. But that is precisely the point; this oddity can only be recognised by drawing inferences in order to produce a coherent text representation. If that happens, though, it becomes unwarranted to speak of a *semantic* tension between a Focus and a Frame, for it is the *pragmatic* goal of achieving a coherent discourse representation which produces the incongruent link between **bird of prey** and **helicopter**; semantically, there is nothing odd about a bird of prey hanging over a crowd. The above remarks may be briefly summarised in one schematic overview:

THREE KINDS OF METAPHOR ANALYSIS IN DISCOURSE

The river betrayed its proximity

Focus: **betrayed**   Frame: **the river X-ed its proximity**
literal referents: **river, proximity**   non-literal predicate: **betray**
topic: **the river**   comment: **betrayed its proximity**

The bird of prey hung ready over the crowd

Focus: **the bird of prey**	Frame: **X hung ready over the crowd**
literal referent: **helicopter**	non-literal predicate: ref **bird of prey**
topic: **helicopter**	comment: **be bird of prey**

I propose that metaphor analysis should not start with the linguistic analysis of sentences in terms of Focus and Frame, but with the conceptual analysis of propositions. Taking propositional analysis as the vantage point for metaphor analysis is the best strategy, I wish to argue, for revealing what is literal and what is non-literal in the stretch of discourse under investigation, as well as in the underlying metaphorical comparison. This starting point also allows for the subsequent analysis of the metaphorical proposition in terms of a topic–comment structure yielding an utterance; it enables the analyst to make a distinction between the two referents **river** and **proximity** in terms of discourse information status. This is a communicative analysis of metaphor as an utterance. The three kinds of analysis – linguistic, conceptual and communicative – correspond with three different kinds of mental representations of text which readers produce during the reading process (Steen, 1994). They can be usefully related to the distinction in Relevance Theory between *what is said*, *what is implicated* and *what is communicated*, although the match is not completely one-to-one.

Contextual implicit metaphor

The implicit metaphors so far discussed are *co-textual*, in the sense that there is an explicit literal referent, but it is located outside the clause concerned. However, there are also implicit metaphors which do not have a referent expressed anywhere in the text; I shall call these *contextual* metaphors. An example from my Dutch corpus of 164 literary and journalistic metaphors (Steen, 1994) is (7):

(7) An old acquaintance arrives on the scene, Mon.

The expression **the scene** is a non-literal expression for an aspect of the situation that the sentence refers to. The aspect can be inferred, but is not put into words in the text. Since every state of affairs presupposes the existence of a location where it is situated, there is no need for the explicit mention of the literal referent to which **the scene** is applied as a figurative predicate. However, from a conceptual point of view, the implicit metaphor in (7) has to be analysed as (8):

(8) Pi (REF SCENE LOCATION)

In other words, I do not take **the scene** as a non-literal predicate primarily relating to the grammatical subject and main referent of the sentence, **An old acquaintance**. Instead, it constitutes a figurative predicate about another referent, which has been left implicit in the text, but which is part and parcel of the situation and the mental model of the situation in the reader's mind.

The question arises whether such propositions should be part of a textbase. This depends on the function of the textbase; if it is seen as an analysis of one kind of mental representation by the reader of the text, which is how it was originally intended, the inclusion or exclusion of propositions like (8) becomes an empirical matter. It is well known that not all possible inferences related to the propositions of a text are actually constructed during comprehension (e.g. Singer, 1994), so that experimental research has to determine whether implicit metaphor construction of the contextual kind actually takes place. However, if one sees the textbase as an instrument for constructing a slightly more explicit version of the meaning of the discourse, then reconstructed implicit contextual metaphors have to be part of it, just as implicit co-textual metaphors are. In that case, it would be useful to have a look at other pragmatic or discourse representation theories, for example at Relevance Theory.

Most implicit contextual metaphors are quite trivial and familiar cases of metaphor with unexpressed referents. Other examples are (9) through (11):

(9) We want some quiet in our home.
(10) This lyric is the beginning of a series of portraits of the *Tusovka*, which, in the Soviet Union, means something like 'the scene' and 'the big mess'.
(11) On Thursday he gave the starting shot for a unique professional training at Utrecht.

Home in (9) is used about a football club, but it could be conventionally used with reference to any company, institution or organisation. **Portraits** in (10) is predicated of a television documentary, but it could also apply to written journalism. **Starting shot** is one word in Dutch and an ordinary term for any symbolic gesture setting off a particular activity. It is one's knowledge of the situation which grounds the analysis of some incongruence between the figurative expression and the implied referent; a football club is no home, a documentary is no portrait, and the minister did not fire a shot. These mismatches do not require a lot of inferencing on the part of the reader in order to work out the intended but implicit referent of the metaphor. They depend on prototypical aspects of situations, as in (7) and (9), or on colourful but familiar expressions for common entities and activities, as in (10) and (11).

If it seems elaborate to devote so many words to these simple cases, consider the following example, where the conceptual structure of the metaphor is similar to (7), but its referential anchorage more difficult to determine:

(12) I see the masked face of space, chiselled and motionless. Behind the mask and almost without noise somebody is sculpting away at the light, which is trembling here and there, exhibiting unnoticeably small cracks, fine like capillaries in the glazing.

Let us look at the entire second sentence. The gist is represented by the following proposition, which is highest in the list of propositions in the text base for the second sentence:

(13) P (SCULPT-AWAY-AT SOMEBODY LIGHT)

In order to reconstruct the complete underlying metaphorical mapping, one at least has to identify the referent for **somebody** on the basis of an unexpressed picture of the situation, the situation model. One has to find a referent in the situation model which does something to the light, as a sculptor sculpts away at stone. Structurally, this is similar to (7), where one also has to find a referent in the situation that has been left unexpressed. Conceptually, however, this is not as easy to do as in (7), and one wonders if it can be done reliably at all.

Summing up, contextual implicit metaphors comprise another class of implicit metaphors. They are characterised by the fact that no mention is made of the metaphor referent in any other part of the text at all. It has to be inferred from the context and not from the co-text, as was the case with (1). In cases like (7) and (9) through (11), there appears to be some mismatch between the literal meaning of the metaphor predicate on the one hand and what is available from the situation model on the other. This is either quite easy to solve, as in the bulk of implicit contextual metaphor, or it can become quite problematic, as in some literary discourse; there may hence be an interaction between the use of particular kinds of implicit contextual metaphor and types of discourse.

Conclusion to this section

One aim of this section has been to order the field for the linguistic analysis of metaphor in discourse. I have argued that it is useful to distinguish between *linguistic, conceptual* and *communicative* metaphor analysis, and that it is best to tackle conceptual metaphor analysis by means of constructing metaphorical propositions. These principles will be used to inform the linguistic checklist to be presented in the next section.

Another result of this section is that we can make the following classification. Metaphors can be implicit in one of two ways. In co-textual implicit metaphors the literal referent of the metaphor may be expressed in the text, but outside the clause containing the metaphor predicate, hence requiring an anaphoric inference to ensure referential and relational coherence between consecutive clauses. However, in contextual implicit metaphors, the referent of the metaphor may not be expressed at all and requires an inference which addresses one's knowledge of conventional language use and the world. Thus both forms of implicit metaphor depend on inferencing to construct the understood metaphorical referent and proposition, providing for a coherent role of the metaphor's predicate in a particular case.

Towards a metaphor checklist

What follows is a provisional linguistic checklist for metaphor analysis. It is primarily meant as a reference section. Readers preferring a less abstract method of presentation should continue with the section on Application, in which all of the variables distinguished here are checked off in the analysis of one particular metaphor.

The checklist

ORIENTATION

A. Conceptual Analysis
> What is the metaphorical proposition: literal referent(s) and non-literal predicate?

B. Linguistic Analysis
> What is the metaphorical expression: non-literal Focus and literal Frame?

C. Communicative Analysis
> What is the metaphorical utterance: literal topic and non-literal comment?

A Conceptual analysis[2]

1 NON-LITERAL PREDICATES

What is the non-literal predicate? Is it simple or complex? If complex, is it restricted to one clause or extended? If restricted, are the terms related at the same grammatical level or in a hierarchical relation? If hierarchical, what is the main word, syntactically and semantically? How many propositions can be derived from the supporting words? If hierarchical, is the domain of reference of the supporting words literal, metaphorical or ambivalent? If extended, does the metaphor extend beyond the clause or the sentence? How many additional metaphorical propositions, clauses and sentences are there?

2 LITERAL REFERENTS

What are the literal referents? Are they expressed or implicit? Are they in the same clause as the non-literal predicate, or somewhere else? If in the same clause, is the metaphor full or reduced? If somewhere else, is the referent preceding or following the non-literal predicate? If somewhere else, does the isolated non-literal predicate produce a second metaphor in the Frame proposition?

3 METAPHORICAL PROPOSITIONS

Does the proposition have a special predicate, such as REF, ISA, MOD and so on? If not, which transitivity type is the proposition: material, verbal, mental, relational or existential?[3] Are all normal participants expressed? Which semantic type is the proposition: abstraction or concretion, animation or personification?

4 METAPHORICAL COMPARISON[4]

What is the underlying comparison statement of the metaphor? What is the underlying analogy of the metaphor? What is the underlying mapping of the metaphor? What, if any, are the related conventional conceptual metaphors of the linguistic metaphor?

B Linguistic analysis[5]

1 FOCUS VOCABULARY

i   What is the word class of the Focus: nominal, verbal, adjectival,

---

[2] See Bovair and Kieras (1985) on the details of proposition analysis; and compare the other contributors to Britton and Black Eds. (1985) for alternative formats.

[3] Transitivity types are discussed by, for example, Halliday (1985).

[4] On comparison statement reconstruction, see Miller (1993); on analogy reconstruction, see Miller (1993) and Sternberg *et al.* (1979); on structure mapping, see Gentner (1982; 1983); on the study of conventional metaphor, see Lakoff (1993).

[5] On the background and further details of many of these terms, see Quirk *et al.* (1985); *cf.* their use in Leech and Short (1981).

adverbial or prepositional? What further subdivision can be made for the word class in question: is the noun count or uncount, and so on? Is the focal word a derivation or conversion of the non-literal predicate in the conceptual metaphor (see A4)?

ii What is the length of the Focus: number of letters, phonemes, morphemes? What is the morphological complexity of the Focus? What is the etymology of the Focus?

iii What can be said about the denotation of the Focus? And its connotation? And its frequency and/or distribution?

2 METAPHOR VOCABULARY

What is the currency of the expression of the metaphorical proposition: is it novel or attested in the dictionary? Does it recur in the corpus? What is the usage value of the expression: is it general, or does it belong to a register, a dialect or a historically older period of the language?

3 FOCUS GRAMMAR

What is the grammatical category of the Focus in the Frame: NP, VP, AdjP, AdvP or PrepP (for implicit, clause and phrase metaphor); N, V, Adj, Adv or Prep (for word metaphor)? What is the grammatical function of the Focus in the Frame: irregular sentence or IC (Subject, Predicate, Direct Object and so on) or constituent of IC (modifier, head, qualifier or complement) (for implicit metaphor); Subject, Predicate, Direct Object and so on (for clause metaphor); determinative, premodification, head, postmodification, complementation (for phrase metaphor);[6] 'Subject', 'Predicate', 'Direct Object' and so on (for word metaphor)?[7] What is the position of the Focus in the Frame: initial, medial or final (for all metaphor)?[8]

4 FRAME GRAMMAR

What is the grammatical category of the Frame: finite or non-finite clause (for implicit and clause metaphor); NP, VP, AdjP, AdvP or PrepP (for implicit, phrase and word metaphor)? What is the grammatical level of the Frame in the sentence: irregular sentence, (semi-independent) clause, IC, constituent of IC and so on (for all metaphor)? What is the grammatical function of the Frame in the sentence: simple, irregular or elliptical sentence; main or subclause (nominal, adverbial, relative); Subject, Predicate, Object and so on;

---

[6] Note that things are different for predicator analysis (but I doubt whether auxiliaries can be metaphorical) and prepositional phrases, for which I refer to Lindstromberg (1996).

[7] Compare Quirk *et al.* (1985: I.60 ff.).

[8] It is also possible to add the further distinction between preposed and postposed foci, or foci which have been extraposed out of the clause.

premodification, head, postmodification, complementation (for phrase metaphor)? What is the position of the Frame in the next category up: initial, medial or final? What is the position of the Frame in the sentence as a whole: initial, medial or final?

C Communicative analysis

1 PRAGMATIC FUNCTION

i   What is the topic of the metaphor? What is the comment? What is the discourse presentation of the topic: given or new? What is the discourse information status of the metaphor topic: given or new? If given, is it also clause, sentence, paragraph or discourse topic?

ii Which presuppositions can be derived from the metaphorical proposition (logical, existential)? Which entailments can be derived from the metaphorical proposition? Which implicatures can be derived from the metaphorical proposition? How many such derivable assumptions are related to the metaphor? Can they be ordered from relatively strong to relatively weak?

iii What is the point of the metaphor? Is it uplifting or degrading? Is it serious or humorous? Is it evaluative or descriptive?

2 RHETORICAL FORM

What is the tropical form of the metaphor: metaphor, simile or analogy? If simile, which signal of non-literal comparison is used (e.g. **as ... as; like; seem, appear, resemble** or **just as ... , ...**). If analogy, which structural formula is used: are three, four or more terms present? What is the order of the terms: A:B::C:D, A:C::B:D and so on? Is the Ground of the metaphor expressed or left implicit? If expressed, does the Ground precede or follow the metaphorical proposition?

3 RHETORICAL WEIGHT

Does the metaphor combine with another trope, such as metonymy, synecdoche, paradox, irony, litotes or hyperbole? Does the metaphor exhibit additional schemes: acoustic, prosodic, lexical or grammatical? What is the rhetorical nature of the additional scheme: repetition, reversal and so on?

4 TEXTUAL FUNCTION

i   What is the text-structural level, position and function of the metaphor? What is the text-generic level, position and function of the metaphor? What is the text-typological level, position and function of the metaphor?

ii Does the metaphor have a particular thematic significance? Are
    there any repetitions, echoes or allusions to the metaphor at
    earlier or later stages of the text? Does the metaphor have the
    function of motif?

Application

To illustrate how the checklist might reveal differences between
metaphors, I will examine a number of metaphors from a lyric by
Bob Dylan, 'Hurricane'. The song contains its own summary, or
Abstract in Labov's (1972) terms:

> Here comes the story of the Hurricane
> The man the authorities came to blame
> For something that he never done
> Put him in a prison cell
> but one time he coulda been the champion of the world   (I, 5–9)

The lyric is a narrative of how Rubin Carter, or the fighter Hurricane,
was falsely accused (framed) for a crime by the police and subsequently convicted in court to serve a prison sentence. The point that
Dylan wants to convey is expressed towards the end of the song, in
Labov's category of *Evaluation*:

> How can the life of such a man
> be in the palm of some fool's hand?
> To see him obviously framed
> Couldn't help but make me feel ashamed
> to live in a land where justice is a game   (X, 5–9)

Dylan's attitude to the story is spelled out in the Labovian *Coda* to
the song:

> Yes that's the story of the Hurricane
> But it won't be over till they clear his name
> And give him back the time he's done
> Put him in a prison cell
> but one time he coulda been the champion of the world   (XI, 5–9)

Let us now examine one of the metaphors in the song and see how it
can be described by using the checklist.

'Justice is a game'

The lines expressing the point of the story quoted above contain the
metaphor **justice is a game**. An orientational analysis yields the
following result:

justice is a game

   literal referent: **justice**   non-literal predicate: MOD **game**
   literal Frame: **justice is a X**   non-literal Focus: **game**
   literal topic: **justice**   non-literal comment: **is a game**

A conceptual analysis of this metaphor shows that the metaphorical proposition is (25):

(25) P (MOD JUSTICE GAME)

The non-literal predicate in this proposition is simple, in that no further content words are involved, either in or outside the clause. The literal referent is expressed, in the same clause as the non-literal predicate, and thus is explicit. Moreover, the metaphor is realised as a clause, making it a full metaphor.

The metaphorical proposition does have a special predicate, MOD, which in this case means that it is to be seen as a reduction of a number of interpretive possibilities for the linguistic expression is; it is taken as an *attributive predicate* (MOD), as opposed to a *classifying predicate* (ISA). Either way, the transitivity relation expressed in the proposition is relational, with both expected participants, carrier and attribute, present. The semantic type of the metaphorical proposition is that of abstraction, comparing one type of activity with another (**justice** being metonymic for **the application of justice**).

The underlying comparison statement would look like this:

(26) (MOD JUSTICE GAME)→(EF) (EG) {SIM [F(JUSTICE), G(GAME)]}

It would have to be read as follows: *there is some property of justice which is like some property of games.* The underlying analogy of the metaphor would probably be (27), explicating the presumed metonymic basis of the expressions:

(27) judge etc : apply : justice :: players : play : game

The underlying mapping of the metaphor could initially take the format proposed by Lakoff (1993):

THE JUSTICE-AS-A-GAME MAPPING
The lawsuit corresponds to the game.
The D.A. and the defendant's lawyer correspond to the competing parties.
The jury and the judge correspond to the referee.
The defendant corresponds to the object played with.
The verdict corresponds to the stakes.
The cross-examination, plea, summing up and pronouncement of the
   verdict correspond to different stages in the game.
The law corresponds to the rules of the game.
Jurisdiction corresponds to the tradition of the game.

This is just the beginning of a fuller structure-mapping analysis of the metaphor, but it may give some indication of the nodes that will be involved in the mapping. Regarding the question of conventional metaphor, many activities are metaphorically talked about as games, the best-known among linguists, of course, being LANGUAGE IS A GAME. However, there is also the conventional metaphor LIFE IS A GAMBLING GAME, discussed by Lakoff and Johnson (1980: 51). This would certainly be a basis for developing the view that 'justice is a game' is at least related to conventional conceptual metaphor, if it is not a specific instance of a classic case.

The linguistic analysis of **justice is a game** would proceed as follows. The word class of the Focus is nominal, **game** being a countable process noun. Its complexity is low and it is from Anglo-Saxon stock. This affects its connotation, turning it into an informal, 'homely' word. Another aspect of connotation to be mentioned is that games are usually positively valued, something which clearly does not apply in the present case, and which may lead to the perception of irony in the metaphor. The denotation of **game** has a number of related and obvious senses, one of which is the following: "a situation that you do not treat seriously" (Collins Cobuild English Dictionary, 1995: 596). It is a frequent word with no particular distribution.

The expression **justice is a game** does not occur as such in the dictionary; however, one example Cobuild lists for the figurative sense of game is **they think life is a game**. Thus the question arises whether this is a novel expression. It does not recur in the corpus and it is not a very special expression in terms of usage value.

Turning to the grammatical side of the checklist, the grammatical category of the Focus, **a game,** in the Frame, **where justice is X,** is NP. Its function is that of Subject Complement, and its position is clause-final; the metaphor Focus receives so-called end-focus, highlighting it as the climax of the metaphor. The grammatical category of the Frame is that of the clause, and its grammatical level in the sentence is low; it is a constituent of a constituent of a constituent of an IC, as is shown by the following schema (28):

(28) Subj(**To see him obviously framed**) Pred(**Couldn't help but make**)
Obj(**me feel** ObjCo(**ashamed** Co(**to live in a land** Mod(**where justice is a game**))))

Its grammatical position in the next category up (**a land** ...) is final, as is its position in the entire sentence. It is not just the Focus which receives end-focus within the metaphor, but it is also the metaphor which receives end-focus within the entire sentence. If the hierarchical position of the metaphor is low, it is balanced, if not offset, by its linear position in a prominent place, at the end of the linguistic expression.

The communicative analysis of the metaphor begins with a reconsideration of its internal structure. **Justice** being a general term, which is the superordinate of a number of hyponyms in the preceding text (**testify, crime, all-white jury, deed, D.A., witness, judge, trial**), it may be concluded that the absence of a definite pronoun does not indicate new status, but allows for given status as well. The discourse status of **justice** is in between given and new, in that it is recoverable from the context by means of a thematic inference. **Justice** also acts as the topic of the restrictive relative clause; but it has not been the discourse topic of the previous discourse, for that was Rubin Carter – see **him** at the beginning of (28).

As to the meaning relations that can be discerned in the metaphor, there is one (uninteresting) presupposition, that there is such a thing as justice. The entailments of the metaphor are that justice is there for fun, that it is based on wilful co-operation between participants, that there are winners and losers, that there are chances for winning and losing, and so on. Also important are its implicatures: if justice is a game, it is to be condemned, and its harmful effects should be revoked – reconsider the coda to the song, quoted above. This naturally leads on to the point of the metaphor, which is to protest against the deplorable state of American justice. It is clear that some of the above assumptions are more relevant than others, and that some sort of ranking can be made between them. Perhaps this would be as good as any definition of point; it is probably the most relevant assumption for the context of use. Other assumptions are less relevant, even if they are strong, such as the presupposition that there is such a thing as justice. Still other assumptions are very weak, but may have an effect, such as the one that justice is there for fun. This could explain why the metaphor is, in a sense, degrading, since it lowers the status of an honourable institution to that of an unimportant activity. The metaphor certainly is serious and evaluative.

The rhetorical form of the metaphor is that of a straightforward metaphor, in the stereotypical formula of *A is B*. The Ground of the metaphor is not made explicit, even though interpretive clues are present in the context; both **fool** and **framed** are indications that justice is compared with games because they are not serious.

The rhetorical weight of the metaphor is considerable; I have pointed out that there is a combination with metonymy (see 16 above) and potentially with irony (see the lexical analysis of the Focus regarding connotation). There is also the rhythm of the full subclause, which is a completely regular repetition of off-beats and beats alternating between syllables. The line ends in a beat on **game,** the Focus of the metaphor, which is drawn out in the actual performance of the song to an emphatic, typically Dylanesque **gaaaaame.**

Finally, there is the textual function of the metaphor. A Rhetorical Structure Theory (RST) approach, such as advocated by Mann and Thompson (1988), to the structure of the text would show that the clause does not figure as an independent element, but is part of the last unit of this section of the text. The metaphor does not have a direct function in the text structure, but only as a constituent at a lower level of more encompassing text structures.

The generic and typological analyses of the text can be dealt with together. The protest song does not constitute a genre with a well-defined structural format, while the 'narrative' text-type allows for various alternative formats with diverging applicability. The present story seems to be very close to the oral narrative as analysed by Labov (1972), and that approach yields the following results for our metaphor. The metaphor is the last remark in the Evaluation section of the story, which is constituted by the complete second half of stanza X. It comes right after the first part of the Resolution, which is the first half of stanza X. In other words, the metaphor is part of the climax of the story. This takes care of the position and function of the metaphor, *level* not being a category that can be applied well in the Labovian framework. It might be suggested that an overall RST analysis of the story would position the evaluation at a particular level in the structure of the story, so that we would achieve a view of the level of the metaphor after all. But this would lead us beyond the scope of the present paper.

The last subsection on the checklist raises the question of the metaphor's thematic significance. It seems that the metaphor sums up at least part of the main point of the protest song, and thus it is not unreasonable to describe it as having clear thematic significance. The question about repetitions, echoes or allusions can now be answered affirmatively by turning to a related metaphor.

Comparison with *the robbery game*

The analysis of **justice is a game** can be usefully compared with another metaphor using **game** as Focus: **robbery game** in stanza VI:

> Four months later, the ghettoes are in flame
> Rubin's in South America, fighting for his name

> While Arthur Dexter Bradley's still in **the robbery game**
> And the cops are putting the screws to him, looking for
> somebody to blame   (VI, 1–4)

The situation is that Rubin Carter has not yet been accused of the armed robbery in which three men were killed, because one of the victims denied that Rubin was the killer just before he died. Therefore the police are approaching one of the two real suspects, Arthur Dexter Bradley, who was present at the scene of the crime, but claimed that he **was only robbing the register, I hope you understand** (I, 4). He is now portrayed as still being **in the robbery game**.

Conceptual analysis of **the robbery game** produces the following underlying metaphorical proposition:

(29) P (MOD GAME ROBBERY)

When we have to answer the question what is the non-literal predicate, a problem arises, for we need to construct a new proposition to be able to see clearly:

(30) Pi (MOD ROBBERY GAME)

Conceptually speaking, it is MOD GAME which constitutes the non-literal predicate, with ROBBERY being the literal referent, and not the other way around. The reversal in the linguistic expression is caused by the reduction of the metaphorical proposition to an NP. The grammatical head of the linguistic expression is not the literal referent, **robbery**, about which something is said by a predicate in a non-literal manner, but it is **game**, the main word of the non-literal predicate, which is grammatically modified by the literal referent, **robbery**. Propositional analysis thus seems to capture the syntactic rather than the semantic structure of reduced metaphors, which causes problems if propositions are seen as conceptual representations of the underlying idea of the metaphorical expression. This point needs to be addressed in future work. However one wishes to deal with it, one difference between **the robbery game** and **justice is a game** is clearly signalled by this kind of analysis.

Turning to the underlying conceptual structure, the comparison statement deriving from the proposition is (31):

(31) (MOD ROBBERY GAME) → (EF) (EG) {SIM [F(ROBBERY),
      G(GAME)]}

It would have to be read as follows: *there is some property of robbery which is like some property of games.* This is similar to the previous comparison statement with **game** (26).

The analogy can be reconstructed as (32):

(32) thieves : rob : $ :: players : play : $

where the '$' acts as a conventional dummy symbol indicating expected but unspecified arguments. In comparison with **justice is a game**, there is a neglect of the role of the Object or Affected in this analogy; one participant in this material process is deemed less important to the comparison (although it is presupposed in its structure). The underlying mapping of **the robbery game** can be usefully compared with that of **justice is a game**:

THE ROBBERY-AS-A-GAME MAPPING
The robbery corresponds to the game.
The robbers and the robbed correspond to the competing parties.
The ??? corresponds to the referee.
The property corresponds to the object played with.
The value of the property corresponds to the stakes.
The breaking-in, actual stealing, and run correspond to different stages in the game.
The ??? corresponds to the rules of the game.
Crime corresponds to the tradition of the game.

Evident but transparent differences in the listing are the lack of a referee and rules of the game in the case of robbery. The relation of **the robbery game** to conventional metaphor would be dealt with in the same manner as **justice is a game**.

The linguistic analysis of **the robbery game** begins to differ from the one of **justice is a game** in the area of Focus connotation; different connotations are relevant here, because robbery is not a positively valued institution, as justice is. Hence **game** does not involve 'not serious' in the same way. Compare another non-literal sense that is listed by Cobuild: "a way of behaving in which a person uses a particular plan, especially in order to gain an advantage", illustrated by **these games that politicians play**, and, notably, **the power game**.

More obviously different is the grammatical function of the Focus in the Frame; it is a complement of the preposition **in** in the PrepP **in the robbery game**. It is also Frame-final, just like **justice is a game**. The grammatical category of the Frame itself is PP, its level being low, as it is an IC of a subordinate clause. Its function is that of obligatory Adverbial Adjunct in the subclause of time. The position of the Frame in the next category up, the subclause as a whole, is final; however, the position of the Frame in the sentence is medial, as the sentence continues with another (co-ordinate) sub-clause after the one containing the Frame. This aspect could potentially make **the robbery game** metaphor less prominent than the **justice is a game** metaphor.

From a communicative point of view, there are some problems with maintaining that there is a topic–comment structure in **the robbery game**. First of all, topics and comments are usually assigned at the level of the clause, so that we need to be clear about the extension of this usage to phrases and words (*cf.* Quirk *et al.*, 1985: 1361). And secondly, if we do go on to apply this kind of analysis at the level of phrases and words, there is the same problem as the one we had above when attempting to analyse the phrase as a proposition; the syntactic structure of the phrase would lead to saying that **game** is the topic and **robbery** is the comment, while the semantic structure would favour the opposite and pragmatically more desirable solution. These are thorny issues which are merely raised for future consideration and are not gone into any further here.

Note that although the entire metaphor is presented as given, *the robbery game*, it is **the game** which is given, not **robbery**. The situation is the other way around when we consider the discourse status, rather than the discourse presentation, of the metaphor topic; in this case it is not **the game**, but **the robbery**, which is given. Finally, neither **game** nor **robbery** is a clause, sentence or discourse topic.

Related observations can be made with reference to presuppositions: **the robbery game** presupposes that there is a game. Compare the entailment that can be derived from the entire clause: if Arthur Dexter Bradley is in the robbery game, then he is in a game. An entailment of the metaphor itself would be that robbery is for fun. One possible implicature of the metaphor would be the following: If robbery is a game, then it is not recognised by robbers that they are committing a crime, which makes their activity all the more objectionable and possibly dangerous. Thus the point of the metaphor could be that, if robbery is a game, then it is not recognised for what it is, so it should be dealt with all the more carefully. It is not clear whether this metaphor should hence be classified as 'uplifting' (Steen, 1994), as it makes a favourable comparison between an illegal practice and something that is there for fun. Nor is it clear whether the metaphor should be taken as serious or humorous. Perhaps these questions can be resolved by looking at the question of description versus evaluation; it may be suggested that the metaphor is descriptive, if considered from the point of view of the criminals.

At first sight, **the robbery game** does not seem to carry as much rhetorical weight as **justice is a game**. It is metonymic, as was pointed out above, but it is not ironic. However, it could be argued to be sarcastic, if one thinks of the possibly descriptive perspective embodied in the expression; if robbery is described as a game by criminals, this description is only 'borrowed' by Bob Dylan in order to suggest its perverted value. From the rest of the song, it is clear that Dylan himself does *not* think of robbery as a game, making the expression **robbery game** best seen as a sarcastic phrase. In that case, the rhetorical weight would only differ from **justice is a game** regarding the lack of any additional schemes. The fact that the clause metaphor seems much more weighty than the phrase metaphor cannot be explained merely by this difference in rhetorical weight; it is also to be accounted for by the grammatical analysis above and its textual function to be discussed presently.

The textual function of the metaphor is comparable to **justice is a game**; it is not an independent unit in RST, either. The fact that it is even more embedded than that clause is significant, but it is accounted for by the grammatical analysis above. The generic and typological analysis of **the robbery game** place it at the beginning of the Complication, but in a much less conspicuous position and with a much less prominent function than **justice is a game** has in the evaluation.

Finally, there is the thematic aspect of **the robbery game**. Game is used in a different context than with 'justice', with a different but related point. This makes it unclear whether **the robbery game** reinforces and supports **justice is a game**, or whether it undermines it, producing a degree of confusion about the latter's point. If **the robbery game** is just easy street-talk, what does that do to **justice is a game**? Or can the two uses also be seen as a sheer textual matter, related metaphors from one semantic field producing a form of cohesion rather than coherence? These are questions which have to remain undecided for now.

Conclusion

Applying the checklist to the analysis of two related metaphors has shown that it can be used as an instrument for the systematic investigation of resemblances and differences between metaphors. Many of the comparisons can probably be made reliably and coded for quantitative analysis of large samples of metaphors. However, there are also variables which require forms of analysis that cannot be formalised as easily, such as the reconstruction of the underlying analogy and mapping. Moreover, reference to such things as conventional conceptual metaphor is to some extent dependent on the state of metaphor research itself. But even here, the checklist can act as a pointer to areas of interest, both in terms of applied metaphor analysis, as well as regarding more fundamental theoretical and methodological research. All in all, I hope that the checklist may function both as a practical tool and as a covert programme for research on the language of metaphor, so that its full linguistic variability may become more clearly visible than it is today.

6 Identifying and describing metaphor in spoken discourse data

Lynne Cameron

What does it mean to know what a game is? What does it mean, to know it and not be able to say it? Is this knowledge somehow equivalent to an unformulated definition? So that if it were formulated, I should be able to recognize it as the expression of my knowledge? Isn't my knowledge, my concept of a game, completely expressed in the explanations that I could give? That is, in my describing examples of various kinds of game; showing how all sorts of other games can be constructed on the analogy of these; saying that I should scarcely include this or this among games; and so on.

(Wittgenstein, 1953: 1–75)

Applying metaphor: issues raised by a 'prosaic' approach

Applied metaphor studies cannot avoid the issue of rigorous identification of metaphorical, in contrast to non-metaphorical, language. Identification through defining, by setting up necessary and sufficient conditions for metaphoricity, produces apparently insuperable problems; identification through knowing and describing, in the manner Wittgenstein suggests, would seem a more promising approach. This chapter describes how, for the purposes of a specific applied research study, the unit of analysis 'metaphor' was established. It argues that metaphoricity can only in practice be identified relative to particular socio-cultural groups and discourse contexts. Rather than trying to find necessary and sufficient conditions for categorising metaphor, identification began by comparing possible metaphors with non-controversial, or typical, instances. Boundary criteria were then used to limit the category by excluding doubtful cases of metaphor. A set of graded descriptors was developed for metaphors through a process of interaction between theory and data.

The need for an operational identification procedure for metaphor arose in my study of metaphor in educational discourse, which aimed to investigate children's productive and receptive experience of metaphorical language. I needed to identify and describe all instances of metaphor in a corpus of spoken classroom interaction, taking into account the point of view of an individual (10-year-old) child within the classroom. The category 'metaphor' was not to be restricted to the highly novel or poetic, but to be open also to prose – after Bakhtin, to "the everyday, the ordinary, the 'prosaic'" (Morson & Emerson, 1990: 15).[1]

The usual initial step of a researcher, of going to the relevant published literature in the field, in order to find established or adaptable definitions, revealed immediate problems. Many of the definitions on offer were based on, or validated through, decontextualised and constructed examples, often restricted in length to sentence-level or below. The definitions were often unsatisfactory too in their completeness, and thus in their operationalisability. The problems inherent in establishing bounded and discrete conditions for metaphoricity, while not dissuading numerous subsequent attempts at solutions, were in fact noted nearly twenty years ago:

> There is an important mistake of method in seeking an infallible mark of the presence of metaphors. Every criterion for a metaphor's presence, however plausible, is defeasible in special circumstances.   (Black, 1979: 36)

> Black, then, seems to be saying that there are no necessary and sufficient conditions for something to be a metaphor, just as Wittgenstein (1953) had argued that there are no such conditions for something to be a game. Perhaps metaphors, too, are related by family resemblances, as Wittgenstein claimed games were.   (Ortony Ed., 1979: 5)

In this respect, the metaphor issue resembles other language categorisation problems:

> Gradation is a fact of language, and in seeking discrete classes we are in danger of misrepresenting the nature of the native speaker's knowledge.
> (Pawley & Syder, 1983: 212)

A prosaic approach to researching metaphor in discourse, however, requires that the identification and classification questions are not put to one side as insoluble, but are tackled head on. Categories of analysis determine what, from all that is observed in the discourse context, is to be accounted for. In this case, they emerged from interaction between the published literature on metaphor and the

---

[1] The term "prosaics" was coined by Morson and Emerson to describe a notion that was a central concern of Bakhtin's work, although not specifically labelled by him as such.

> Prosaics encompasses two related, but distinct, concepts. First, as opposed to "poetics", prosaics designates a theory of literature that privileges prose in general and the novel in particular over the poetic genres. Prosaics in the second sense is far broader than theory of literature: it is a form of thinking that presumes the importance of the everyday, the ordinary, the 'prosaic'. (Morson & Emerson, 1990: 15)

research purposes of the study, an interaction which produced two particular sets of problems that are dealt with in this chapter:

1 *The problem of conflating different types of metaphor analysis.*
2 *The problem of differential metaphoricity* – some metaphors are more metaphorical than others.

Clarification of the precise nature of each of these problems will reveal implicit assumptions underlying some definitions or descriptions of metaphors common in the literature. Once Problem 1 is dealt with and types of analysis are clearly separated, necessary conditions for metaphoricity, and thus preliminary identification procedures, are set up. The gradedness of metaphor can be described through a set of descriptors that serve the particular research aims. I will thus argue that Black was perhaps wrong to suggest that seeking definitional criteria is *per se* a mistake, and that the way forward lies precisely within the "special circumstances" that form the context of investigation in a given research study. By confronting the complexity and creativity of metaphorical language in everyday, contextualised talk and text, a prosaic approach to metaphor in discourse can be provided with the analytic tools of identification procedures and descriptive categories.

The chapter begins by returning briefly to the "levels of analysis and representation" discussed in Chapter 1, in order to help clarify the distinction between metaphors that depend for their identification and description on empirical evidence, and metaphors that can be defined at "theory level". After consideration of the nature of empirical evidence of metaphor, I then explore how, at the theory level, the particular demands of the discourse context of a research study can constrain identificational criteria, and how a researcher can set up category boundaries for metaphor through explicit decision-making. The chapter then moves to illustrate the construction of a set of features of typical metaphors, and a set of graded descriptors of metaphor, which were used in the analysis of discourse data.

Levels of analysis of metaphor as a mental phenomenon

The identification question can be formulated as: *Is X a metaphor?*, where X is a stretch of language in a particular discourse context. An answer to this question might require, as an initial (and roughly stated) necessary condition (following Kittay, 1987) that a metaphor include at least one lexical item (the Vehicle term) referring to an entity, idea, action etc. (the Topic), and that the Vehicle term belongs to a very different, or incongruous, domain from the Topic. However, as soon as we take a real stretch of language, such as **I can read your lips** (Author's data), it is clear that it is possible to disagree in at least two quite different ways about metaphoricity, by appealing to different ways in which a domain incongruity can be said to exist. Firstly, it can be argued that, although **lips** and 'printed symbols' may, in some theoretical way, belong to distinct domains, these domains were not, on the particular occasion being considered, individually activated and processed. Secondly, disregarding what may have happened in a speaker's or listener's mind on a particular occasion, it can be argued either that the expression *is* a metaphor, because an individual claims to always think of 'reading' as involving printed symbols that belong in a very different domain from **lips**, or, conversely that the expression is *not* a metaphor because it reflects a conventionalised way of describing the process.

The first disagreement around the identification question confounds two levels of analysis – the processing level and a more abstract and general, 'theory' level – while the second disagreement reflects a lack of a distinction *within* the theory level, between the individual and some norm of language use. As argued in Chapter 1, the level at which questions are asked determines the nature of the evidence required to generate answers or hypotheses, and the data that will count as such evidence. It is thus important to clarify the levels of analysis appropriate for the study of metaphor, and to maintain clarity in this respect at all stages. In Chapter 1, I separated the theory and processing levels of analysis, following Marr (1982), and it was noted that, in general,

- at the theory level, theoretical frameworks should be fine-grained enough to fit the research demands;
- operationalisation requires congruence between levels;
- discourse context needs to be taken account of within each level.

The first type of disagreement about metaphoricity can then be formalised by establishing a distinction between two kinds of prosaic metaphor, at different levels of analysis, and that will require different identification procedures:

Process metaphors: identified through work within the processing level, as processed metaphorically by a discourse participant on a particular occasion;

Linguistic metaphors: identified through work within the theory level, as stretches of language having metaphoric potential.

The use of the term *linguistic metaphor* follows Steen (1994), although it is not restricted here to manifestations in language of conceptual metaphor, as it is by Lakoff and Johnson (1980). I now proceed to discuss the identification of, firstly, process metaphors, and, secondly, linguistic metaphors.

Identifying 'process' metaphors

The category of process metaphor contains those instances of language processed analogically across distinct domains, also labelled "psychological metaphors" (Steen, 1992) and "novel metaphors" (Pollio & Pickens, 1980). It will contain linguistic metaphors which have not only been identified as having *potential* for metaphorical processing, but which have actually *realised* this potential, by being interpreted, in real-time, through an active process of analogical reasoning across two distinct concept domains. However, the category of 'process metaphor' is more than simply a subset of linguistic metaphors, and will include instances of language that might be judged non-metaphorical by an analyst working at level 1, but which are in fact, for some individuals, processed metaphorically. An example from my own data would be **spell**, in the weather forecaster's **hot spells**, which was interpreted by a child as connected to the domain of 'witches'.

Necessary conditions for process metaphors might be formulated as follows:

A stretch of language in its discourse context is said to be a **process** **metaphor** *if a discourse participant perceives an incongruity between two domains referring to the same topic and, in processing, resolves the perceived conceptual incongruity, so that some meaning is transferred across domains.*

The identification of 'process metaphor' is clearly an empirical matter, and a very different operation from the identification of linguistic metaphor. The category is constructed anew for each individual during each discourse event,[2] and there is a major problem in finding observable behaviours from which metaphorical processing can be reliably inferred (see, for example, Steen, 1994, on the use of Think-Aloud techniques). In my study, I claim some evidence for process metaphor from Think-Aloud protocol analysis and from

[2] The term *discourse event* is used, partly to parallel Hymes' speech event as "activities, or aspects of activities, that are directly governed by rules or norms of the use of speech" (Hymes, 1972: 56), but also to signal the inclusion of norms of behaviour and interaction, and of written language as well as spoken. Examples of discourse events in a school context would include "News Time", "school assembly", and specific subject-based activities such as "writing", as in "on Mondays we do writing".

explicit discussion of metaphoricity by participants.[3] In Extract 1 below, a group of five pupils talk with the researcher (R) about 'metaphors' they have collected over the week. They explicitly identify and elaborate the incongruity between **traffic** and **jam** (as made from fruit), thus providing some evidence that **traffic jam** might be processed as a metaphor.

EXTRACT I EXPLICIT DISCUSSION OF
METAPHORICITY OF TRAFFIC JAM

Pupils – P1, P2, . . . P5; P = unidentified pupil; R = researcher

    1 P1: traffic jam
       P2: traffic jam?
       P3: it sounds more like you're eating the traffic out of a jam pot
       P: yea

       . . .

    5 R: . . . why (.) why is (.) could traffic jam be a metaphor?
       P: it's
       P4: traffic all getting in a jam
       P: in a jam
       P: really a jam pot
   10 R: it's not really jam
       P2: it's all jammed up together (.) like in a jam pot
       R: ⌊ so why would it (.) why would it be
          like a jam then?
       P: because it's (.) all squashed up
   15 P3: jam's all squashed up (.) all crammed up
       P2: it's all crammed up to a space
       P: it would be though (.) cos it's so hot (.) you'd get sticky
                                                              laughter

In Extract 2, two pupils are reading aloud a text on how the heart works, and thinking aloud about each sentence. When they encounter a problem with an unknown concept, **muscular walls**, they seem to deal with it by attempting a metaphorical interpretation of **walls**, identifying an incongruity between the soft heart and the rigidity of walls (line 14), and trying to resolve the incongruity through interpreting **walls** as a Vehicle term for **ribs** (line 16). Although they then

---

[3] There is not space in this paper to discuss the methodology and limitations of Think-Aloud research (see e.g. Ericsson & Simon, 1984; Ericsson, 1988). In my study, sentence-by-sentence concurrent reporting carried out jointly by two pupils is used to gain insights into the interactional construction of joint understanding, and the research methodology is claimed to reflect many aspects of normal classroom interaction.

go on to dismiss this interpretation of **walls** (line 19), the Think-Aloud protocol does, I suggest, provide some evidence that "muscular walls" is a process metaphor. It further demonstrates that readers may try metaphoric processing as one strategy for dealing with interpretation problems.

EXTRACT 2 THINK-ALOUD PROCESSING OF MUSCULAR WALLS

Louise (L) and Ellen (E) engaged in a Think-Aloud task, reading sentence by sentence *The Heart*:

"It has four chambers with muscular walls."

 1 L: (*reads*) it has four chambers with (*v. quietly*) muscular walls
      (1.0) muscular walls
   E: (*whispers*)
   R: what's what?
 5 E: what has four chambers? (*laugh*)
   L: it's not telling you what has four chambers and
   R: well read the sentence before again and see if that helps
   E: (*reads previous sentence*) at the centre of this system is your
      heart (.) it has four chambers (.) oh th (.) does that mean
10   the *heart* has four
   L: muscular walls
   E: oh the heart has four chambers with muscular walls (.) to
      protect it probably
   L: muscular walls (.) walls is (.) quite a strange word to use for
15   your body (.)
   E: could be your ribs (*laugh*)
   R: mmm
   L: cos your ribs (.) protect your
   E: ⌊ your ribs aren't like a wall though
20 L: yea
   R: what's a chamber?
   L: it's like (.) it sounds like a dungeon
   E: I always think of a
   L: things are stored
25 E: I always think of like a big (.) sort of (.) chamber y (.) ri (.)
      like Louise ca
   R: like what?
   E: like Louise um thinks of it
   R: like a dungeon?
30 E: yea (.) sort of sounds (.) like it

R: so what's muscular mean? (2.0)
L: sounds as though it's like all your (.) muscles and
E: ⌈ strong
L: things put together (.) it's a very strong wall

While heeding Gibbs' warning (in Chapter 2) that different processes are involved at different temporal points and that care must be taken in making inferences about on-line processing from *post-hoc* explication, as in Extract 1, or from Think–Aloud evidence, as in Extract 2, these examples do suggest that it *is* possible to find evidence of process metaphor by employing suitable research methodology.

Identifying linguistic metaphor

I now consider alternative ways of identifying linguistic metaphor theoretically (i.e. at level 1): firstly, by moving, via generalisation and abstraction, from processing level 2 evidence to level 1, and secondly, through operations internal to level 1.

Definitions at level 1 derived from level 2

Metaphoricity at the theory level 1 can be established through a process of generalisation from multiple instances at the processing level 2, revealed through introspection, tests of recognition, paraphrasing or other experimental methodology (see e.g. Pollio & Smith, 1980). The category of metaphors thus identified are averaged across the population sampled at level 2, whether that be a speech community or some subset. When people argue over the metaphoricity of a particular stretch of language, such as **I can read your lips**, by appealing to their own introspected processing, they can be seen as questioning the validity of inferring individual behaviour from a generalisation. Barsalou warns of the potential dangers of assuming too much of such "analytic fictions" at the theoretical level; he writes about similar work in cognitive psychology:

Instead of being actual representations that people sometimes use in a particular context, these theoretical constructs are averages or ideals of representations abstracted across a wide variety of people and contexts.

(Barsalou, 1989: 86)

It is important to remember then, in analogy with this point, that the category of theoretically identified metaphors does not consist of actually occurring metaphors, but rather, of abstracted "averages or ideals" of metaphors. They are abstracted and generalised, and thus defined, *relative to particular groups and types of discourse context*, which may not always be explicitly acknowledged. Without knowing specific details of the sample, we cannot know how widely the level 1 theory can be applied to other groups or individuals. Problems of validity may arise if the theoretical constructs used in a research study are derived relative to very different groups and/or discourse contexts. The more individuals differ from the norm used at level 1, the greater the potential problems for researcher and analyst. So when we try to study metaphor in the language of children, whose partial world knowledge inevitably means that individual mental conceptualisations will often deviate from assumed adult norms (Vosniadou, 1989), we would ideally want to build up theoretical constructs to identify metaphor by abstraction and generalisation from level 2 processing evidence related to children. Keil (1979; 1983) tries to do exactly this, predicting development in metaphor comprehension from empirical evidence concerning children's acquisition of domain boundaries. Most other child studies of which I am aware do not make such a distinction, and relate children's use and comprehension of metaphor to adult norms.

Internally derived definitions at level 1

Some theorists appear to be working within level 1 when they derive their definitions of metaphor. However, on closer scrutiny, decisions are again being made according to unstated norms, which may lead to problems if adopted by researchers working outside those norms. An example can be found in Black's 1979 paper, in which he progressively restricts his concerns to the sub-category of metaphors described as both "active" and "strong". "Active" metaphors are contrasted by Black with those that are extinct (i.e. where the original meaning was different from the current meaning and is now lost), or dormant (i.e. where the original meaning is not active, but could be activated). Active metaphors are those "that are, and are perceived to be, actively metaphoric"; they are "recognized by speaker and hearer as authentically 'vital'" (Black 1979: 26). Although Black's criteria for identifying active metaphors appear to be level 2 processing criteria, no conditions for deciding how to operationalise recognition procedures are suggested; instead, what is and is not vital appears to be judged by the implicit native-speaker norms of the analyst. Black hints at the use being made of such norms when he claims of the example **falling in love**, that the expression would not seriously be taken as metaphorical by a "competent reader". He further confounds etymology with synchronic norms at this point, by adding that: "it is doubtful whether that expression was ever more than a case of catachresis" (1979: 26). Thus, Black, as "competent reader" as well as writer, appears to identify a group of examples as 'metaphors' according to his own, unstated, etymologically-informed, highly-educated, native-speaker norms. The use of such normed criteria for identifying metaphor in educational discourse would, apart from omitting many prosaic metaphors, limit the research to the investigation of children's experience of language that is metaphorical for educated, adult males. It would *not* allow the investigation of all the language that might in fact be processed metaphorically by children.

With both explicitly and implicitly normed definitions, the analyst must beware of assumptions about how individuals relate to norms. At the very least, those assumptions need to be explicit; they should ideally also be tested out empirically. In work with children, the assumption that individual knowledge corresponds to adult norms is unacceptable, unless empirically validated. Indeed, much that is of interest and importance in child metaphor studies derives from the differences evidenced between individuals and adult norms.

Choice of criteria for the identification of linguistic metaphor

There is then a clear need for studies of children's (and other non-standard) language to decide and state explicitly whether their definitions and descriptions of metaphor adopt adult norms, create age-related norms (and the risk of disorder and lack of cross-study comparability that might ensue), or deal in some other way with the idiosyncrasies of children's use. There are (at least) four sets of criteria by which 'domain incongruity', and hence metaphoricity, can be identified, and the nature of the discourse context being researched will motivate a choice between these different sets of criteria.

A stretch of language can be identified as metaphorical –

1   *on etymological criteria*, e.g. **salary** can be said to be metaphorical because it originally referred to salt given to Roman soldiers.
    (i.e. metaphoricity is a matter of history)
2   *relative to speech community norms*, e.g. **hot spells** is not a metaphor because that is how the concept is normally encoded, with no incongruity apparent to producers or receivers.
    (i.e. metaphoricity is a matter of convention and probability)
3   *relative to individual background knowledge*, e.g. **hot spells** is a metaphor because a particular child links it to **witches**.
    (i.e. metaphoricity is a matter of individuality and experience)

In addition, at level 2, processing evidence would allow identification of metaphorical language,

4. *relative to what is activated by an individual on a particular occasion*, e.g. **I can read your lips** may or may not be a metaphor depending on the activation of **read** as symbolic and thus incongruous with **lips**.
   (i.e. metaphoricity is a matter of activation during processing)

When theorists use decontextualised, constructed or selected non-controversial exemplars of metaphors, individual knowledge and processing (as in 3 and 4) is assumed to be representative of shared norms (as in 1 and 2). In theories of metaphor such as Black's, and often in empirical studies based on them, statements that appear to be linked to 3 or 4 are often based on criteria 1 and 2.

The aims and methodology of a research study can motivate the selection of identification criteria. A researcher who wishes to construct examples of metaphor and non-metaphor in order to test subjects' competence with metaphorical language in some way, can work with non-controversial central examples (for which 2 and 3, and possibly 1, coincide), discarding borderline cases at the piloting stage, and only general criteria, related to etymology or community norms, are needed to classify sample stretches of language as metaphorical. On the other hand, researchers who wish to identify metaphors in text or talk must work with more precise criteria, both for what counts as metaphor, and for what does not count as metaphorical, facing up to the problems of borderline cases ex-plicitly. Not to do so would risk losing potential candidates for metaphor, and, by preventing replicability, would risk invalidating the study.

In my particular study, etymology is of no central concern, except in so far as it may be assumed to be common knowledge that would be subsumed under speech community norms of 2. I thus included as potential linguistic metaphors all those stretches of language that satisfy criterion 2, i.e. those that according to my judgement of those current speech community norms – triangulated where possible – could be interpreted metaphorically, and taking the speech community to include both adults and children. The relation of 3 to 2 is also of concern, since the role of metaphor in equipping children with adult cultural norms is to be investigated. The set of metaphors identified by criterion 3 would be those that, with knowledge of the individual discourse participants, seem likely to be processed meta-phorically. Metaphors that can be identified using these criteria will also be included, although this last set is grossly underdetermined;

processing evidence, Think-Aloud protocol analysis, and development of children's explicit awareness of metaphor, may allow it to be determined more fully in a move, via generalisation and abstraction, from 4 to 3 with respect to the specific group of children involved in the study.

Identifying and describing linguistic metaphors in discourse data

Ortony, quoted in the first section, suggests that metaphor description might be better addressed by a family resemblances approach. Wittgenstein's analogy between metaphors and games will help get started on the task of identification and description. Metaphors, like games, are pervasive in human society; they are social and cultural in their use and invention. New media, such as the video and CD-ROM, give rise to new types of games. New situations lead to new metaphors: for example, the privatisation of public utilities produced the new metaphor of **fat cats**, to refer to directors with huge salaries. As categories, both 'games' and 'metaphors' are extendible and unpredictably open. There is wide potential for activities to be interpreted as games, even though they might not have been originally intended as games. As with metaphoricity, the 'game-ness' of a game depends to a large extent on how it is actually used. Wittgenstein points out that, as between members of the same family, there is among games perhaps no property that is common to all, but

a complicated network of similarities overlapping and criss-crossing: sometimes overall similarities, sometimes similarities of detail
(Wittgenstein, 1953: 1–56)

By following the 'game' parallel, the prosaic metaphor identification problem can circumnavigate the insoluble issue of finding a watertight definition and set about the task of identification through processes of analogy, exclusion and description. Prototypical cases of metaphor are used analogically to locate other possible examples in a first trawl through the data to find samples of talk that look like 'typical' metaphors. This trawl produces a set of potential linguistic metaphors, which can then be examined from the perspective of the discourse context, including likely knowledge and assumptions of participants, to establish that domain incongruity is justified and to exclude doubtful cases. To avoid the possibility of inappropriate inclusion of stretches of language as metaphor, Kittay (1987: 84) suggests checking possible candidates for linguistic metaphor against the following contra-indicating circumstances:

– the speaker is making an error
– speaker and listener are communicating *within* a constructed discourse world, in which the language is not metaphorical although it may appear so when viewed from the outside.

The remaining set of linguistic metaphors can then be described linguistically, ideationally and interpersonally. The list below summarises identification procedures for prosaic linguistic metaphor. It is immediately clear how important it will be, especially in the last two steps, to be explicit about how decisions are made, since they may be arbitrary, or at best "motivated" decisions (Lakoff 1987a).

1 Trawl through the data looking for metaphor-like uses of language.
2 Use necessary conditions to identify a set of potential linguistic metaphors.
3 Remove as non-metaphors apparent incongruities that arise from error.
4 Remove as non-metaphors apparent incongruities that arise from shared understandings within the discourse context.
5 Impose boundary conditions to exclude certain types of potential metaphors from the set.

Trawling to find metaphors analogically by form

In the first stage of identifying linguistic metaphors, I worked analogically to find stretches of talk that 'looked like' uncontroversial examples of metaphor, as presented in the metaphor theory literature to illustrate theoretical discussions. In preference-rule terms (see Jackendoff, 1983), these metaphors can be seen as 'typical' cases, and examination of these exemplar metaphors produces the following set of typicality conditions:

T1 The Topic term is stated explicitly, or its referent is visible in the discourse context to both producer and receiver.
T2 The Vehicle domain is (assumed to be) familiar to both producer and receiver.
T3 The producer intends the utterance to be interpreted metaphorically.
T4 The high level of incongruity between Topic and Vehicle makes it likely that the receiver will interpret the stretch of language metaphorically.
T5 The form is not negative: **Juliet is the sun** is more typical than **I am not a smile** (Sylvia Plath).

T6 Certain syntactic forms are typically used, in particular the
A is B form.

Necessary conditions

The basic necessary conditions for linguistic metaphors are taken to
be domain incongruity and potential transfer of meaning (after Kittay,
1987). An incongruity must be found between the domains of a lexical
item (the Vehicle) used to refer to some other idea (the Topic), which
may or may not be explicitly lexicalised in the stretch of talk. The
incongruity needs to have the potential to be resolved and to produce
an understanding of the Topic in terms of the Vehicle. Identificational
criteria are thus shifted on to the identification of incongruity between
underlying domains, seen as collections of various types and levels of
information and meanings that may be activated on encountering the
Topic and Vehicle terms. Domains activated in discourse contexts are
thus unavoidably situated within individual minds, deriving from past
experiences and knowledge, although, as we have seen, in practice,
generalisations may have to be made about domains averaged across
individuals. Basic necessary conditions for metaphor are set out below
(drawing on Kittay, 1987).

These conditions will produce a very broad category that will
include many stretches of language, including metonymy, idioms and
extended meanings. The unpredictability of children's interpretations
of language makes it important for a study of educational discourse
to have available such a broad category, in order not to miss any of
the metaphorical language opportunities open to children.

A stretch of language is said to be a linguistic metaphor if:

N1 it contains reference to a Topic domain by a Vehicle term (or
terms) and

N2 there is potentially an incongruity between the domain of the
Vehicle term and the Topic domain and

N3 it is possible for a receiver (in general, or a particular person),
as a member of a particular discourse community, to find a
coherent interpretation which makes sense of the incongruity in
its discourse context, and which involves some transfer of
meaning from the Vehicle domain.

Excluding incongruities that arise from errors and shared discourse worlds

Phonological and lexical errors may produce stretches of talk that may look something like typical metaphors. For example:

a *slither* of rock
the apostrophe *becomes* before the S   (Author's data)

However, the anomalous terms in such cases appear to arise from lexical accessing problems, rather than from particular lexical choices, and are thus omitted from the set of metaphor Vehicles.

In a second type of exclusion, language that appears metaphorical when viewed from *outside* the shared discourse world of speaker and listener, is not justifiably categorised as metaphor *within* it. Such constructed worlds include the fantasy worlds of the theatre, stories and children's play. An example of non-metaphor would be the utterance **This pillow is my spaceship**, produced by a three-year old (Marjanovic-Shane, 1989a). From its surface form, this would appear to be classifiable as a metaphor, with a clear Topic and Vehicle, unconventionally collocated; yet, when the context of production of the utterance, alongside knowledge of the individual, is taken into account, I am led to agree with Marjanovic-Shane (1989a) that this should not be classed as metaphor, but rather as a relabelling. The child who produced the utterance was creating a parallel fictional world and constructing an imaginary play scenario, in which she found roles for various everyday objects (and people); the particular role assigned to the pillow was to act as the spaceship. The spaceship does *not* work as a metaphorical Vehicle for **the pillow**, by giving producer and receiver a new perspective, from which to understand **the pillow** in terms of the meanings and associations of a spaceship. This would be equivalent to proposing that when Henry V is played by the actor Kenneth Branagh, Henry V functions as a metaphor for Kenneth Branagh.

Constructed worlds include technical discourse worlds where lexical items have an agreed specific sense, different from the non-technical. Examples from the technical discourse of mathematics include the following:

difference (between 6 and 4 is 2)
simultaneous (equations)
make (2 and 3 make 5)

In my study, such technical discourse worlds overlapped with the shared discourse world of the classroom, resulting in simplified mathematical language that might resemble linguistic metaphor, but could not be included as such:

bring down the other four
sixteen *into* a hundred and twenty-four?
... doesn't quite *go*   (Author's data: maths lesson)

Boundary decisions: the example of verb metaphors

The need to have identification procedures that apply across the complexity of prosaic discourse presents a further problem when we move beyond uncontroversially distinct domains that produce metaphors such as **Juliet is the sun**, and deal with borderline cases of metaphor, where there might be disagreement on categorisation. The source of disagreement is the location of boundaries of Topic and Vehicle domains, in terms of what exactly is "taken to be salient for that language community" (Kittay, 1987: 19). For example, I might claim that **in** in **How many 9s in 909?** (author's data) is being used metaphorically, because the conventional domains of the Noun Phrases collocated with **in** are objects and containers, and numbers and physical objects/containers belong in clearly distinct categories. Someone else might argue that numbers have become conventional categories to be linked with **in**, and so there is no possibility of metaphor. What we disagree about is the, largely intangible and unmeasurable, degree of conventionalisation of categories and its relation to how we, as individuals, think. Resolution of conflict between two different assessments of what is conventional, and the resulting uncertainty over domain distinctiveness, requires the imposition of category boundaries that are to some extent arbitrary, in order to proceed with attempts to delimit and categorise metaphorical language.

Verbs provide one such challenge to the identification of metaphor. While it is uncontroversial and straightforward to postulate incongruity between two conceptual domains underlying highly specific Noun Phrases, as in,

the *rottweilers* (= barmaids) **behind the bar**
    (Author's data, adult. The discourse makes no other reference to dogs)

a *dead* rainbow   (Author's data, 7-year old)

where lexical items are unarguably drawn from domains distinct to the producer, verbal metaphoricity needs to rely on judgements made about collocated Noun Phrases and their domains, and thus seems particularly open to question and disagreement. The best guard against such potential problems seems to be explicitness in respect of those judgements, as I will try to illustrate.

'Delexicalised' verbs (like **make, put, have** or **do**; Sinclair, 1991: 113) in particular, seem to have very little intrinsic meaning, but very many potential meanings or, at least, possible uses. The precise sense of such delexicalised verbs in use is determined in relation to the immediately collocated Noun Phrases, or the Subjects and/or Objects implied by the discourse context. The notion of an independent first-order meaning, inappropriate in the discourse context, but needed to access a metaphorical interpretation (Kittay, 1987), seems to have been almost completely lost. There are two ways forward. One way would be to decline to classify any uses of these words as potentially metaphorical. This does not remove the problem but rather defers it, since we then need to decide on exactly which verbs are included in the set of those precluded from the possibility of metaphorical use. If **have**, as in **have a good time**, is kept as literal, would **see**, as in **I see what you mean**, be literal? And then what about **push**, as in **she pushed the deal through**? The alternative solution also involves an arbitrary decision, but, in this case, which uses of any particular verb will count as metaphorical is decided on by defining which uses will count as first-order, primary or 'literal'. It is tempting at this point to invoke the concept of an intrinsic 'central' meaning (McCarthy, 1990: 24) (or 'congruent forms'; Halliday, 1985) that would act as first-order meaning, and against which some level of incongruity between conventionally collocating NPs of the given verb and the NP in question could be established. But this in turn is an arbitrary, or perhaps at most motivated, distinction, since 'central' meanings are not those that are the most frequently used (Sinclair, 1991) and may not be, etymologically, the oldest. We need instead to be *explicit* about the choice of one set of meanings, out of the range of possible meanings of delexicalised verbs, which is classed as non-metaphorical, so that the others may be classed as metaphorical. For example, the verb **go** is used very frequently and with many collocates. If we take as essential to its non-metaphorical meaning a sense of physical progress or movement, then collocated words or phrases that do *not* fit with this sense, but in which some sense of progress is implied, e.g. **go mad**, may be held to warrant the label 'linguistic metaphor'.

In establishing metaphoricity in this way, each delexicalised word first needs a statement describing its own separate primary, non-metaphorical meaning(s), along with criteria for deciding whether or not it is that sense that is being employed in an utterance. So, for example, we could propose that **go** + *some physically real destination* is primary and non-metaphorical, whereas **go** + *non-existent destina-*

tion is counted as metaphor; **have** (core meaning of 'possessing/experiencing') + *concrete object/event* is primary and non-metaphorical, whereas **have** + *non-concrete object/event* is categorised as metaphor; **get to** + *physical location* is primary and non-metaphorical, whereas **get to** + *other* NP may be metaphorical.

To see how this procedure works with actual data, I look more closely at the example of **have**. This was the fourth most frequent verb (after **is, was, do**) in one of the sets of classroom data. 20 occurrences of **have** and 14 of **had** were followed by Object Noun Phrases such as **singing practice/dinner.** Eliminating concrete nouns left the following:

have +   *a)*   **a backlog** *(of flights)*
　　　　　b)   **an awfully good innings**
　　　　　c)   **Skiddaw** *(= the trip to Skiddaw)*
　　　　　d)   **a go**
　　　　　e)   **a look**
　　　　　f)   **a think**
　　　　　g)   **a read**
　　　　　h)   **a few minutes**
　　　　　i)   **half an hour on the computer**
　　　　　k)   **fire**

Phrases (b) and (c) refer to events, with **Skiddaw** being used metonymically to refer to 'a trip to Skiddaw'. Phrases (d) – (g) with nouns derived from action verbs, can also be construed as events, as can (h) and (i) when their following prepositional phrases are considered too. Two possible contenders for identification as linguistic metaphors then remain: **have a backlog** and **animals have fire**, this latter coming from a story read aloud. This second example points to the necessity, as a last step in the metaphor identification process, of checking collocated Noun Phrases for other possible causes of incongruity, such as ellipsis or metonymy deriving from shared discourse knowledge. **Fire** here refers metonymically to 'the power to create and use fire for light, heat etc.', although in another sample from the data **we had the bonfire** referred to 'the event of lighting a bonfire, standing around it etc.' It is the analyst's decision at this point as to whether **have** + *abstract nouns for ideas, skills, powers etc.* should be classified as linguistic metaphor or not. If it is decided that the primary, literal meaning does not extend as far as abstract nouns for ideas, powers etc., then (a) is classed as metaphorical, as would similar phrases such as for example **have a good idea; have the power to cast spells.**

It is important to note that, as with more highly lexical verbs, metaphorical meaning seems to spread from the verb across into the collocated nouns, as abstract nouns such as **backlog** or **idea** take on, metaphorically, some of the characteristics of an event or possession. The procedure then for identifying verb metaphors is as follows:

1 Identify the conventional collocating Subject or Object Noun Phrases of the verb. If the verb is so delexicalised as to make this identification process debatable, then make an explicit statement of the primary, non-metaphorical meaning being assigned to the verb, and its prototypical Noun Phrase collocations.
2 Identify a domain incongruity between the Noun Phrases collocated in the particular instance, and those identified in 1.
3 Check for possible errors or for interaction within constructed worlds, that rule out metaphor as a possible cause of the incongruity.

The metaphoricity of prepositions presents a similar boundary problem, amenable to a similar solution, by taking primary senses as spatial (following Quirk & Greenbaum, 1975: 153 [*in*], and Lakoff, 1987 [*over*]). While such decisions are of course open to disagreement, they are at least explicit; explicitness, I argue, must replace correctness or 'truth' as a goal for the analyst.

In my study, identification procedures for linguistic metaphors in the corpus of data were set up in this way, with each boundary decision being explicitly recorded. Having identified a set of linguistic metaphors in the data, some quantitative analysis could then be carried out on the density of linguistic metaphor in various types of discourse event, on the range of linguistic forms of metaphor, and on the range of types of metaphor. For this last research aim, it was necessary to establish features of metaphorically used language that would be used to distinguish 'types', and it was in this part of the research process that the notion of gradability was applied.

Graded descriptors of metaphor

A review of the key literature on metaphor produced a set of nine graded dimensions of metaphor from various suggested defining conditions. This theory-level set was revised and adapted in the light of its use with the linguistic metaphors found in the data, to produce a set of graded dimensions that have required theory-processing congruence. Theorists usually work with only one or two dimensions, and the attempt here to be (more) comprehensive is thus innovative and will hopefully provide a new tool for analysts.

A review of theory showed that, for example, both Black and Kittay stressed the importance of the distinctiveness of the domains of Topic and Vehicle (Black, 1979; Kittay, 1987), and the degree of incongruence this distinctiveness generates when Topic and Vehicle are brought together in a metaphor. In Ortony's work (Ortony, 1975), the effect of familiarity of the Topic domain is highlighted, and to this can be added the familiarity of the Vehicle domain. The density of domains is discussed by Black under the label "richness" (Black, 1979), which Kittay deals with as the internal systematicity of domains (1987). The work of Aristotle and writers who draw on his ideas (e.g. Aitchison, 1987) emphasises the degree to which a metaphor can be rephrased without the use of metaphorical language. Each of these features was used in the construction of the initial set of graded descriptors.

Graded dimensions do not need to be independent of one another, but they should be independently applicable. For example, *cognitive demand* will not be independent of *familiarity*, but it will be possible to categorise Vehicle terms as high in familiarity but low in demand, or high/low in both. Since graded conditions are partly determined by the research aims, they also do not need to be exhaustive or independent; they can be added to or altered as required.

G1   THE DEGREE OF INCONGRUITY BETWEEN TOPIC AND VEHICLE

This includes the continuum "transparency/opacity" used in relation to idioms to refer to how clearly and specifically the Topic and Vehicle are related. In theoretical debates (see Chapter 1) not a great deal of progress has been made in clarifying the concept of 'distance' between the Topic and Vehicle domains. Discussions often end up grounded on fundamental issues, such as the nature or existence of similarity as a psychological reality (e.g. Rips, 1989) or the identification of 'domain' boundaries. Attempts to apply this feature to interactional data produced further difficulties at a theoretical level, although as we saw in the third section, it is possible to demonstrate empirically that some T–V anomalies are noticed by receivers of a metaphor.

The distinction between what may be identified theoretically as incongruous, and what empirically appears to participants to be anomalous, can be seen particularly clearly in the use of idioms. Theoretical analysis of the data for Topic–Vehicle domain incongruity would result in idioms such as **keep the kettle boiling** or **come up trumps** being categorised as highly incongruous T and V domains. However, there is usually no reaction to them from the receivers, suggesting that they are not perceived as highly anomalous.

Analysis of prosaic metaphor shows that incongruity is to some extent context-dependent and relative to the expectations of discourse participants and their shared contextual knowledge. For example, the teacher in a Geology lesson exemplifies the idea of 'classification' by grouping the children and commenting:

then we've got another classification (1.0) they're still human (.) so we can put them in *a big circle* that *says* human (.) but we can also **put them in two** *smaller circles* (.) that *say* (1.0) male female

(Author's data: Geology lesson)

Outside the particular school context, the use of **put them in a big circle/two smaller circles** to refer to classifying and sub-categorising might seem to make use of a Vehicle domain (big and small circles) that is highly incongruous with the Topic domain. The use of phrase-internal metaphor Vehicle **says** to refer to the Topic domain of labelling or naming a category also draws on a fairly remote domain when viewed out of context. However, interpretation within the specific context required pupils to recall previous shared activity in which they had categorised objects by physically placing them inside plastic hoops that represent set boundaries, and labelled them both orally (**says**) and in writing. For the pupils and teacher **circles/says** do not come from remote domains but from recent shared experience, so that the incongruity is not enormous.

The converse of this context-dependence of incongruity may well operate too, with lack of shared knowledge leading to perceptions of incongruity different from that intended by the producer of a metaphor. The child who picked up the teacher's **where does the time go?** and replied **I know where the time** *goes* ... **into the past** noticed the incongruity between the Vehicle domain of place and motion, and the Topic domain of time. It is doubtful that the teacher would have intended the original question to be strikingly anomalous rather than simply idiomatic.

Interactionally, discourse participants appear to make use of variation in incongruity/anomaly in the explication of ideas through metaphor. For example, in a Geology lesson, talk around the Topic of the nature of volcanic lava, the Vehicle terms employed for the same Topic domain seem to shift along a cline of decreasing incongruity/anomaly:

sticky treacle – runny butter – wax (Author's data)

Incongruity in prosaic metaphor is thus graded, and is dependent on both context and on background knowledge.

G2 NOVELTY/CONVENTIONALITY OF TOPIC–VEHICLE LINK

G2–1 Idiomaticity: the degree of conventionality of a particular Topic–Vehicle combination.

G2–2 Vitality: novelty/conventionality of a particular choice of Vehicle, given the particular Topic domain.

For example, **kick the bucket** is idiomatic in the sense of 2–1, but other Vehicle terms, such as **sleep**, are more commonly used for the domain of **death** (2–2).

G3 ATTITUDINAL IMPACT

Aristotle's work first raised the issue of the 'paraphraseability' of metaphor as the degree of ease with which the meaning of a metaphor can be explained in literal language. The importance of this factor in processing metaphor in discourse context was not immediately obvious; it was not clear whether being able to explain the meaning of a metaphor could correlate meaningfully with ease of comprehension (rather than interpretation, see Gibbs, Chapter 2) or production, since an understanding of a metaphor might equally well be reached through non-verbal means, such as imaging, non-algorithmic thought (Penrose, 1989) or internal speech (Vygotsky, 1968). Paraphraseability was initially retained as a graded condition, since it was felt that explicit explanation of metaphors might occur, or even be useful, in educational contexts, and, in that case, the paraphraseability of a metaphor might affect outcomes.

Searle comments on paraphraseability that, at a trivial level, it can be seen as either completely impossible or always possible (1993: 109), and that the essence of paraphraseability lies in the accessibility to participants of the extra understanding or the shared "intimacy" that results in the use of a particular metaphor (Cooper, 1986: 163). The data showed clearly that the ideational content of much prosaic metaphor is explicated in interaction around the metaphor. Further extra content conveyed by metaphor lies in the connotative power and in the interpersonal function of metaphor, which was seen particularly clearly in the use of metaphorical language in giving feedback to pupils and in classroom control sequences. Three dimensions of interpersonal content were adapted from Graumann (1990) and shown to be useful in analysis, adequate and gradable:

Positive – negative evaluation
This is seen in the choice of lexical item and in frequency of systematic use of particular Vehicle items:

Teacher to pupils: **I think you all deserve a medal**
(Author's data: Dance lesson)

Alignment – distancing
The alignment function was seen in metaphorical language that involved the use of humour and use of 1st person pronouns to express solidarity across power differentials. Degrees of formality could also be seen as contributing to alignment/distancing:

Teacher to pupils: **my brain can't manage that** (Author's data: Maths lesson)

Emphasising – de-emphasising
This was done through pre- and post-modification:

Teacher to pupils: **make a little mental note** (Author's data: English lesson)

and through the choice of Vehicle lexical item relative to participants' expectations:

Teacher: **rock … becomes like sticky treacle** (Author's data: Geology lesson)

These graded dimensions are included as a cluster relating to Attitudinal Impact:

G3–1 positive – negative evaluation
G3–2 alignment – distancing
G3–3 emphasising – de-emphasising

These can be construed at both a theoretical and a processing level; there can be congruence between the construals of them at the two levels, and, between them, they take some account of paraphrase-ability. Other aspects of paraphraseability may be taken account of by Connotative Power (G8) and by the degree of explication metaphors receive when used (G4). The results of the study demonstrated quite clearly that the comprehension demands of metaphors are usually supported by explication in the talk surrounding the metaphor, which paraphrases the metaphor in close discourse proximity of its use. Analysis of the discourse data suggests that, while explication is normal practice, the nature and type of explication is affected by both, how a producer perceives the needs of receiver, and by the ability of a producer to actually perform the explication task. Gradedness was found in the extent and nature of explication of specific metaphors for specific discourse participants. "Explication" is thus suggested as a graded dimension G4, that can be operationalised both theoretically and empirically.

G5 FAMILIARITY

G5–1 of Vehicle domain to producer and/or receiver
G5–2 of Topic domain to producer and/or receiver

Both types of familiarity may be empirically determined for specific individuals, but may well have to be estimated for particular groups, such as, in my case, 10-year-old children in a rural British school. When used in conjunction with other conditions, such as G2–1 Idiomaticity, we have a way of relating an individual's knowledge to conventional norms.

G6 COGNITIVE DEMAND OF TOPIC AND VEHICLE TERMS AND DOMAINS

Cognitive demand was expected to be a multiple dimension, emerging from the interaction of factors including the internal structure of the conceptual categories concerned, the linguistic form of the metaphor, the level of abstraction of the conceptual content of Topic and Vehicle, and the open-endedness of the link, also called the *richness* of the analogical mapping (Gentner 1982, 1983) or *resonance* (Black, 1979).

One of the aims of the research study was to further delineate this dimension as it applies in educational contexts. The cognitive demand of a metaphor for receivers arises from both Topic and Vehicle. Investigation of how metaphor is used in classroom instruction showed that the cognitive demand of metaphor Topics varied along sub-dimensions of familiarity, abstraction, generality and complexity. The same dimensions can be applied to Vehicle terms and concepts, and to the two combined in a particular metaphor. So, religious metaphors such as **the Lord is my Shepherd** may have Topics that are more cognitively demanding than their Vehicles, whereas a metaphorical idiom such as **keep the kettle boiling** may combine relatively undemanding Topic and Vehicle.

Familiarity is separately included as a graded dimension. The other three dimensions can apply at both theoretical and processing levels and were added into the framework as a cluster relating to the broader notion of cognitive demand:

G6–1 *abstraction* of Topic, Vehicle and combination
G6–2 *generality* of Topic, Vehicle and combination
G6–3 *complexity* of Topic, Vehicle and combination

G7 EXPLICITNESS OF METAPHOR: THE RECEIVER'S CONSCIOUS AWARENESS OF THE PRODUCER'S METAPHORICAL INTENTION

At the theoretical level this feature related to the signalling of metaphorical similes by the words *like, as* etc., and the signalling of metaphor explicitly with a marker such as **metaphorically**. In the empirical study there were no occurrences of this latter signal although, interestingly, the converse was found when non-metaphorical uses of a verb were marked with **actually,** as in

you can actually see the new structure   (Author's data: Geology lesson)

The use of such terms might suggest that a need to guard against metaphorical interpretations was subconsciously perceived.

Candidates for less explicit signals of metaphoricity include the positioning of metaphor Vehicles consistently in rheme position in the clause, and pausing. This graded feature thus can function both theoretically and at a processing level.

G8 CONNOTATIVE POWER OF THE VEHICLE TERM

While this may be impossible to measure precisely, it is intended to capture the notion of culturally shared associations linked to a lexical item. In

the moon was a ghostly galleon   (Alfred Noyes)

galleon has historical connotations that are more restricted, but more specific and richer than those of, say, **ship**

G9 SYSTEMATICITY: THE EXTENT TO WHICH THE SAME METAPHOR OR VARIATIONS ON IT ARE USED IN DISCOURSE, LOCALLY OR GLOBALLY

G9–1 *local systematicity* of metaphors within a particular discourse event

G9–2 *discourse systematicity* of metaphors within use in specific discourse communities

G9–3 *global systematicity* of metaphors across a range of discourse types and content

This dimension relates to the ways in which one metaphor may link with another across a single discourse event or across many discourse events (see also Chapter 1, this volume). A metaphor may be used just once in a discourse event, but often the same metaphor is repeated, or variants of the metaphor are used, both within and across discourse events. Some linguistic metaphors for success or failure in love for example are found in a wide range of songs, films and poetry: e.g. **a broken heart; my heart is on fire**. Other metaphors may be invented and used several times or in several ways, but just within a single discourse, e.g. **my love is an arbutus / that grows by the stream** (Burns), making no further appearances, intertextually or otherwise. The dimension of metaphor systematicity described here in discourse is external to the metaphor, in contrast with systematicity as used by Gentner (1989) to refer to the internal systematic nature of the semantic field of the Vehicle term.

Local, discourse and global systematicity were found in varying degrees in the interactional data, confirming that this feature is graded and works at both theoretical and processing levels.

The list below summarises the graded dimensions used for describing metaphor in the spoken discourse data.

G1   Incongruity between Topic and Vehicle domains
G2   Novelty / conventionality of Topic–Vehicle link
    2–1   Idiomaticity
    2–2   Vitality
G3   Attitudinal impact
    3–1   Positive – negative evaluation
    3–2   Alignment – distancing
    3–3   Emphasis
G4   Explication
G5   Familiarity
    5–1   of Vehicle domain
    5–2   of Topic domain
G6   Cognitive demand
    6–1   Level of abstraction of Topic and Vehicle
    6–2   Level of generality of Topic and Vehicle
    6–3   Complexity of Topic and Vehicle
G7   Explicitness of metaphorical intention
G8   Connotative power
G9   Systematicity
    9–1   Local systematicity
    9–2   Discourse systematicity
    9–3   Global systematicity

Application of the identification and descriptive procedures

To illustrate the potential of combining the metaphor identification procedures of the previous two sections with the set of gradable dimensions, I briefly consider three types of potential metaphor:

Idioms

Metaphorical idioms are stretches of language that satisfy the necessary conditions for linguistic metaphors, that are high in G2–1 (Idiomaticity), but variable in other graded conditions.

Strong metaphors

These are linguistic metaphors that are highly likely to produce new ways of thinking and analogical reasoning. They should therefore be expected to have high degrees of:

G1   Incongruity
G2–2 Vitality
G6   Cognitive demand
G8   Connotative power in Vehicle term

with low degrees of

G2–1 Idiomaticity

and varying degrees of the other graded conditions.

Similes

This category is defined by its surface linguistic form i.e. the inclusion of **like** as in

My luve is like a red, red rose

Beyond that, the linking of terms may or may not result in a conceptual incongruity and its resolution, necessary conditions for classification as metaphorical. The example above satisfies these criteria, whereas a simple comparison, such as **This apple juice is like cider**, does not.

We can then have a sub-category of (potential) linguistic metaphors called *metaphorical similes* which fulfil the necessary conditions for metaphor, and to which typical conditions and gradable descriptors can be applied, but with the added necessary condition:

N4 Topic and Vehicle terms are linked with the word **like** or equivalent term, such as **as**.

Conclusion

This chapter has illustrated how an applied study of metaphor in prosaic discourse can establish identification procedures and descriptive categories as analytic tools, relativised within given research and discourse contexts. It has been argued that a clear separation must be maintained between theoretical and processing levels when identification procedures are being drawn up, and that care is needed in explicitly identifying the particular socio-cultural groups or discourse communities who provide samples or evidence of metaphorical language. I have illustrated how metaphors in discourse data can be 'known' through processes of identification by analogy and exclusion, and description by clustering of graded dimensions. The graded dimensions of metaphorically used language which have been produced operate in relation to discourse context and participants, thus allowing contextualised analyses of discourse data. They can be used to describe linguistic metaphor in discourse data in a subtle and detailed way, allowing for example, exploration of how different types of metaphor are combined in interactional sequences to ensure shared understanding of ideational and interpersonal content.

PART III

ANALYSING METAPHOR IN NATURALLY
OCCURRING DATA

7 Who framed SLA research?
Problem framing and metaphoric accounts of the SLA research process

David Block

Introduction

This paper takes its initial inspiration from the work of Schön, who over 15 years ago offered the following explanation of what he calls "problem framing":

> There is a very different tradition associated with the notion of metaphor, however – one which treats metaphor as central to the task of accounting for our perspectives on the world: how we think about things, make sense of reality, and set the problems we later try to solve. In this second sense, 'metaphor' refers both to a certain kind of product – a perspective or frame, a way of looking at things – and to a certain kind of process – a process by which new perspectives on the world come into existence.
>
> (Schön, 1979: 254)

It is important to examine in detail the two-part function of metaphor in this quote. First of all, there is metaphor as process, that is "metaphors as central to the task of accounting for our perspectives on the world" and "as a process by which new perspectives on the world come into existence". In this paper I shall adopt the stance that metaphor is an ongoing process by which we constantly assimilate input by comparing and contrasting it with representations of previous experiences which we retain in our memories. It thus constitutes an interplay between top-down and bottom-up processing. The roots of this view of metaphor are to be found in the work of Neisser (1976) who describes what he calls the "perceptual cycle" (pp. 63–70). This perceptual cycle resembles in many ways the earlier work of Piaget (1952), in that it begins with an individual interacting with the environment. Piaget, dealing with children, sees the cycle as necessarily beginning with an overt action such as touching; Neisser, on the other hand, argues that the cycle may be triggered by watching or listening as well. The cycle also ties in with what Cameron, in Chapter 1, calls the "conceptual processing level" of metaphor, in that it is concerned with "the activation of concepts, as constructed through interaction between individuals and their socio-cultural environment" (Figure 1).

In Schön's theory of framing, the cycle begins with watching and listening, and in this paper, it will be this type of interaction with the environment which will begin the framing process. The initial interaction with the environment leads to some form of assimilation of incoming information into existing schemata (the information is altered) and then to the accommodation of these initial schemata to incoming information (the schemata are altered). This assimilation/accommodation is in effect what I would call *metaphorisation*, the making sense of incoming information by seeing it as similar to already existing schemata, which in turn are altered by this information.

The second notion of metaphor for Schön is metaphor as product. In this case, metaphor is a linguistic artefact produced by professionals as they attempt to make sense of their day-to-day activity, which we can describe, discuss, analyse and evaluate. This view of metaphor ties in with what Cameron (Chapter 1) calls the "theory level" of metaphor, which follows Kittay's (1987) necessary conditions for linguistic metaphors. Cameron describes these necessary conditions as follows:

A stretch of language in its discourse context is said to be a linguistic metaphor if it contains a reference to a Topic domain by a Vehicle term (or terms) and there is potentially an incongruity between the domain of the Vehicle term and the Topic domain.   (Cameron, p. 118)

It is assumed that someone encountering the stretch of language would be able to resolve the incongruity through some transfer of meaning from Vehicle to Topic. The frames dealt with in this paper meet these criteria, as they contain conceptual incongruity which, at the same time, is resolvable by the listener/reader.

Over the years, Schön has applied his theory of problem framing to a variety of situations and experiences. His work ranges from an examination of how the US government's view of public housing changed over the 30-year period from the 1950s to the 1970s (Schön, 1979, 1983), to an edited volume on the application of his theories to various educational contexts (Schön Ed., 1991), and finally to a more recent book on the pragmatic resolution of seemingly insoluble disputes, such as early retirement programmes in Germany, the state of the homeless in Massachusetts and the introduction of new technology in an educational context (Schön & Rein, 1994). In all his work, Schön describes a process consisting of three key steps which he claims motivates professionals' decisions about solutions to problems which they perceive to exist in their areas of work. First, a situation or experience is problematised; that is to say, it is interpreted as problematic or troubling in some way. Second, a frame is created for the experience or situation. This frame is based on a fundamental metaphor of seeing **A as B**, a metaphor which Schön terms "generative" because of its capacity to generate solutions. The generation of solutions constitutes the third stage in the process.

Schön constructs the entire process of problem framing and solution generation by listening to the 'stories' which people tell about their problem situations:

When we examine the problem-setting stories told by the analysts and practitioners of social policy, it becomes apparent that the framing of problems often depends upon metaphors underlying the stories which generate problem setting and set the direction of problem solving.

(Schön, 1979: 254)

Schön is thus working within the tricky realm of positing underlying metaphors to account for surface discourse. Such interpretation, as Gibbs points out, is not widely accepted as valid in cognitive psychology circles:

Most generally, there are limitations to inferring anything about scientific concepts and culture from an analysis of what people say. The primary limitation is that shared by most linguistic research; namely, the problem of reaching conclusions about phenomena based on the individual analyst's own conclusions. Cognitive psychologists, for example, are generally skeptical of hypotheses about human conceptual knowledge that are based on a theorist's intuitive speculations, even when such speculations are based on a systematic analysis of linguistic structure and behavior. To many, the idea that conceptual metaphors underlie our everyday experience or motivate our use and understanding of different linguistic expressions cannot be accepted as "psychologically real," because such a theory is based on intuitive explanation.   (Gibbs, 1994: 202)

Curiously enough, Schön himself has never really addressed this issue head-on; however, I have, albeit in modest fashion. At the end of an article I published several years ago (Block, 1992), I defend the positing of underlying metaphors to account for comments which language teachers and language learners made about their respective classroom roles. While recognising that a degree of faith was in order if readers were to accept my analysis, I rejected the view that I had merely 'read metaphors into' the data I had collected and analysed. I appealed to Lakoff and Turner's (1989) views on poetic interpretation, which I claimed might equally apply to the interpretation of language in general:

When a reader gives a highly unusual or idiosyncratic construal of a poem, he is sometimes accused of 'reading meanings into' the poem that are not 'really there'. But, because of the nature of language, all reading is reading in. Even if one sticks to the conventional, shared meanings of words, one will necessarily be evoking knowledge of the schemas in which words are defined. And in using one's natural capacity for metaphorical understanding, one will necessarily be engaging in an activity of construal. All reading involves construal.   (Lakoff & Turner, 1989: 109)

I went on to make the case that researchers who posit underlying metaphors should not underestimate their ability to construe meanings which are remarkably similar to those which other members of the research community might construe. Stating the case in inverse fashion, I concluded that if my interpretations were simply idiosyncratic, then every individual examining my data would be likely to come up with a different construal, and nobody would be able to understand my analysis. There would exist a situation of almost total incommensurability.

Interestingly, Schön has dealt with (and rejected) the possibility of an 'anything goes' approach to problem framing, according to which there would be an infinite number of possible frames created for the same problematised situation. Schön points out that framing is carried out by individuals who are part of the same culture and, this being the case, the frames they devise will make sense not only to themselves as individuals, but also to other members of the community. The framing imagination is therefore constrained by what is allowed or accepted, as well as what is *not* allowed or accepted by a particular community. This argument does not in any way rule out the existence of more than one frame for the same problem. Indeed, as we shall see in a moment, it is generally the case that there are competing frames for the same objective problematised situation (see Deignan, in this book, Chapter 9, and Lakoff, 1987a, for examples of the parallel case of competing conceptual metaphors).

Having presented Schön's model of problem framing, I should now like to move on to conduct an analysis of an area of social activity with which I am familiar: second language acquisition research (SLAR). In the section which follows, I shall reconstruct what I would claim is a fairly common frame for the current state of SLAR, namely one which envisages multiple approaches to the nature of research as something negative and undesirable. I shall base the reconstruction on selected quotes from selected authors and, in doing so, demonstrate how I have adopted the framing technique for my own area of professional activity.

Framing SLA research

I shall begin this section with a discussion of what Wheeler (1987) has called the "inferiority complex" in the social sciences, which leads some researchers to reject the idea of multiple approaches to the exploration and explanation of social phenomena. I shall then describe how several influential applied linguists exemplify this inferiority complex, through three key lamentations which they make about SLA. These lamentations are:

1 The existence of multiple theories is a sign of scientific immaturity.
2 The existence of multiple theory evaluation criteria leads to irrational anarchy.
3 The notable lack of replication studies in SLAR is unscientific.

I wish to argue that these three lamentations constitute a frame which Wheeler would call *monotheistic* (one god, one reality) in nature. Wheeler challenges the appropriateness of this frame for the social sciences, suggesting that social scientists might do better to adopt a *polytheistic* frame (multiple gods, multiple realities) – a concept I shall discuss in the next section.

The inferiority complex

In her 1987 article entitled 'The magic of metaphor', Wheeler describes what she calls the "inferiority complex" of the social sciences, *vis à vis* so-called 'true sciences'. According to Wheeler, this inferiority complex exists because social scientists insist on evaluating what they do according to criteria borrowed from 'true' science. It is based on the belief that if the physical sciences have attained a certain degree of success, and a resulting recognition and status in society, the only way for social sciences to achieve the same result is to follow an identical route to truly scientific practice. When under the influence of this belief, social scientists typically convert the description of characteristics of their fields into lamentations about key problems or weaknesses. Thus, the objective state of the social sciences is problematised and its key characteristics are framed in a negative light.

If we examine the current state of SLAR, we see that the inferiority complex which drives this process is alive and well in some circles. I should now like to examine a set of comments from the SLA literature, which serve as examples of the three lamentations. This done, I shall discuss how the lamentations reflect a particular frame for SLAR.

Lamentation 1: *The existence of multiple theories is a sign of immaturity*

Lamentation 1 begins with the recognition of the existence of multiple theories of SLA (although exactly how many theories exist is not completely clear). Beretta (1991) describes the situation as follows:

> Long (1985a) ... referred to the existence of "some 15 to 20 so-called theories, models, metaphors, perspectives in the current [SLA] literature" (p. 389). Five years later, the number rose to ... more than 40 (Larsen-Freeman & Long, 1991, p. 227). McLaughlin (1987) evaluated 5 of them; Larsen-Freeman (1983) considered 4; and Larsen-Freeman and Long (1991) considered 5. Ellis (1986) reviewed 7 that he considered to have assumed a central place in SLA research ...   (Beretta, 1991: 495)

The existence of multiple theories is seen by some authors as a sign of immaturity. This view of the situation draws on what Wheeler calls the "child metaphor", which is directly linked to the work of Kuhn (1970) and his talk of "mature science". Two examples follow:

> An apparent problem of multiple rival theories (and their perennial lack of convergence) is that, according to some philosophers at least, the already successful sciences do not have them (except perhaps when 'paradigms' compete during a period of paradigm shift [Kuhn, 1970]), and it is frequently pointed out that it is a clear indication of the weakness of theories in the human sciences that the pluralism exists. (Beretta, 1991: 497)

> The existence of a dominant theory (or paradigm) is necessary if a new field is ever to attain that state of grace known as 'normal science' (Kuhn 1970, 1977; Newton-Smith 1982). Normal science takes place when the domain(s) of interest, relevant questions, and methods of going about answering them have been specified by a theory to the general satisfaction of researchers in a field (hence, the theory's acceptance by most of them), such that they can get on productively with their work, at peace with themselves and each other over basic issues in the philosophy of science. Research becomes cumulative, details can be attended to, and applications of theory can be harvested. The work is done efficiently and economically because the theory tells researchers the relevant data to collect. It is theory-governed, organized, cooperative effort.   (Long, 1993: 230)

Beretta sees the existence of multiple theories as a "weakness", and the elimination of multiple theories as the achievement of 'successful science' status. Long begins with the idea of a dominant theory and develops a frame for 'normal science' which seems almost evangelical in nature (his reference to the final goal of "that state of grace known as 'normal science'"). He devotes several lines to the development of the concept of research as a security blanket which guides the researcher from the beginning of the process to the end, telling him/ her what the domain is, how it should be researched and in the end, where the results of his/her studies will find a home. There are keywords of harmony in Long's proposal, such as "the general satisfaction of researchers", "the theory's acceptance", "get on pro-ductively", "at peace with themselves and each other" and the highly utilitarian goal of "[r]esearch becomes cumulative", "applications of theory can be harvested", and "[t]he work is done efficiently and economically", all according to a "theory-governed, organised, co-operative effort". The image which comes to my mind is a group of directed – albeit satisfied, accepting and productive – farm labourers working together to harvest and accumulate knowledge, like so much wheat emerging from fertile fields. What is interesting in both of these comments is the way that the objective state of multiple theories is framed as weak and undesirable, and a situation where one dominant theory exists is framed as successful and desirable.

Lamentation 2: The existence of multiple-theory evaluation criteria leads to irrational anarchy

The second lamentation makes direct reference to the existence of multiple criteria for deciding that particular theories are valid. Ellis (1994) sees this situation as ideal, as it means that theories are more or less valid *vis à vis* the source discipline from whence they came. Thus SLA researchers working in the Universal Grammar (UG) tradition can make decisions about the validity of their research, by making reference to developments in the source field of theoretical linguistics. Similarly, variationists such as Ellis might look to socio-linguistics for a barometer for their work. However, the same authors who find multiple theories to be a problem (see the previous section), not surprisingly find multiple criteria for evaluation hard to accept as well. Two exemplary comments follow:

This means that poetry, voodoo, religion, and nonsense are no less valid bases for belief than "science". This nihilism seems to leave science paralyzed. SLA researchers may as well tell their stories in rhyming couplets as carry out an experiment to test a hypothesis, since there is no means of attributing more value to one than the other.   (Beretta, 1991: 501)

Elsewhere, Long (1990) adopts a similar attitude towards those who are not bothered by multiple theories:

Proponents of an extreme relativistic, "anything goes" view of the growth of knowledge (e.g., Feyerabend, 1975) argue that voodoo magic, or religious beliefs are held no less certainly than are scientific beliefs, and that scientific beliefs are different, not superior.   (Long, 1990: 656)

The authors cited here appeal in common for unity of evaluation criteria in the face of potential academic anarchy. Elsewhere, authors such as van Lier (1994), Block (1996) and Lantolf (1996) have discussed and critiqued the use of relativism as a strawman to attack. An important point made by all three of these authors is that the extreme nihilism which Beretta and Long attack is little more than a caricature of relativism, a relativism so extreme that it is questionable whether it is genuinely embraced by anyone involved in research. Nevertheless, their comments are important in the context of this paper, as they reflect the framing of the objective existence of multiple criteria of theory evaluation as something to be repudiated on rational grounds, and hence as a problem for which solutions will need to be found.

Lamentation 3: The notable lack of replication studies in SLAR is unscientific

The third lamentation begins with the observation that in SLAR there is a notable lack of replication studies and ends with the negative framing of this situation. Santos (1989) presents the positive side of the coin, pointing out the virtues of a replicating field of academic enquiry:

The most obvious benefit of replication is to the discipline. Research is an accretive process; it is the accumulation and consolidation of knowledge over time. Replication of research confirms or calls into question existing findings; without it, a discipline consists of scattered hypotheses and insufficiently substantiated generalizations.   (Santos, 1989: 700)

Elsewhere, the editors of the journal *Studies in Second Language Acquisition* have made a call for more replication studies, and in the process present the negative side of the coin – the fact that very few SLA researchers feel attracted to the prospect of replicating other researchers' work:

The way to more valid and reliable SLA research is through replication. Rerunning the experimental studies under different conditions while maintaining central variables constant promises to eliminate much uncontrolled variance ... To be sure, in replication one loses the aura of glamour and the exhilaration of innovation. But it is the type of activity so basic to scientific enquiry and so prevalent in the so-called sciences that one wonders why it is so disdained in our field.
                    (The Editors of *Studies in Second Language Acquisition*, 1993: 505)

Thus replication is presented in two different lights. Santos sees it as "discipline" which will lead SLAR to "the accumulation and consolidation of knowledge", and away from the anarchy ("scattered hypotheses and insufficiently substantiated generalizations") which results from a lack of purpose and discipline. The editors of *SSLA*, on the other hand, brand it as a loss of "glamour and the exhilaration of innovation", while expressing their wonderment at why it is so prevalent in "the so-called sciences", but so rare in SLAR. Both share a view of replication as the best way for a field to move closer to the 'truth' and both once again show how an objective circumstance, in this case the virtual inexistence of replication studies in SLAR, can be framed in a negative way and seen as a problem to be dealt with.

Conclusion to this section

Taken together, the three lamentations make up what I suggested earlier is an influential frame for the current state of SLAR.[1] The frame is summarised in Table 1 (p. 144).

As Wheeler (1987) points out, this particular view of a social science (here, SLA) leads to an inferiority complex and according to Wheeler, the explanation is painfully simple. Social scientists create their own inferiority complex because they insist on seeing what they do in the mirror of "true science" and because they cannot conceive of a different frame for what they do. She writes:

The notion of the social sciences as inferior arises from evaluating them from a particular perspective, the metaphor of one reality. A different set of notions would result from considering social science research through the metaphor of multiple realities.   (Wheeler, 1987: 225)

---

[1] One obvious question which arises here is how influential this view of SLA research is at present. With reference to the September, 1993 Special Issue of *Applied Linguistics*, entitled 'Theory Construction in Second Language Acquisition', the editors of the journal have the following to say:

> While details in their positions differ, the authors of the Special Issue papers generally share the essentially rationalist epistemology which predominates in contemporary SLA/applied linguistics. (The Editors of *Applied Linguistics*, 1994: 347)

Elsewhere, Ellis (1994) uses different terminology to make a similar point:

> A brief examination of some of the current journals that publish L2 acquisition research (for example, *Language Learning, Studies in Second Language Acquisition* and *Second Language Research*) will reveal the current primacy of theory-led, experimental-type research. (Ellis, 1994: 2)

Following these authors, I maintain that the view of SLA research which I discuss in this paper is at least important in the field, if not predominant or primary, as Ellis and the Editors of *Applied Linguistics* suggest.

Table 1. *SLA problematised*

Situation	Framed as
Multiple theories co-exist.	This is a sign of immaturity; 'true sciences' do not function in this way.
Multiple criteria for evaluating theories.	Irrational anarchy results, as there are no criteria for deciding that one theory is more valid than another.
There are very few replication studies.	There is no lineal accretion of the facts and proof(s) needed to move the field ever closer to the 'truth'.

According to Wheeler (following Hillman, 1981), the social science inferiority complex, such as that outlined above, is so common among social science researchers because these researchers have bought into a monotheistic view of the world (the belief in single reality), as opposed to a polytheistic view (the belief in multiple realities). Moreover, they have tried to impose this monotheistic view on an area of enquiry which, as I shall argue in a moment, is more consistent with a polytheistic approach. Wheeler describes monotheism as follows:

Monotheistic religions regard god as a single unity, the ultimate god, the one true god. Other gods are not just lesser, but false, and must be forsaken. These religions tend toward rigid, fixed beliefs to which believers must adhere exclusively. Likewise, monotheism as the metaphor of one reality posits a single, exclusive, and absolute truth about the phenomenon; any other ideas are false and must be forsaken. ... Monotheism, according to Hillman, values unity, generality, and integration. It strives for simplification and elimination and is concerned with absolutes and ultimates.   (Wheeler, 1987: 226)

The lamentations described above all fit in with the monotheistic view. The calls for unification around one theory are consistent with the need for adherence to rigid and fixed beliefs. The fear of anarchy, which arises from multiple criteria for theory evaluation, is natural in a quasi-religious system, which values single and absolute truth, simplification and the elimination of ambiguity. Finally, replication as 'truth finding' arises from the need to forsake lesser and false gods and from the striving for ultimate and absolute truth.

But need social scientists such as SLA researchers feel bad because of the present state of the field? My answer to this question is No.

The key lies in moving outside the monotheistic frame which forces us to see SLAR in a particular way, getting out of the trap of what Wheeler calls "automatic metaphor confirmation" (p. 228), where the problem is that a given phenomenon fails to exemplify the vision of the world provided by a particular metaphor; in this case, social sciences do not exemplify the monotheistic view of what a field of research should be. The alternative is to see the metaphor itself as a problem, as being 'out of synch' with the phenomenon it is being mapped onto. According to this logic, the misfit between 'the way SLAR is' and 'the received monotheistic model' suggests that SLA researchers need a different metaphor to frame their research. In the next section, I shall explore a polytheistic frame, which would allow us to see SLA in a different way, a way which I believe is more appropriate for the field.

The polytheistic frame

Wheeler differentiates polytheism from monotheism as follows:

... the polytheistic religions with which I am familiar not only acknowledge many gods, but tend to be loose, adaptable, and undogmatic about the inventory of gods and their characteristics, as well as about other ideas connected with the religion. These religions do not regard themselves and other religions as mutually exclusive, and often incorporate new gods and ideas as they encounter them in other religions and cults. Likewise, polytheism as a metaphor of multiple realities involves an open-ended array of perspectives on the world, each one equally valid, not mutually exclusive with others, and not as assigned in an absolute sense to categories such as "true" and "false", "correct" and "incorrect", or "reality" and "fantasy" ... Polytheism esteems diversity, plurality, complexity, and representation. It leads to an involvement with the details of experience, with context, and with relativism.   (Wheeler, 1987: 227)

Such a frame would lead us to an acceptance of the current state of play in SLAR, where multiple theories exist. Returning to the three lamentations about SLAR outlined in the previous section, we see that a polytheistic frame allows us to see them in a very different light. The existence of multiple theories is in line with what Wheeler calls "perspectives on the world" which are "equally valid [and] not mutually exclusive". The multiple criteria for theory evaluation are consistent with the lack of "categories such as *true* and *false* or *correct* and *incorrect*". From being a sign of inadequacy, the lack of replication studies comes to be seen as proof of the difficulty of making uniform what is diverse, plural and complex and which "leads to an involvement with the details of experience, with context, and with relativism". To sum up, the polytheistic frame allows us to see the current state of play in SLAR as a reflection of the complexity of the phenomena it attempts to elucidate, and not as a shortcoming.

What is perhaps most important is the way monotheists can only see polytheistic plurality in terms of a monotheistic world. When pluralism crops up, it is a problem to be dealt with and eventually eliminated, for there cannot be more than one valid way to see a phenomenon at a given moment. By contrast, polytheists accept plurality, and accommodate it by creating parallel schools of thought within one field. The monotheist somehow cannot even consider that the very existence of multiple perceptions might be taken as empirical evidence that the object of study may be approached and understood from more than one angle. What monotheism does, instead of trying to understand multiple perspectives, is to refer back to 'true sciences' and see plurality as the failure of the field to unite. The error therefore lies among practitioners, not in the world view of monotheists.

Wheeler also considers the accusation that social sciences "lack progress". She points out that this is yet another problem of conflicting problem-framing. If one can only envisage progress as movement along a line towards a single goal, then this is perhaps a valid interpretation. It is also a concept deeply embedded in the Western mindset: that of manifest destiny and the final goal achieved. However, if one considers the collective experience which the whole of the social sciences have gathered over the years, it is easy to entertain the thought that another way of establishing a field's worth is perhaps by bulk, as opposed to reaching a point on a line. In other words, a field might be evaluated according to how much knowledge it has accumulated, or how much has been understood about a particular area of human existence, and not in terms of where it has managed to get on a line supposedly leading to absolute knowledge of the 'truth'.

The discussion of different frames for the same state of affairs begs a discussion of whether or not individuals or groups of individuals can consciously change their frames. In other words, is it possible to generate a new frame for a particular situation, which in turn generates a new solution, or new solutions? Schön adopts the view that individuals *can* re-problematise phenomena which they encounter during their day-to-day activities. Indeed, his work with professionals is based on this very idea. For example, in one of his earlier publications (Schön, 1979), he describes how a group of product development researchers threw off their traditional frame, based on the metaphor of a paintbrush as a stiff and brittle instrument used to spread paint across a surface, and embraced a new frame, whereby a paintbrush was metaphorised as a pump, which moved a liquid from the brush onto the surface being painted. Schön shows how the new frame led to the further generation of suggestions about how to adapt and improve the design of the paintbrush bristles.

To my mind such changes in frame can only take place in professional atmospheres where practitioners are regularly encouraged to see phenomena in different lights. And I would argue that such professional atmospheres are much more consistent with an overarching polytheistic frame of reality than they are with a monotheistic frame. The former is more accepting and ultimately more respectful of plurality, while the latter tends towards the stifling of plurality.

Conclusion

I began this paper with a presentation of Schön's concept of framing and then went on to suggest that this mode of analysis might be carried out on the discourse of SLAR. Several excerpts from SLA literature were presented in an attempt to show that a common framing tendency in the field is what Wheeler would call monotheistic (the belief in a single reality). I suggested that a more appropriate metaphor frame for SLAR would be polytheism (the belief in multiple realities).

For me, this paper is but the beginning of a new area of metaphor enquiry. I see it as different from recent applications of modern metaphor theory to research in that it represents a move behind the scenes to examine the metaphors *of* research as opposed to metaphors *in* research (e.g. Gentner & Grudin, 1985; Leary, 1990; Soyland, 1994). Such a move towards the study of the metaphors, which frame research and (following Schön) eventually lead to decisions about practice, is needed in SLAR, which has only begun to address the philosophical underpinnings of its research programmes in the past several years.

In their recent book on hidden assumptions in the behavioural sciences, Slife and Williams (1995) suggest that there are three conclusions which one can draw about theory:

First, we cannot escape theory. Even in wanting to escape theory, to be open-minded, or [in] wanting to believe that theorizing was unimportant to science, we would be practicing a theory. Second, all theories have assumptions and implications embedded in them. Theories stem from cultural and historical contexts that lead them to meaning, and influence how they are understood and implemented. Third, these hidden influences have important consequences. They can lead to discrimination, poor science, and ineffective practitioners, just to name a few.

(Slife & Williams, 1995: 9–10)

I would like to suggest that we could say the same thing as regards the framing of research. If we substitute a form of the word **frame** each time the authors have used a form of the word **theory**, we get the following result:

First, we cannot escape [framing]. Even in wanting to escape [framing], to be open-minded, or [in] wanting to believe that [framing] was unimportant to science, we would be practicing a [frame]. Second, all [frames] have assumptions and implications embedded in them. [Frames] stem from cultural and historical contexts that lead them to meaning, and influence how they are understood and implemented. Third, these hidden influences have important consequences. They can lead to discrimination, poor science, and ineffective practitioners, just to name a few.

Thus, whether we decide to explore them or not, framing metaphors are there behind the actual research which is carried out. A field of study can survive without exploring them; however, I would suggest that this is a field populated with researchers who are not acting in as reflective a manner as is perhaps desirable.

8 Bridges to learning

Metaphors of teaching, learning and language

Martin Cortazzi and Lixian Jin

'A metaphor is the bridge to reality' A classical Arabic saying

Introduction

A metaphor can easily be seen as a bridge, etymologically 'carrying over' from one side to another. It links and comprises the known and the unknown, the tangible and the less tangible, the familiar and the new. As "a bridge enabling passage from one world to another" (Shiff, 1979: 106), metaphors enable learners "to understand and experience one kind of thing in terms of another", to paraphrase Lakoff and Johnson's (1980: 5) notion of the essence of metaphor. In this paper, we explore teachers' and students' metaphors of teaching, learning and language. The generation of metaphors in such professional contexts as learning how to teach, and learning about language in speech therapy and communication courses, is, we will argue in this paper, a bridge to the 'reality' of the professional or technical world.

Outline of the study

In this study we examine metaphors from four sources:

1 spontaneous metaphors arising in experienced UK primary teachers' accounts of learning;
2 elicited metaphors about teaching and language collected from postgraduate students on primary education courses in the UK;
3 elicited metaphors about language collected from undergraduates studying linguistics on speech therapy or human communication courses in a UK institution; and finally
4 cross-cultural elicited metaphors about 'good teachers' from university students in five other countries. The four sets of data overlap sufficiently to allow the metaphors to be seen as bridges to learning, albeit in different ways.

Our primary interest is to explore the cultural – cognitive elements of metaphor use. More specifically, since metaphors are frequently encountered in inter-cultural learning contexts, studying them may reveal aspects of different cultural orientations to communication and learning. Metaphors may also have a useful function in teaching, by helping to raise learners' awareness of key concepts, models and issues. Similarly, raising teachers' awareness of their own metaphors may help them to reflect on their own experience and to develop professionally. Our research questions are, then:

Q1 What sorts of metaphors do teachers and students use to refer to learning, teaching, language and good teachers?

Q2 In what ways may these metaphors be bridges to learning?

Q3 What similarities or differences are there across the groups of subjects?

Q4 What implications are there concerning any differences, either between teachers and students, or across cultural groups?

We explore metaphors along the line taken by Lakoff and Johnson (1980), and Lakoff (1987a). Our view is thus that the everyday talk of students and teachers is thoroughly imbued with metaphor and the proper locus of metaphor is the conceptual system. A study of the conceptual metaphors produced by teachers and students should, as a result, prove revealing, telling us something about their professional perceptions, their thinking and their learning. This is an applied linguistic interest, in the sense of using linguistically oriented approaches to address the problems of knowing about teachers' and learners' thinking about learning and of how to raise their awareness about language, teaching and learning.

The subjects of this research are 128 UK primary teachers (who all teach English as a core element in the National Curriculum); 140 British postgraduate students undertaking primary education courses (who train to teach English among other subjects); 140 British undergraduate students of Communication studying English linguistics (who train professionally as speech therapists, or who study psychology); and 113 Chinese, 104 Turkish, 93 Japanese, 90 Lebanese and 60 Iranian university students of English as a Foreign Language (some of whom intend to become EFL teachers). Common features linking these subjects are that they all teach or study English, as a first or other language, and they can all be assumed to have a reasonable awareness of metaphor. They are all university students, except the teachers, who have all completed tertiary education. The first set of data was gathered in the late 1980s, the remaining data were gathered in 1994–1995.

There are, of course, differences in these subjects' linguistic and cultural backgrounds, and it is one of our aims to explore these by examining some of the metaphors across linguistic or cultural groups. It may be that some, at least, of the generic-level metaphors are culturally specific, or that they are given a different emphasis in different cultures. If, as Lakoff and Johnson claim, the most fundamental values in a culture are "coherent with the metaphoric structure of the most fundamental concepts in the culture" (1980: 22), and if some "can vary from culture to culture" (p. 14), then the fundamental metaphors of teaching, learning and language are worth investigating, both within one culture (e.g. to study the occupational culture and beliefs of teachers) and across cultures, as part of a study of cultures of learning.

There are also some differences in the subjects' focus and type of data. In the data gathered from the British teachers, the metaphors came from narratives which arose in interviews focusing on teachers' experiences. It is unlikely that the subjects had any particular awareness of metaphors at the time of speaking, beyond the normal awareness which native speakers might have in spontaneous speech. In contrast, the rest of the data involves elicited metaphors obtained by asking subjects to complete a sentence stem: '*Teaching is ...*'; '*Language is ...*'; or '*A good teacher is ...*'. Subjects were encouraged to give metaphors; stems completed without a metaphor were not included as data. The methodology here necessarily draws subjects' attention to metaphors, but this factor is constant across all the data sets (except the teachers' metaphors). Since the British teacher trainees were working in primary schools for teaching experience, it was natural to ask them to complete a sentence stem about teaching; the idea was that this could easily be related to their professional context. This set complements the first set, which focuses on primary children's learning.

In the third set, it seemed more natural at the time to ask about language, which was the direct subject of study of these British undergraduates, than about teaching. In retrospect, we should perhaps have asked about teaching, or teachers, to afford a more direct comparison with the fourth set of data, in which groups of students from a range of different countries were asked about teachers. This fourth set formed part of a wider questionnaire study, but it would not have been appropriate to ask about language, even though all the students were studying EFL. This fourth set was thus to some extent opportunistic. The data sets are therefore not as directly comparable as we would wish, but this study explores several related directions simultaneously.

Several questions regarding validity arise, concerning how metaphors might be bridges to learning. These are in fact similar to the problems faced by Block in Chapter 7: How do we know if (or whether) metaphors are linked to learning, thinking and behaviour? What kind of evidence will be acceptable to judge that metaphors are bridges to learning? How 'real' are the metaphors: are they only verbal devices, or do they have cognitive and social validity for students and teachers?

While it may not be possible to give conclusive answers to these questions in an exploratory study, there is a range of corroborative evidence which might be sought, to ascertain the role of metaphors in these contexts: the frequency of occurrence of the same, or very similar, metaphors in the data; the number of speakers who give these metaphors; the use of these metaphors in significant contexts of teaching and learning; what subjects themselves say about activities in which metaphors play a central role; the fact that verbal metaphors are accompanied by related actions or behaviour; change in actions or behaviour through/following the metaphors. The most convincing evidence would be to show clear relationships between teachers' metaphors (or those of students) and students' learning outcomes, or to relate particular sets of metaphors to different types of classroom behaviour and different approaches to learning. However, at present, these are distant goals. A first step is to explore possible bridges between teachers' and students' metaphors and their learning.

Related research: metaphors in education

Metaphors are held to have a general value in education to assist in reflecting and organising social thought and practice in schooling (Scheffler, 1960: 62). Metaphors have been regarded as having a crucial role in the development of a number of disciplines. This is seen in such book titles as *Physics as Metaphor* (Jones, 1983) and *Psychology as Metaphor* (Soyland, 1994). Familiarity with the dominant metaphors or models of major schools of thought can clearly facilitate students' understanding of a subject. In linguistics, for example, much has been made of such dominant metaphors as: *Language is a game of chess* (Saussure, 1960: 110); *Language is growth; language is an organ* (Chomsky, 1978: 205); *Language is an instinct* (Pinker, 1994: 18); *Language is a resource* (Halliday, 1978: 17). In at least some of the discussion about language by prominent linguists the use of such metaphors seems to be a conscious striving for understanding: 'If we want a reasonable metaphor we might perhaps talk about *growth:* language seems to me to grow in the mind, rather in the way familiar physical systems of the body grow' (Chomsky, 1978: 205).

Metaphors often carry over from one discipline to another. A good example is '*scaffolding*'. This neo-Vygotskian metaphor was coined in psychology (Wood *et al.*, 1976; Bruner, 1978) to describe a form of guided discourse and cognitive support given by adults, or more skilled peers, which is progressively withdrawn as the learner moves towards mastery of a particular skill or activity. The **scaffolding**, as a specific kind of **support**, is **constructed** by an adult and later gradually **removed**, as the **structure** of the child's learning is gradually **built up**. The metaphor has been widely taken up in education to encourage ways to develop pupils' talk (Edwards & Mercer, 1987; Wood, 1986) and this has been extended to literacy in Reading Recovery projects (Clay & Cazden, 1990) and literacy development for second language readers (Boyle & Peregoy, 1990). The *scaffolding* metaphor has become closely bound to other widely accepted metaphors of **constructing** talk (Newman *et al.*, 1989; Mercer, 1995) and **constructing** literacy (Cook-Gumperz Ed., 1986; Wells & Chang-Wells, 1992) through an **apprenticeship** (Rogoff, 1990) or **dialogue** (Meadows & Cashdan, 1988), which involves a **hand-over** by the adult and a **take-over** by the child, all this within a general **constructivist** framework of learning. Among language and literacy teachers, this set of metaphors is now widely used. It is doubtful if many teachers are aware of the specific nature of the original metaphors; some teachers now simply use them to refer to any kind of support for any learning activity. However, it can be argued that the metaphors, encountered on in-service courses, have themselves 'scaffolded' the teachers' awareness of aspects of language and learning; teachers have 'taken over' the metaphors in their own way. When this happens – and we have heard teachers in several countries claim that this has happened to them – the metaphors are a bridge towards internalisation of concepts and towards changes in the practice of teaching.

It has also been argued that such metaphors, even when understood in context, can be barriers as well as bridges. Smith (1987), for instance, has shown how metaphors of literacy (literacy as **information, process, skill, levels** and **stages**) can mislead as much as they lead. Metaphors motivate action, as seen in the powerful presentation of progressive education in terms of such images as **growth, nurture** or **play**, for instance, in the Plowden Report on British primary education (Central Advisory Council for Education, 1967). This has also been criticised (e.g. Dearden, 1968) in that the image-making is favoured above analytic thinking; metaphors can become empty slogans.

Nevertheless, it is periodically advocated that metaphors should be used in direct classroom instruction, to aid children's understanding of subject content through analogy between familiar experience and new concepts (Gordon, 1966; Williams, 1983) or to raise learners' awareness of specific everyday uses of language, for example by exploring metaphors in science (Sutton, 1992; Low, in Chapter 3). One reason for the effectiveness of metaphor as a teaching device is that understanding a metaphor involves active mental participation to link target and source domains. Gibbs, in Chapter 2, distinguishes four aspects of understanding: *comprehension*, the immediate moment-by-moment process of creating meanings for utterances; *recognition*, the conscious identification of the products of comprehension as types; *interpretation*, the analysis of the early comprehension as tokens, perhaps understanding a particular set of entailments; and *appreciation*, an aesthetic judgement given to a product as a type or token. The act of interpretation or appreciation is a collaboration (Davidson, 1979: 29) with the metaphor-maker – who may be the teacher – which completes a cycle of imagination. The interpretation reflects as much on the interpreter as on the originator. This remains true of the researcher attempting to categorise metaphors; every classification is an interpretation.

In fact, classroom activities which focus deliberately on the use of metaphors have shown metaphors to be central to aiding student understanding of the nature of subject disciplines. Good examples have been discussed in science education, where teachers draw learners' attention to the "creative function of metaphor in the nascent phase of the scientific imagination" (Holton, 1984: 96) by showing how eminent scientists used metaphors as an apparently necessary part of the process of investigation and model building (Holton, 1984; Sutton, 1992, 1994). Through such historical examples and discussion of their own metaphors for concepts, students may come to understand how out of metaphors "many new thoughts have arisen, and new areas of subject matter have been developed ... " (Sutton, 1994: 64). Holton emphasises the necessity of metaphor in bridging 'gulfs' between research areas, arguing that a metaphor is a "means for bridging an apparent gulf ... The bridge is of gossamer. It breaks often, but sometimes it carries us across the gulf; and in any case there is nothing else that will" (Holton, 1984: 97–98).

Related research: metaphors in teacher education

A number of researchers in teacher education have demonstrated that metaphors represent cognitive and affective distillations of teachers' fundamental beliefs about teaching. The study of teachers' metaphors appears to be a fruitful, indirect way to study important aspects of teachers' cognition: for example, how teachers plan or make decisions, or how they give meaning to their experience (Munby, 1986). Researchers have concluded that some of the more significant thought processes of teachers consist principally of images constructed from classroom events and that these images (including metaphors) are central to how teachers know students and classrooms (Elbaz, 1983; Clandinin, 1985). Much of this research focuses on the development of practical classroom knowledge of student teachers, or of pedagogic content knowledge, by interviewing and observing small numbers of novices (Clandinin, 1985; Connelly & Clandinin, 1988; Bullough, 1992; Grant, 1992; Johnston, 1992). Generally, this is held to be a necessary qualitative approach to studying the development of teaching skills and teachers' knowledge and control of classroom processes which, at the same time, aids new teachers to formulate partial explanations for processes which as yet they do not fully understand (Miller & Fredericks, 1988; Bullough, 1991). The elicitation and discussion of student teachers' own metaphors for their classroom practice, and subsequent reflection on how their metaphors and practice develop, have a direct pedagogic function to promote awareness of professional practice and of self-image, in a process of continuing professional development. For some (e.g. Clandinin, 1985; Nias, 1989), a teacher's image of personal or professional self is not simply an idealised goal, nor merely a reflection of practice, but is an over-riding framework which shapes practice in specific directions. Some of the images found turn out to be similar to classical metaphors used to describe teachers and teaching, as De Castell (1988) notes: *teacher as midwife* (Socrates); *teacher as artist/scientist* (Dewey); *teacher as technician* (Skinner); *teacher as researcher* (Stenhouse).

Each of these metaphors, or student teachers' own metaphors, could be seen as conceptual metaphors, subsuming many verbal expressions and several semantic fields. Munby (1986: 203–206) exemplifies this by analysing one teacher's metaphor as THE LESSON IS A MOVEMENT: for example, **Keep it moving somehow smoothly; We move along faster; We were slow at getting started today; Well I keep going; They won't follow along, they're behind.**

Larger scale studies of student teachers' metaphors include Marchant's (1992) statistical analysis of over 100 subjects which yielded eight generic metaphors (he calls them similes): TEACHER AS AUTHORITY: **judge, police officer, prison warden;** AS

CAREGIVER: **parent, doctor;** AS DIRECTOR: **movie director, orchestra conductor;** AS CAPTIVE: **prisoner;** AS PARTY HOST; AS PERSON ON TRIAL: in **a courtroom,** waiting for the verdict of the **jury;** AS REFEREE; and AS AGENT OF CHANGE: **advocate** of change. These can be compared with our own findings summarised below.

In the field of language teacher training, a number of writers advocate the use of metaphors and analogies which centre on both *teaching* and *language* in order to raise trainees' (or language learners') awareness of language learning processes (e.g. Dubin & Olshtain, 1986; Thornbury, 1991; Scott, 1994; Ponterotto, 1994). Thus Scott (1994: 99) asks EFL teachers: "What in your teaching or studying of TEFL is similar to an egg?" To which one group replied: **growth of language acquisition; the fragility of learners' self-esteem; the yolk of vocabulary and the white of context; the hatchability of input theory.** More broadly, Woodward (1991) demonstrates the applicability of what she calls *loop input,* whereby trainee teachers undertake one classroom activity and are then led to see it in terms of another: for example, a vocabulary game about language teaching terms, or a substitution table about lesson warm-ups, or a substitution table about metaphors for teachers and learners.

Advocates of all these uses of metaphors in teacher training certainly do *not* see the generation of metaphors for teaching, language or oneself as teacher as a verbal game. Rather they see metaphor activity as a bridge to talking meaningfully about practice, to understanding practice, and, crucially, as part of practice itself. Thus, in an elaboration of one method, Connelly and Clandinin directly address both pre-service and in-service teachers telling them to pay attention to 'metaphors we teach by':

We understand teachers' actions and practices as embodied expressions of their metaphors of teaching and living. It makes a great deal of difference to our practices, for example, if we think of teaching as gardening, coaching or cooking ... How can metaphors be identified? Perhaps the most direct way is to listen to speech. How do you talk about your teaching? ... We think it is more telling for you to examine your practices, interview material, stories and journals to capture your metaphorical concepts of teaching. To do this we suggest you need ... to contextualise your metaphors within your experiences and to see them played out in your practices. Our intent is not to have you see this way of understanding practice only as a way of talking about practice, but also as part of your practice.

(Connelly & Clandinin, 1988: 71)

Results of the study

Breakthroughs in learning

If indeed metaphors are bridges to learning they should occur in teachers' accounts of learning, either of their own learning or of their students' learning. In fact, this is what we have found; teachers' accounts of significant learning events are deeply and widely pervaded by metaphors.

In research interviews, Cortazzi (1991) obtained 128 teachers' oral narrative accounts of classroom experiences of children's learning. These accounts were shown to be very similar to accounts found in normal teacher-to-teacher interaction (e.g. in staffroom conversation) and the data are therefore naturalistic, in the sense that the interviews were not designed to elicit metaphors; the metaphors occurred in narratives in normal running speech. Cortazzi (1991) found that 85 teachers, in recalling 'breakthroughs in learning', used metaphors repeatedly in the evaluation sections of their narratives (*cf.* Labov, 1972; Cortazzi, 1993; Cortazzi & Jin, 1994). The evaluation indicates the main point of a narrative and often reveals the speaker's attitude to what has been recounted. The teller gives marked emphasis to this part of the narrative through choice of lexical items, exclamations, repetition or distinctive uses of pitch and intonation. In the evaluation, the speaker is basically indicating how the narrative should be interpreted. This can be seen in the following accounts of two learners given by the same teacher:

One boy that I've had a lot of trouble with, his reading is not good, but his number work was appalling. He couldn't count, he couldn't recognise any numbers, and then all of a sudden in the space of about two weeks it seemed to click and I could see him beginning to go. He's now beginning to understand it. And then another little boy who just did not understand addition at all. I tried it all ways. You name it, I tried it, and then all of a sudden he just came in one day and [clicks fingers] it seemed to click and I could really see the breakthrough.

These narratives are, in the teacher's own terms, about 'breakthroughs' in learning (itself a metaphor) which are evaluated using the dramatic adverbials **all of a sudden** and **suddenly** but more particularly, through the key metaphors **it seemed to click, beginning to go**, and **it came on**. The **click** is itself underlined by physical finger-clicking in the second mention. This sound and the physical gesture acting out the metaphor could be seen as corroborative evidence validating the notion that the metaphors are used consciously and that there are some clear links between metaphors and teachers' thinking. The click might further be seen as an example of revivifying a conventional metaphor (Pettit, 1982).

A further example, with key metaphors italicised, will give a clearer idea of how metaphors are used in these teachers' accounts of memorable examples of children's learning and will provide a context for the lists of recurring examples we will cite later.

One particular girl, she suddenly realised she *was making headway* and the whole of her outlook on school work changed dramatically because of that, and her achievements *went up in leaps and bounds*. It may have had something to do with teacher expectations as well. She *has suddenly taken off* with her reading and other things. I was sat there, I must have looked daft because I had a silly grin all over my face and I was so pleased with this and that was my reward for the day that she had achieved and that she had somehow managed *to get herself going*. I think any little thing that a child doesn't understand and is genuinely worried about and comes to you and says to you, 'I don't understand this. I can't make head or tail of it.' And if they go away and they can understand it, you can see *the light dawn on their face* and that to me is worth – well, you can't put a worth on it in financial terms.

Such narratives commonly conformed to a schema of: the struggle of a child with learning; the teacher's thoughts about lack of progress; a metaphor describing the moment of learning (a breakthrough); the joy of both the learner and teacher; the teacher's thoughts about this; the teacher's comment that such moments make teaching worthwhile. The teachers often have no explanation for the learning (no theories of learning are cited in any of the narratives), or, as seems possible, the metaphor *is* the explanation or, at least, a striving to explain.

The metaphors seem to capture the essence of the learning event in images of moments of, apparently sudden, learning. Teachers use these metaphors as a symbolic commodity, which can be exchanged in talk with other teachers who have experienced similar moments, but apparently these others also have no particular explanation. Many of the narratives (surprisingly, since the teachers' main role can be considered to bring about learning) explicitly comment on the unplanned, unexplained nature of the breakthrough. It is **accidental, by coincidence, for no apparent reason, unbelievable, unpredictable.** It is **a mystery, a miracle, there's no reason . . . it just happens.** The click, for example, comes to symbolise this mystery. The conclusion that the metaphoric expression *is* the subject of reflection and a kind of shorthand jargon in teachers' thinking is further supported by evidence from teachers' writing, such as the following extract from an academic assignment, in which a teacher discusses young children's learning:

How do children learn to make sense of the written material around them? We often hear the excited teacher, having spent weeks with young David struggling over his words and sentences, saying, "I think it's finally *clicked*". Magically he's found the key to make sense of all the black shapes on a page. Did it just *click* in a flash of understanding, or did he have to go through a number of stages to get there? What process has he been going through in his mind for it to '*click*'?

Evidently, the metaphors are often used in strong affective contexts (*cf.* Lerman, 1984). Indeed, in 36 instances, immediately after using a metaphor, teachers expressed strong emotional reactions to seeing the child's learning: **I was so thrilled, It was amazing, Fantastic, Terrific, Marvellous, You can't put a price on it.** These reactions are themselves frequently expressed in metaphors of a journey or upward movement: **I was riding on a cloud, I was up in the air, I was over the moon.** Significantly, from the viewpoint of studying metaphors in occupational culture, in 33 narratives the use of the metaphor was followed by clear statements that such moments made primary teaching worthwhile: "That, for me, is the reward this year", "That's what makes the job worthwhile".

The teachers' metaphors are clearly placed at the high point of the narrative. They are deeply evaluative of the recapitulated experience. They frequently precede expressions of affect and important job evaluations. It might be concluded from our study of these 85 accounts that for the teachers these incidents, small as they may seem to outsiders, mark out the cognitive and affective meaning of what it it is like to be a teacher and what the rewards are. It is noteworthy that the incidents were recalled as examples of learning which stood out in the teachers' minds.

The dominant generic metaphors in these narratives, all of which in their original context refer to moments of learning, are as follows (numbers in brackets indicate the total number of examples which occurred in the corpus):

LEARNING IS A CLICK (28)
it just clicked together; it's clicked in his mind; he has clicked; it all clicked straight away; the words clicking and the number clicking
LEARNING IS LIGHT (18)
the light dawns; he's seen the light; the light in his eyes; her face lit up; a spark; this sort of flash going straight through
LEARNING IS MOVEMENT (50)
it's come; he came on; she came from nothing; they're beginning to go; they're not going to move that much; they all seemed to be moving; she's gone; she just goes straight through; he got off on his reading; a couple really have pushed through; this sudden leap; we really have got lift off

point with her; he was off, he was off; they zoomed away; you can see a spurt forward

Two less frequent generic metaphors were: LEARNING IS A JIGSAW (3): **the pieces came together; it all sort of came into place,** and LEARNING IS TAKING (5): **he suddenly picked it up; it takes the thing into its head.**

These metaphors are commonly occurring, yet the range of teachers' metaphors in these spontaneous accounts is greatly restricted. Surprisingly, the metaphors seem to replace any technical terms for learning. Considering that these kinds of narratives are often exchanged among teachers in school staffrooms, the metaphors seem to have the status of being key elements of a folk theory of learning. Alternatively, they might be interpreted as frames, following Schön's stages (described by Block, in Chapter 7): the existing situation of teachers attempting to account for children's 'breakthroughs' is seen as problematic; it is framed as **clicks, light** or **movement,** which preserves elements of mystery and joy but absolves the teachers from responsibility; these metaphors are then exchanged in staffroom talk, often performed or acted out. This performance (with gestures, intense facial expressions, changes in pitch and intonation, whispers and imitations of child voices), presumably to underline the teachers' emotional reaction to the child's learning, and the quoted 'thoughts' in such accounts, corroborates links to behaviour and cognition.

The 'movement' metaphors were frequently deictic, oriented towards the direction of the teacher, (e.g. **come on, come round, reaches forwards and meets you.**). They echo Munby's (1986) examples cited earlier. Some subcategories showed: LEARNING IS A JOURNEY where children made **steps** and **great strides,** reaching **milestones** and **peaks;** THE LEARNER IS A ROCKET where children had **lift off** or **take off** and **zoomed away;** LEARNING IS MOVEMENT THROUGH WATER where children moved by **spurts, surges** or **making headway.**

Why do teachers use metaphors?

Teachers seem to use metaphors in accounts of learning for at least seven reasons (*cf.* Low, 1988; Ortony Ed., 1979).

First, using metaphors may help teachers to *identify for themselves what they actually experience* (Provenzo *et al.*, 1989: 556). Using a metaphor enables teachers to verbalise what is unknown or difficult to describe in other terms. The metaphor frames a problem by putting it into words, thus defining its parameters (Schön, 1979). The metaphor is 'the solution of the enigma' (Ricoeur, 1979: 144).

Second, metaphors may have the performance function of *adding dramatic effect* to the narrative of children's learning told in the staffroom or in a research interview (Cortazzi, 1991).

Third, metaphors may *express the meaning more concisely* than a prolix non-metaphorical equivalent. At the same time, metaphors capture multiple meanings in experience (Ricoeur, 1978).

Fourth, metaphors *invite interaction* (Scheffler, 1960: 48; Black, 1962: 38) by forcing listeners to work out the relevant resemblance between target and source domains.

Fifth, metaphors have a function of *organising systematic concepts* (Lakoff & Johnson, 1980) in teachers' cultural-cognitive models of learning. The metaphors in accounts of learning occur especially at points where the teacher interprets the children's learning, in the evaluation of the narrative (Cortazzi, 1991).

Sixth, some metaphors may be core clichés through which tellers *transform images into models*, which are manipulated through performance to develop critical themes (Scheub, 1975: 377).

Seventh, it is difficult to be sure whether the context, interpretation or narrative account organise the metaphor, as a key element of the teller's evaluation of an event, or whether the metaphor, as a central image of learning, *organises the teacher's interpretation of learning* and the subsequent account of it. It is possible that both processes are involved.

Teaching is ...

The above spontaneous metaphors for one kind of learning can be contrasted with further data elicited from 140 British postgraduate students undertaking primary teacher training. Between them they generated 236 metaphors in response to being asked to complete the sentence stems of *Teaching is ..., because ...* Some students did not respond with metaphors, others wrote several. Since they had recently completed a teaching practice in schools, the stems implicitly also elicited *Learning to teach is ....* While the range of metaphors is much wider than the 'breakthrough' metaphors, they can be readily grouped into generic types. Many showed wry humour and mixed emotional reactions to the complexity and difficulties they had encountered when teaching.

The metaphors are classified below according to our interpretation of what the conceptual metaphors are. Our classification is based on the metaphor itself, the entailments (reasons) given by the students themselves, and similarities with other metaphors. We set a minimum number of five tokens before considering accepting candidate conceptual metaphors, i.e. we are interested in some degree of commonality among the students and frequency of citation, and five tokens seemed a fair figure to represent this. Generally this minimum was substantially exceeded. Numbers in brackets give the total number of tokens for each conceptual metaphor; each type is illustrated by two examples only, with the reasons given (see Table 1 opposite).

Further examples were TEACHING IS ART; TEACHING IS FIRE; TEACHING IS A CREATURE; TEACHING IS A MACHINE OR TOOL; TEACHING IS COMMUNICATION; TEACHING IS A SOURCE; TEACHING IS A TEXT.

Where teaching was MOVEMENT, sometimes a JOURNEY, learning was also a JOURNEY. The nature of the data does not allow further comparison of the subjects' interpretations, since in the teachers' spontaneous metaphors the 'reasons' are not given.

The TEACHING IS GROWTH metaphor, with 20 tokens from these postgraduate students, echoes much rhetoric from the 1960s in Britain from the Plowden report (Central Advisory Council for Education, 1967) and subsequent public debate (Dearden, 1968), which may be evidence that some of these metaphors have considerable endurance. On present evidence, we cannot say whether such metaphors are reinvented, transmitted through a reading of the many references to growth-related concepts in child-centred literature, or whether they are transmitted in an enculturation process as new teachers enter schools.

Some students voluntarily took this metaphor activity further. This may be evidence that they found it useful and that, for some, it affected their actions. One group produced a series of paper cut-out models of vehicles and maps to illustrate JOURNEY metaphors, another group produced a huge wall collage of visual representations of GROWTH metaphors. Others discussed metaphors in schools and reported that they realised that experienced teachers had different metaphors from their own and were unsure if theirs would change while teaching.

In a teacher education programme it seems worthwhile to explore such metaphors further with student teachers, and to look at: their applicability; their limits; their professional, personal and emotional validity; how they may combine or complement each other; and how they may change over time. It would also be interesting to compare these metaphors from intending primary teachers with those from secondary trainee teachers, or to compare metaphors from teachers of different subject areas.

Table 1. *Teaching metaphors from trainee teachers*

Teaching is:	Because (reasons) ....
TEACHING IS A JOURNEY. (N=44)	
An endless journey	Everyone (including the teacher) is always learning.
A mystery trip	You know where you are starting from but not where you'll end up.
TEACHING IS FOOD / DRINK / COOKING. (N=22)	
Making bread	It requires lots of ingredients, time to prove and very delicate handling.
A coconut	Tough on the outside, nice and soft on the inside.
TEACHING IS PLANT GROWTH AND CULTIVATION. (N=20)	
An oak tree	It needs firm roots to bear fruit.
A tree	Children's knowledge branches out into more and more complexity.
TEACHING IS A SKILL. (N=19)	
Juggling	Keeping many things going at once, sometimes you drop one.
Spinning plates	There are so many simultaneous things to do.
TEACHING IS AN OCCUPATION (OTHER THAN TEACHING). (N=16)	
A judge	Fair, implements rules
A priest	Relaxed, wise, pleasant, 'improving'
TEACHING IS ENTERTAINMENT. (N=15)	
Acting	Putting on an act, taking many roles, being on stage
A comedy hour	Fun, but only with good preparation and good relationships
TEACHING IS SEARCHING FOR TREASURE. (N=14)	
Mining	The teacher is always chipping away trying to find understanding.
A priceless jewel	Generally under-valued and sometimes in the wrong setting
TEACHING IS FAMILY RELATIONSHIPS. (N=13)	
A respected aunt	Approachable, kind, friendly
A responsible uncle	Wants you to do well, but can tell you off
TEACHING IS WAR. (N=6)	
War	It's a battlefield out there.
Arming the troops	Giving children weapons of learning, questions to defend themselves
TEACHING IS CONSTRUCTION / (PART OF) A BUILDING. (N=9)	
An open house	It welcomes and accommodates all people, but it needs building.
Building a wall	You need firm foundations for a good result.

Language is ...

Further metaphors on the theme of language were collected from first- and second-year undergraduates studying Linguistics as part of Psychology or Speech Therapy courses in a department of Human Communication. Here, 140 students completed the open-ended sentence stem, *Language is ... , because ... .* to yield 412 metaphors for language. Again, there is a wide range of responses and again most metaphors fell into fairly clear generic types. Others remain tricky to classify; should they be classified by the word and its relations to other words in an obvious set, or classified by reasons which are the point of comparison? Since students elaborate reasons differently, giving varying numbers of reasons, giving more or less detail, giving obvious points of comparison or not, a comparison of the reasons is not always clear. The metaphors are listed in Table 2 opposite, with total numbers of responses for each group and two examples only of the metaphors, with the reasons as given.

Other conceptual metaphors were: LANGUAGE IS AN INSTI-TUTION (the State, Law, Religion, Education, Politics, Power) (17); LANGUAGE IS A BIOLOGICAL ACTIVITY (death, life, dream, sleep) (15); LANGUAGE IS BODY PARTS (body, brain, heart) (7); LANGUAGE IS FINANCE (money, bank, stock exchange) (5).

The concepts revealed from the students' metaphors reflect two main themes: that language is structural (seen in the source domains of 'buildings', 'society', 'body parts', 'institutions'); that language is functional (reflected in the source domains of 'tools', 'leisure', 'everyday life', 'relationships', 'cloth'). However, when the reasons given for these metaphors are further investigated, while some have obvious close links between source and reason, others show a more open relationship between target and source which is much less obvious until the reason is stated.

Thus, in the more obvious cases, when language is a 'jigsaw puzzle' (13 responses) this is only because **the pieces fit together;** when language is 'the sea' (8 examples) the reason is always because of **depth** or **change;** when it is 'a game of tennis' (6 mentions) it is because of **interaction** and **bouncing meanings;** when it is 'a tree' (12 instances) it is because of **growth** and **having a trunk and branches;** when it is 'a flower' (8 examples) it is similarly because of **growth** but also **variety** and, for one student, **to brighten up someone's day.** Such obviousness is still important – these are perhaps cultural paradigms, but some British students also seem to have interpreted the elicitation task as a quest for originality, which resulted in more epigrammatic

Table 2. *Language metaphors from undergraduate students*

A language is:	Because (reasons):
LANGUAGE IS NATURE. (N=84) (e.g. river, sea, flower, tree, sky, galaxy, weather, etc.).	
A thunderstorm	It is unpredictable and varies in size, dimension, region and strength.
A spider's web	Because of its complexity, regarding its structure.
LANGUAGE IS LEISURE. (N=80) (e.g. Music, Sport, Play/ing, Art or a Game)	
A piece of music	It is made up of the same set of notes but in a never ending number of ways.
A game of draughts	Each move depends on the other player.
LANGUAGE IS A TOOL OR OBJECT. (N=75)	
A tool	It gets used by people to achieve an objective.
A slightly faulty radio	It is reliable, clear and understandable 99% of the time but when you need it the most it will break down/fail you.
LANGUAGE IS EVERYDAY LIFE. (N=41) (e.g. Food, Drink, Shopping, Medicine)	
A supermarket	Everyone uses it, but no two people achieve the same trolley full of shopping
A recipe	It consists of many different ingredients.
LANGUAGE IS (PART OF) A BUILDING OR BUILDING MATERIALS. (N=25)	
A pile of bricks	We use individual signs to construct any desired sentences.
A nuclear power station	It's colossal, complicated and necessary in order to give power to the nation.
LANGUAGE IS SOCIETY, RELATIONSHIPS OR PEOPLE. (N=23)	
A family	It builds relationships between people.
Love	There are a limited number of people but an infinite number of possibilities.
LANGUAGE IS CLOTHES, CLOTH OR JEWELLERY. (N=12)	
A big, baggy jumper	'One size' fits lots of different people and you can stretch it to fit your own shape or 'identity'.
A wardrobe of clothes	You can change the way you speak like you change the clothes you wear for different occasions.
LANGUAGE IS A JOURNEY. (N=10)	
A motorway	It is a simple means of getting from A to B but the more cars (words) that travel upon it the more congested and harder to follow it becomes.
A mystery tour	New ways of communicating through language are created daily without prior thought or planning being given to what will be said.

replies. Thus language is 'a calendar' ("It has order, but only the order a culture gives it"); 'the stock exchange' ("There are many different voices talking at the same time and all waiting to be listened to"); 'a crime' ("sometimes you get away with what you say and sometimes you don't"); 'my piggy bank' ("It's limited"); and even 'a wife' ("One is enough"). Interestingly, for the spontaneous metaphors (the teachers' learning breakthrough metaphors) the target–source relationship is clearer than for many of the elicited ones (when the students wrote down the metaphors *and* the reasons). This may be because some students saw the task demand in creative terms or because the spontaneous metaphors occurred in face-to-face interaction where the speaker had normal conversational feedback: if the metaphor had been seen as *not* being understood, the speaker would presumably have explained it.

Some of the students' metaphors may appear to emphasise structural aspects of language, but the reason given may reflect functional aspects (or *vice versa*), or the reason may include both functional and structural aspects. Thus, when language is 'a house', it is because it has structure but "it can be decorated to suit taste, culture and experience"; when it is 'a wall', this is mainly because it is "a barrier separating different groups" but also because "each new word gives us new steps up to the top".

Above all, many metaphors from all source domains indicate an overriding view of language; it is complicated, varied, mysterious, constantly changing and developing. Few metaphors are found which can be categorised as communicative, although the students show a clear understanding that language is for communication and interaction. It would be interesting to repeat the elicitation exercise towards the end of their course to investigate possible restructurings in the most common metaphors.

Since some students found the task difficult, they were shown an example, *Language is a game of chess*. This had an unforeseen consequence; first-year students with little background in language study tended to give similar structural examples, whereas second-year students tended to give more informed, functional examples. The task itself was useful to promote reflection and discussion on the nature of language and to raise language awareness, as some students explicitly stated. Similarly, we have found that discussing the breakthrough metaphors with experienced teachers promotes reflective thinking on such professional issues as how children learn and how teachers think about, talk about and promote this learning.

An interesting feature of these results is that there are some parallels and overlaps between the metaphors for *teaching* and *language*, produced by different groups of students. Both, for example, are seen in terms of JOURNEYS. It is not clear whether this is because, for the students in question, both concepts involve *learning*: that is to say, one group of students is learning to teach, the other is learning about language and linguistics.

Cross-cultural data

The British data considered earlier can be compared with further examples of metaphors of A GOOD TEACHER IS ..., which were elicited from 113 Chinese students, 106 Turkish students, 93 Japanese students, 90 Lebanese students and 60 Iranian students. In each case the participants were in their own country, except for the Turkish group, who were on a summer visit to Britain. Each group was asked to complete the sentence stem *A good teacher is ...* individually, as part of a wider questionnaire study, which was administered face to face by the researchers or assistants. The data are thus elicited, rather than spontaneous.

There are some cautions: the data were obtained in English, which is a foreign language for all the students. Although the students were studying English at university and had completed at least six years of English at school, this could clearly present difficulties, since few of them were English majors. About half of the Lebanese students had attended English-medium secondary schools, but again English was not their first language, nor was it used much outside school. Secondly, many students did not readily respond to the task, as the British students had done. In fact, some students in all groups did not complete it at all. Reasons given for non-completion included the feeling that the task was too difficult in English, and that the point of the task was not clear. A small number wrote more than one metaphor; others said that they had "*only written common metaphors which everyone knows*". We return to this point later, since it provides a clue to how some participants saw the task; although all groups were given identical tasks, as the British students had been, we cannot be certain how the task was interpreted in different cultures. We will discuss the Chinese examples in some detail and briefly report the metaphors of the other groups.

From previous cross-cultural studies which compare Chinese and English metaphors it is not clear whether one should predict similarities or differences, or whether this depends on the lexical field selected. Yu (1995) shows that both languages share many underlying conceptualisations of anger (e.g. ANGER IS HEAT) and happiness (e.g. HAPPINESS IS UP, HAPPINESS IS LIGHT), but that there are differences in sub-categories which can be explained with reference to cultural models. Scollon (1993), in contrast, shows that when metaphors of self and communication are compared, Chinese has a quite different underlying base from English and that it is important to understand this in inter-cultural contexts.

In the present data, out of a total of 95 Chinese metaphors, the dominant metaphor is, A GOOD TEACHER IS A FRIEND (42): **a respected friend, a close friend, a strict friend, a kind friend.** Also important is A GOOD TEACHER IS A PARENT (16): **a strict father and a patient mother, my mother, a father but with patience.** These were sometimes combined: **a friend and parents, a father and a friend, a strict mother and a good friend.** Other important examples are A GOOD TEACHER IS A SOURCE OF KNOWLEDGE (5); A GUIDE (3); A MODEL OR MORAL EXAMPLE (3); A GARDENER (3); AN ACTOR (2). Only a few showed humour or originality: **a salesman, a gold digger, a hen laying eggs, a UFO** ("I have no idea of it").

To some extent these metaphors seem strange. Much writing about Chinese attitudes towards the teacher (Harvey, 1985; Yum, 1988; Dzau Ed., 1990; Wang Ed., 1990; Ross, 1993; Young, 1994) indicates that students follow a long-standing tradition of holding teachers in respect, as authorities, in a somewhat formal relationship. While this seems to be consonant with the TEACHER IS A SOURCE OF KNOWLEDGE metaphor, it hardly accounts for the TEACHER IS A FRIEND, or PARENT. Yet a closer reading of such sources shows that since Confucius' time the teacher–student relation has been one of five key relationships; this is a close and enduring relationship of reciprocal responsibility in which teachers are expected to exercise a role of strong parental care. This has been found in a recent analysis of 135 Chinese students' essays and in interviews (Cortazzi & Jin, 1996). It is also seen in the common saying, *'My teacher once, my parent forever'.* Traditionally, knowledge, and the teaching of knowledge, have been regarded as the most important qualities for a teacher. Further corroboration of the link between these metaphors and people's thinking in China, at least in the public domain, might be found in official metaphors used as titles for teachers which have been widely promulgated in public campaigns in recent years. Thus the TEACHER IS A SOURCE OF KNOWLEDGE, the TEACHER IS EXPERT or the TEACHER IS GARDENER are metaphors which commonly occur in official speeches, documents or newspapers. Again, however, a closer reading of official titles since 1949 reveals that these have, in fact, changed to reflect (or perhaps to create) public attitudes, as official policies have changed. Buley-Meissner (1991) summarises them according to national developments in China. During Reconstruction (1949–1957) teachers were 'gardeners' and 'brain-power labourers'; in the First Five Year Plan (1953–1957) they were 'people's heroes', 'advanced producers', 'engineers of the soul'; in the Great Leap Forward (1958–1959) they were negatively known as 'obstacles', or positively as 'common labourers'. Subsequently, in a period of Retrenchment (1960–1965) the industrial metaphors were again popular and teachers were 'machine-tool makers' and once more 'engineers of the soul'. In the polarisation of the Cultural Revolution (1966–1976), negative metaphors were 'freaks', 'monsters' or 'stinking number nines' (i.e. at the bottom of a list of 'enemies of the people'), while positive ones included 'warriors' or 'weapons in the class struggle' and 'red thinkers'. In the 1980s the industrial metaphors were back in favour; teachers were 'technicians', 'machinists' and again 'people's heroes'. In the 1990s teachers have been 'candles', 'lamps', 'golden key holders' and remain 'engineers of the soul'. With the development of the market economy, there are new metaphors; many workers and teachers have **xia hai** or 'plunged into the sea' of private business and some, particularly English language teachers, **chao geng** ('stir-fry night'; **geng** means both 'a dish of food' and 'night') and go in for evening work, or they **lao wai kuai** ('use a sieve or net, extra money'; **kuai** means both a measure word for money and 'fast') and are busy making extra money, with overtones of moonlighting. There are parallels here (though the context and metaphors are different) with the 'marketization' of educational discourse in Britain (see Fairclough, 1995: 130–166) where students become 'clients' or 'customers', courses are 'sold' and 'delivered', institutions are 'marketed'. In both cases, the ambience of teaching and learning is being reframed, but, as far as we can tell, this process has not yet affected the core metaphors for teaching and learning.

The exact connection between such metaphors and action and belief is difficult to specify. The metaphors are numerous. Most have been introduced, or at least disseminated, by those in authority. They are, indeed, examples of framing (see Block in Chapter 7), with periods of frame shift and frame polarisation. They have frequently been used in public discourse, in the media and in schools over nearly five decades by many millions of people in China under complex and often difficult circumstances, as the nation as a whole and specifically the education system has developed (Cleverley, 1985; Lin, 1993; Lewin *et al.*, 1994). Certainly these metaphors have accompanied large-scale significant action. Often they have been a spur to action, although we cannot know how such action might have occurred without them. Given the number of metaphors and the number of speakers involved, it seems likely that the use of *some* metaphors must have led directly to *some* action.

In practical terms, when teachers in China have been observed and interviewed while teaching and training, further metaphors are also found to be influential: for example, TEACHER IS VIRTUOSO or TEACHER IS PERFORMER, with entailments of acting, practice, imitation, apprenticeship and rehearsal (Paine, 1990; Cortazzi & Jin, 1996). It is our impression that these teachers' metaphors are important guides and goals of Chinese teacher behaviour, but it is of interest that they are *not* the metaphors of students, which may be why they are not evident in our student data.

The long-running TEACHER IS RED AND EXPERT metaphor expresses a basic polarity in China (Ross, 1993; Schoenhals, 1993; Paine, 1992) between the teacher as expert, authority and source of knowledge, which is important for modernisation, and the teacher as 'red', a model not only political, but, equally, moral and social. (The positive connotation of red is more than political; it is associated with luck, happiness and weddings.) 'Red' and 'expert' represents a strong example of the polarisation of framing: at various times, the solution to problems of one pole has been to emphasise the frame of the complementary pole. Thus 'redness' has been important in nationalisation. The two poles are shown in the two most common Chinese expressions for 'teach': **jiao shu** or 'teach the book' and **jiao ren** or 'teach people'. Paine (1992) argues that it is central to the success of current reforms that the EXPERT aspect takes on characteristics of creative thinking, problem solving and independent work. There is some evidence of change in this direction (Cortazzi & Jin, 1996) but this has not appeared in the metaphors discussed above. However, in the Chinese students' metaphors for teaching, while the KNOWLEDGE metaphor relates to the EXPERT or 'teach the book' aspect, the FRIEND, PARENT, MODEL, GUIDE metaphors all relate to the RED or 'teach the people' aspect. Numerically, the Chinese students' metaphors seem to favour this aspect, which may index a social change of emphasis or an instant of reframing.

The detailed realisations of these metaphors will be related to key notions of *cultures of learning* and *cultures of communication* (Cortazzi & Jin, 1996) in our conclusions. Meanwhile we briefly examine data from other cultures.

The Japanese metaphors are sparser – apparently the students found the task difficult. Out of a total of 41 metaphors given, the most frequent metaphors were: A GOOD TEACHER IS A

FRIEND (14): **a good friend, a warm-hearted friend, a sympathetic friend;** AN AROUSER (10): **an arouser of students' interest, a prod to make students eager to learn;** A SOURCE OF KNOWLEDGE (9): **a deep well of knowledge, a fountain of knowledge.**

The teacher as a MODEL (3) was **a model for study and morals.** There were only two mentions of the teacher as a PARENT. We had expected more similarities with the Chinese metaphors and had anticipated a wider range, following the findings of Hiraga (1995), and Berendt and Mori (1995). They showed that while there are overlaps with such English conceptual metaphors as LEARNING IS A JOURNEY or LEARNING IS A COMMODITY, Japanese also has distinct metaphors: LEARNING IS RAISING A BIRD, which stresses practice – a bird practices flying by repeatedly moving its wings – and LEARNING IS CARVING AND POLISHING. More common in Japanese than in English are EDUCATION IS WAR, particularly during examination periods, and LEARNING IS IMITATING A MODEL or LEARNING IS AN AREA. These are seen in such Japanese sayings as 'Follow your master seven feet behind so that you don't step on his shadow', 'Knock at the gate of learning', 'enter the gate', and 'Enter by imitating the model and later exit out of the model'.

This raises a methodological point. Hiraga (1995) and Berendt and Mori (1995) used mainly Japanese textual sources (dictionaries, books of proverbs and sayings, books and essays on learning) to investigate conventionalised metaphors, rather than eliciting or collecting spontaneous metaphors. In our case, the elicitation method in English may have inhibited expression of what is clearly a rich metaphor tradition. It is also possible, if less likely, that because students were asked to write in English, they understood the task to require metaphors from English-speaking cultures.

Among the larger number of Lebanese metaphors, 106, the range was greater. This might be explained by the fact that some students had been to English-medium secondary schools and probably had a wider range of vocabulary. The following metaphors predominate. A GOOD TEACHER IS A PARENT (31): **an understanding parent, a good father, a mother who gives from her heart;** A FRIEND (30): **a real friend, a knowledgeable friend, a reliable friend, a mature friend;** A SOURCE OF KNOWLEDGE (15): **a source of knowledge, a deep well of knowledge.** Others included A MODEL (5); A GUIDE (4); A LOVER (3); FOOD (3) (e.g. **a juicy fruit, fresh food, bread**); and there were also metaphors of A CATALYST, A MEDICINE, AN ANCHOR and AN ARTIST.

The Turkish group gave 98 metaphors, including: A GOOD

TEACHER IS A FRIEND (44): **my best friend, a good friend, an older friend, a friend who wants good for me, a friend but also there must be a distance;** A PARENT (19): **a strict father, a merciful mother, a kind parent.** Closely related is a SIBLING (7), (**an older brother, a sister**), which again draws attention to difficulties of categorisation. Clearly, a RELATIVE would be a candidate for the generic metaphor, but there were very few mentions of 'brother' or 'sister' elsewhere, and for more specific comparability PARENT seems to be the relevant term. Again, a SOURCE OF KNOWL-EDGE (9), a GUIDE (5) and a MODEL (4) seem important, although mentioned with different frequency than by the other groups. Uniquely, the Turkish students included A SUNNY DAY (7) and A COMIC (5), i.e. a source of humour.

The Iranian group gave a much lower number of metaphors, namely just 18. The students were very reluctant to fill in questionnaires or sentence stems for metaphors; we are not certain of the reason for this. However, even though they are sparse, these data follow the trend of the other groups. The predominant metaphor is: A GOOD TEACHER IS A FRIEND (13): **a good friend who understands and cares, a good, wise, knowledgeable, older friend, a friend who tries to transmit his knowledge to the students.** As these examples show, some Iranian students linked FRIEND to KNOWLEDGE. Other metaphors included A PARENT (1), and **a money-hunter.**

Conclusions

Clearly further investigation could focus on British (or other) students' developing metaphors over their immersion in a linguistics course, to track their knowledge and awareness of language. The development of teachers' cognition about teaching could also be tracked, in both quantitative and qualitative approaches, using similar procedures. Asking students, or teachers on in-service courses, to make metaphors may engage them in acts of making meaning, by looking for points of commonality between source and target domains. Depending on how participants interpret the task, it may also involve searching for the essence or key characteristics of a topic, besides elements of originality or humour.

In education, the use of metaphors has been receiving attention for some time (Taylor, 1984). In courses for the professional development of teachers, especially in pre-service courses, it is now common to attempt to get teachers to identify their own metaphors for teaching, the classroom, learning, etc. as part of a reflective process of helping them to reconceptualise the processes of teaching and learning through self-critique and through appreciation of multiple perspectives. The development of alternative metaphors related to evaluating actual practices is part of this. Usually, research studies monitoring the use of metaphors in such professional development are small-scale but often in-depth (Munby, 1986; Connelly & Clandinin, 1988; Bullough, 1991, 1992; Grant, 1992; Johnston, 1992). Others, to obtain metaphors from larger numbers of teachers, use elicitation procedures (Provenzo *et al.*, 1989; Marchant, 1992; Scott, 1994). The present study draws on larger samples of teachers and students, and focuses on both spontaneous and elicited metaphors.

A number of points can be made to summarise our findings regarding the validity of the salience of these metaphors in speakers' cognition and in their social and professional worlds, using the criteria mentioned earlier. Many of these metaphors occur frequently enough, across a good range of speakers and in significant contexts of teaching and learning, to warrant a conclusion that they are important in teachers' and students' talk about learning. Some of the students' metaphors for language and teaching, and certainly the teachers' metaphors for learning, are highly consistent; a small range of metaphors about central topics of learning are repeatedly used by many speakers in similar linguistic contexts. It remains an inference that this reflects actual teaching or learning, but there is some evidence from the teachers, British postgraduate students and from China that at least some of these metaphors accompany behaviour and action, and sometimes changes in action. From the British undergraduates, there is evidence that the students' metaphors about language change over several semesters (since first- and second-year students' metaphors were different), indicating that the metaphors reflect learning. For researchers, then, this study of metaphors is a bridge to learn more about teachers' and students' metaphors of learning. This is true for the tutors and mentors of the trainee teachers and the undergraduates studying language; tutors who examined our data felt that such study helped them to understand students' learning.

The British teachers' spontaneous metaphors for learning were limited in range, but seem to have a key role in narratives of learning. The 'breakthrough' metaphors come from oral accounts of significant learning; teachers notice and remember breakthroughs while other kinds of learning may pass unobserved; they gain personal and professional rewards by observing and recounting such moments. The metaphors were usually placed in the crucial position of the evaluation part of narratives and they were often performed with rhetorical and paralinguistic underlining. All this gave the metaphors a strong affective tone; while listening to the tapes it was clear that the metaphors reflected personal and professional relationships between teachers and learners. The metaphors are bridges between teachers too; they are typical of staffroom conversation as a vicarious exchange of meaningful experience among teachers who rarely see each other at work. The metaphors may thus represent a mutual striving to explain the mystery of why and how children learn. An alternative interpretation, following Lerman (1984), is that because teachers are responsible for children's learning, yet cannot explain it or apparently control it, the metaphors are used as distancing devices or masks to avoid direct talk on the matter. This interpretation would seem appropriate if the metaphors were given in more negative tones or contexts, but it does not seem to fit in with the strong positive affective tone of the teachers' narratives of children's learning.

The British students' elicited metaphors were wide ranging but showed some common elements. They showed that the students, in their study of language, were well aware of 'structure', 'function', 'rules', 'variety', 'complexity' and 'change' (though hardly of communicative aspects), yet for many students the metaphors stressed the unknown and mysterious aspects of language. Although it was evident that some students saw the elicitation task as a challenge to create innovative metaphors, the high number of particular types of metaphors is surprising. Similar points could be made about the postgraduate students' metaphors for teaching. However at the time of completing the metaphor task, they had recently been teaching in schools, and, like the 'breakthrough' metaphors, many of the student-teachers' examples showed warmth, achievement and challenge. Both the student-teachers' and experienced primary teachers' metaphors showed awareness of their professional culture and commitment to teaching and learning. A parallel sense of commitment to language study is not particularly evident in many undergraduates' metaphors and reasons, which perhaps reflects their student culture. Yet for some postgraduates, the metaphor task promoted the kind of reflection which is a bridge to professional culture, since the metaphor activity helped them to identify their professional selves and to see how others identify theirs. At the simplest level, it was useful for both groups of students to realise how varied the metaphors could be and therefore, as they concluded, how varied concepts of teaching and language are. The metaphor activity helped university tutors to assess informally their students' understanding, and feelings, about teaching and language. The metaphors bridged the student–tutor gap and were used by tutors to facilitate what they believed was useful discussion.

The metaphors from the other groups were limited in both quantity and range. They were written in English and, although the students were all at advanced levels, the language of the task may have had an effect. However, it is also likely, given these students' cultures of learning, that they saw the task less as a creative challenge (British students may treat the task as an act of individual innovation) and more as a statement of commonly accepted views. It is tempting to interpret this further by suggesting that Britain is high on indices of *individualism* while the other countries would appear to be more *collectivist* (Hofstede, 1991; Triandis, 1995) and that this might affect both perception of the metaphor task and perhaps the uses of metaphors in different cultures. However, this research is exploratory, and this interpretation must remain tentative. The obvious extensions are to continue this research by eliciting metaphors in students' first languages; to exercise caution in elicitation procedures; to check elicitation results with text-based research; and continue to wrestle with problems of classification, validation and corroboration.

There is a predominance of FRIEND and PARENT metaphors for teachers among the Chinese, Japanese, Lebanese and Turkish groups, compared with the much lower frequencies of these metaphors in the British data (there are only 13 instances of *'parent'* and none of *'friend'* among 236 British metaphors), although this must be interpreted with caution because the elicitation stems are different. Overall differences in metaphors may be a clear signal of different cultural frames and these may lead to differing cross-cultural interpretations. While TEACHER IS FRIEND or PARENT is common, it is apparent that the frequencies between groups are different and it is likely that the cultural associations may have different emphases and different sources. Thus, these metaphors are very strong in neo-Confucian traditions of relations-based approaches to social life, including education, which would readily apply to current Chinese and Japanese contexts (King & Bond, 1985; Bond, 1991), but hardly to those in the Middle East, where the metaphors stem from other cultural sources.

As an example of applying these insights, we have found (Jin & Cortazzi, 1993, 1995; Cortazzi & Jin, 1997) that there are cultural gaps which need to be bridged when Chinese students require help from British teachers. The metaphors for teaching and learning may directly relate to students' or teachers' cultures of communication in the classroom. The students see the teacher as *friend* or *parent* and, following their culture of learning which stresses mutual responsibility and reciprocal relations, they expect the teacher in the friend or parent role to be sensitive to students' needs and to offer help when it is needed. However, the British teachers, working within different conceptual metaphors and a different culture of learning, expect the students to be more independent and to ask for help when it is needed; if there is no such request, they presume the student has no problem (teachers would help if they were asked to). All too often, the consequence is that when help is needed, it is not asked for, nor is it offered or given. This may leave frustration and disillusion on one side and false presumptions of student independence or competence on the other. If differing metaphors for teaching and learning are known to all participants in inter-cultural educational contexts, then awareness of differing interpretations may build another bridge across cultures of learning.

Acknowledgements
We give many thanks to the following teachers who helped us with data gathering: Zheng, Rongxuan of Nankai University, China; Wang, Zhiru of Hubei University, China; Nola Bacha of the Lebanese American University, Lebanon; Karen Fedderholdt, of Toyama University, Japan; Fikret Yasar of Surat Company, Turkey; and Rahman Sahragard of Shiraz University, Iran.

9 Corpus-based research into metaphor

Alice Deignan

Introduction

In this paper I discuss a corpus-based approach to the identification of metaphorical expressions in English and consider the insights which can be gained through such an approach. The approach described here has its roots in lexicography, and is influenced by models of language and thought developed by research within cognitive linguistics by writers such as Lakoff and Johnson (1980) and Gibbs (1994). I begin by arguing that the study of large corpora can give information about the frequency and use of linguistic metaphors which is otherwise difficult to access. I then discuss decisions which must be made in order to develop a sound methodological framework for research into metaphor. I give examples of some aspects of linguistic metaphors which can be investigated using corpora, and finally list some limitations of a corpus-based approach.

A computerised corpus is a large collection of texts held in electronic form, which can be accessed using various types of software packages; for the purposes of language description, these are often concordancing programs. A concordancing program enables the researcher to study a word form (or forms) by looking at large numbers of citations of that word form with its linguistic contexts. (To see how this data is presented, see the extract of the concordance of **heated**, below.) Citations can be sorted in various ways, enabling the researcher to examine different patterns of structure and collocation. Concordancing has obvious applications in lexicography, which has long recognised the importance of considering citations from language in use. The centrality of corpus work for modern lexicographers is demonstrated by the fact that almost all of the most recent generation of English dictionaries for the non-native speaker market claim to have been based to some extent on corpora – see for example the prefaces to the *Cambridge International English Dictionary* (1995), the *Collins Cobuild English Dictionary* (1995, 2nd edition), the *Longman Dictionary of Contemporary English* (1995, 3rd edition) and the *Oxford Advanced Learner's Dictionary* (1995, 5th edition). Interest in corpora for other areas of language description is also growing rapidly; these include the analysis of specific registers (see for example Thomas & Short Eds., 1996), and grammatical descriptions (Francis *et al.* Eds., 1996).

A computerised corpus can enable the researcher to detect patterns of usage more quickly than either the use of intuition or the analysis of individual texts, as words or expressions are automatically retrieved from the corpus and sorted. This can also, arguably, lead to a less subjective analysis. Sinclair is one of several linguists who argue that the systematic study of large corpora yields information about language use that is not available to unaided intuition:

> ... the contrast exposed between the impressions of language detail noted by people, and the evidence compiled objectively from texts is huge and systematic. It leads one to suppose that human intuition about language is highly specific, and not at all a good guide to what actually happens when the same people actually use the language.   (Sinclair, 1991: 4)

Corpus-derived insights into language frequently strike the researcher as familiar once made, because they confirm information that is part of the competent speaker's linguistic knowledge, and, as a result, these insights may be dismissed as trivial or obvious. Such linguistic knowledge can nonetheless be difficult to access using intuition alone, prior to corpus investigation, as many lexicographers will confirm (Summers, 1996: 263). Given the possibility that 'obvious', but hitherto unnoticed, facts about use may be unearthed, it seems logical to attempt to apply and adapt techniques that have evolved for consulting large corpora to the investigation of linguistic metaphors.

Corpus-based investigations of a slightly different kind have already been carried out in the field of metaphor and critical discourse analysis; see for example, van Teeffelen's study of metaphors used to write about the Palestine–Israeli conflict in popular fiction (1994), Rohrer's work on the metaphors of the Gulf War (1995), Patthey-Chavez *et al.*'s discussion of metaphors in women's erotic fiction (1996) and Block's work on SLA research (this volume). For each of these studies, the writer built his/her own specialised corpora; such corpora are small in scale in relation to general corpora such as the British National Corpus, or the Bank of English, which was used for this study.[1] The aim of the above

---

[1] All concordance data cited in this paper were taken from the Bank of English, a corpus of approximately 323 million words (at the time of writing) of current written and spoken texts. The Bank of English is held at COBUILD, which is a division of

writers' research is primarily ideological: to tease out underlying attitudes and make explicit various persuasive devices, by identifying metaphors and unpacking their assumptions and entailments. The type of research discussed in this paper is different from the work of these writers; it differs in that it uses large, non-specialised, machine-sorted corpora, and in that its aims are primarily linguistic: to study the syntactic, collocational and semantic patterning of linguistic metaphors.

One of the first observations that can be made through studying the concordances for many words is the frequency of occurrence of their metaphorical senses. While non-metaphorical senses may be psychologically primary and historically prior, contemporary corpus data show that metaphorical senses of some words are used as frequently as, or more frequently than, their non-metaphorical senses. This is unsurprising where a non-metaphorical sense is only detectable through studying etymology, as in Lakoff and Turner's example of **comprehend** (which is derived from the Latin word for 'take hold' (physically) but which does not have this sense in English) (1989: 129). It may be less expected where the non-metaphorical sense is still current however. To exemplify this point, a concordance of **shreds** is looked at in order to establish the relative frequency of the concrete and non-concrete uses of the plural noun. A sample of 400 citations was taken, of which 16 were discounted because they were either unclear or were proper names. 15 verbal uses were also disregarded. Of the remaining 369 citations, 207 had concrete referents, and 162 had non-concrete referents. Typical citations of **shreds** with non-concrete referents include:

1. So far she'd managed to cling to **the shreds of** her pride.
2. Her nerves are **in shreds.**

This suggests that the metaphorical use of **shreds** is more frequent than might have been predicted using unaided intuition. In the case of some structures the non-concrete uses are more frequent than the concrete uses; there are 48 non-concrete citations of **shreds of** compared with 39 concrete uses in the sample discussed here, with, for example, **shreds of patience** being a more frequent collocation than **shreds of cloth**.

This is not to suggest that metaphorical senses of any given word are always of this order of frequency, relative to non-metaphorical senses of that word; in some cases they are a great deal more

HarperCollins Publishers, and is based within the School of English at Birmingham University. The concordancer used was developed by COBUILD and is not commercially available.

frequent, while in other cases the reverse is so. It does suggest however that intuition is not a reliable guide to frequency, and that the frequency of use of metaphorical senses of many words might often be overlooked. It seems unlikely for example that many speakers could predict even approximately the relative frequencies of the metaphorical and non-metaphorical senses of the various structures in which **shreds** appears.

Shreds is a relatively straightforward word form to study, as citations can be grouped depending on whether they refer to a concrete or non-concrete entity with reasonable ease, once the verbal uses have been identified and discarded. It is also relatively uncomplicated because, with the exception of the concrete/non-concrete sense division, it is not, broadly speaking, polysemous. It will be seen later that it is not always easy to make decisions on meaning division, and that it can often be difficult to decide which citations of some words are metaphorical; this decision will depend on the definition of metaphor used.

It will be clear from the discussion so far that the direction of investigation in corpus linguistics is generally from word to meaning. In the case of metaphor, patterns can sometimes be traced from linguistic evidence through to a possible underlying metaphor functioning at the level of thought: a conceptual metaphor in Lakoff's terminology (1987a). It is not possible to work the other way round; that is, there is no automatic way of discovering the linguistic realisations of any conceptual metaphor, because a computer cannot tell the researcher anything about speaker meaning. Concordances will show the researcher words in their context, but he or she has to process this information. The researcher uses informed intuition to decide whether a particular citation of a word is metaphorical, within his or her own definition of metaphor. Intuition is also needed to decide whether a linguistic metaphor is a realisation of a particular conceptual metaphor. Further, the computer cannot tell the researcher which word forms to study. Concordancing is a powerful observational tool, but no more than a tool; a researcher is needed to decide what to examine and how to interpret the resulting data.

Developing a methodological framework

In this section, two examples of concordance data are discussed. The first is given in order to demonstrate what the data look like, and the second is shown in order to exemplify three major problems which have arisen in developing a classificatory framework for linguistic metaphors for this research.

Concordance data appear in the form of a list of citations containing the word being studied, or *node*. The citations can be sorted in various ways; in the following extract they have been sorted alphabetically by the word immediately following the node **heated**. (Sorting in this way makes it easier for the researcher to identify the items which are modified by **heated**, as, if the same item occurs in several citations, these citations will be grouped together.)

1.   For instance, I found myself in **heated** argument the other day over the
2.   \<p\> I vividly remember having a **heated** debate with my boss, 23 years ago,
3.   by air-chilling the surface of a **heated** glass sheet to create strain
4.   the night, make sure his room is **heated** independently. \<p\> A cold baby's
5.   likes to laugh.\<p\> Pro: can be **heated** like a hot water bottle in winter,
6.East Germany. The issue has caused **heated** political argument, as Igor
7.   I rose at 5 a.m. to battle with **heated** rollers and the few remaining
8.orrison was behind schedule. \<p\> A **heated** telephone exchange between Goldm
9.   conducts electricity poorly; when **heated**, though, it turns into a metal-lik
10.   special offers every month on **heated** towel rails and selected suites.
11.   site near London. Tyres are **heated** up to 1080 degrees C in a high-
12.Thank God for a small house which **heated** up quickly. Rosie sat down wit

(\<*p*\> signals the start of a new paragraph in the original text.)

It is relatively straightforward to make a statement about the non-literal use of **heated** based on this data; even from this very small sample it is clear that **heated** can be used metaphorically to modify words which refer to a spoken exchange, and this is confirmed when the full concordance is studied.

The following extract from the concordance for **deep** is more problematic:

1. h.\<MOX\>They're about nine inches **deep**. And really you couldn't you've got
2.   for in this weekend's lottery. **Deep** below the Royal Bank of Scotland in
3.   most pressing item. After taking a **deep** breath, we write a cheque, post
4.   mauve markings. \<p\> Lord Bute: **Deep** burgundy with pink edging.
5.   ingrained stains or not, I use this **deep** cleansing scrub about twice each
6.   if Germany pulls out. There is **deep** concern that the billions of pounds
7.   have to close, or at least make **deep** cuts in their workforces. This m
8.   oil and cocoa butter to promote a **deep**, even tan whilst keeping the skin
9.ce I had spotted comic Angie Le Mar **deep** in conversation with an
10.   cold blue eyes that seemed to bore **deep** into her soul. All at once she
11.   ement of my local culture and to a **deep**-seated root in my family's
12.   that its preferred site for **deep** storage of intermediate and low-

(*MOX* in Citation 1 signals a change of speaker.)

The grammatical category of each citation will not be considered at this point, although, as will be argued later, the different syntactic behaviours of a word-form can sometimes signal differences in metaphorical frequency and use.

Three major problems which arise in the study of metaphor using naturally occurring data are exemplified in this extract. All three involve distinguishing metaphor from closely related linguistic phenomena: firstly, establishing a point at which dead metaphor is so well established in the language as to be regarded as a literal sense, related to other senses of the same lexeme by a relation of polysemy rather than metaphor; secondly, dealing with the metaphors which occur in regularly occurring, relatively fixed phrases which might be better described as idioms; and thirdly, handling the boundary between metaphor and metonymy. These problems are looked at in turn here.

Firstly, while some citations seem unarguably either metaphorical or non-metaphorical, others lie in the less clear-cut area of 'dead' metaphor, a term which can potentially cover a wide range of metaphors (Lakoff, 1987b). At one extreme 'dead' metaphor can refer to any metaphor which is not completely innovative, while at the other it may be taken to refer only to lexical items whose metaphorical origins are no longer detectable in current English. However, to begin with those citations which do not seem to present such difficulties; the uses of **deep** in Citations 1, 2, 5 and 12 above seem to be unequivocally non-metaphorical in that the sense used "having great extension downward; extending far inward from the outer surface or backward from the front" (*SOED* 1973: 504) is the earliest known use and is probably psychologically core for most speakers. Also relatively uncontroversially, the uses in Citations 6, 7, 9, 10 and 11 seem to be metaphorical, as mapping from the core use onto other domains is involved and can still be reconstructed by current speakers.

Problems arise with the analysis of lines 4 and 8, where **deep** refers to intensity of colour (although it would be possible to argue that in line 8 it refers to a tan which penetrates several layers of skin). The 'colour' sense is listed as figurative in the *Shorter Oxford English Dictionary* (1973: 504), having originated as an extension of 'physical' **deep**. The earliest citation of this sense found by the editors dates from the sixteenth century. This sense is now so well established that it seems unlikely that many speakers would perceive it as dependent in some way upon the 'literal' sense of **deep**. This may also be due to the fact that it describes a concrete rather than an abstract quality. Because of this, I personally prefer to categorise this sense as non-metaphorical, despite its etymology. I would therefore regard the relationship between the 'colour' sense and the 'measurement' sense of **deep** as one of polysemy, polysemy being a more general relationship which can include conventionalised metaphors and their literal counterparts but which can also include other types of relations between senses of a lexeme (see Moon, 1987, for a discussion of types of sense relations distinguished by lexicographers). This attempt to categorise the 'colour' sense of **deep** demonstrates the difficulties which arise in making decisions on individual senses of individual words. Such decisions may seem intuitively sound to the individual researcher, but they may strike others as purely subjective and *ad hoc*.

To get around the problem of making intuitive decisions about individual citations, it is necessary to establish an objective cut-off point at which dead metaphors can be regarded as non-metaphorical, and to attempt to implement this consistently. Lakoff sets out one model for categorising 'dead' and 'live' metaphors, in which four criteria are key: the existence of the original 'literal' sense and of linguistic mapping between domains in current English, and the existence of the original image and of conceptual mapping between domains in current speakers' conceptual systems (1987b). Researchers might want to use this model or develop another one, adapting or dropping some of these criteria and possibly adding further ones. One such further criterion might concern the notions of concrete or abstract reference; while these seem to be implicit in Lakoff's discussion of 'dead' metaphor, they are not formally included in his categorisation. Another additional criterion might concern the nature of the referential function of the metaphor. This last point will be particularly of interest to those concerned with the role of metaphor in discourse (see Steen, this volume). The type of model developed will depend on the research goals. Whatever these are, the issue of dead metaphor is a central one which needs to be resolved before any consistent analysis of concordance data can proceed.

The second problem listed above, that of distinguishing idioms from metaphors which occur in fairly fixed collocations, is exemplified in Citation 3 (and, to a much lesser extent, in Citation 7). In Citation 3, metaphoricity is not attached to **deep** as an individual lexical item but to the expression **take a deep breath** as a whole. The fixedness of the expression seems to make this use of **deep** different in nature from its use to mean 'important or serious' (Citation 6), which is more or less free-standing, combining with a range of lexical items in the corpus. **Take a deep breath** is idiom-like in two ways; it is syntactically fixed (**a deep breath was taken** is not used with the same meaning, for example) and lexically fixed (near synonyms are not usually substituted for any of the component lexical items). The classification of **take a deep breath** as an idiom is dubious however, as a third quality often associated with idioms, semantic opacity, is not present; that is, the meaning of this expression as a whole is reasonably easy to deduce through the meanings of its parts. Between free-standing metaphors (such as **deep** = important or serious) and clear-cut cases of idiom (such as **let the cat out of the bag**), there is a grey area of collocations such as **take a deep breath** which share some features of each type of expression. The researcher needs to be clear whether he or she is interested in just a part of this cline, or the whole spectrum. Even in the second case, where the researcher wishes to include idioms in his or her understanding of metaphor, some kind of categorisation is probably still desirable.

This same citation also illustrates the third problem mentioned above, that of distinguishing metaphor from metonymy. This can be seen more clearly when a wider context is examined:

3. Most of us sit down glumly from time to time and deal reluctantly with the most pressing item. After **taking a deep breath**, we write a cheque, post it and then relax in the knowledge that one payment, at least, is behind us.

To take a deep breath has developed a figurative meaning which could be paraphrased as 'to decide, with reservations, to embark upon a course of action'. It is unclear from this citation whether the physical sense is intended, or the figurative sense, or indeed both. This difficulty arises in the analysis of citations of many idiomatic expressions which refer to parts of the human body (Moon, R.E., personal communication, 1995). Kittay gives a similar example, in which **His hands were tied** can be interpreted literally, metaphorically or both (1987).

It has been argued in this section that a preliminary definition of metaphor must be developed before citations can be categorised in any way. This definition will vary depending on the researcher's interests, but must deal in some way with the three issues raised here: the status of different types of 'dead' metaphors, the treatment of figurative fixed strings as opposed to freely combining one-word metaphors, and the treatment of metonyms, in particular those which retain a literal use. For the purposes of the studies discussed here, I have excluded historical metaphors, such as the colour use of **deep**, and have noted fixed strings and metonyms separately.

In the next section I look at some features of linguistic metaphors which can be investigated using concordance data.

Linguistic metaphors: areas of investigation

Syntax

Theories which treat metaphor as primarily concerned with the organisation of thought, rather than as a purely linguistic phenomenon, nevertheless have implications for the study of language. Indeed, much of the evidence for such theories is found in the existence of conventional linguistic expressions. However, such theories have not attempted to be predictive of language use; Lakoff and Johnson (1980) note that metaphorical mapping is normally only partial. This is consistent with the corpus data discussed here; the research, while at a very early stage, seems to show that the occurrence of linguistic metaphors and their structural patterns are not fully explained by the existence of conceptual metaphors. Although it seems likely that conceptual metaphors motivate much figurative language, they cannot be used to predict it because there is a degree of apparent arbitrariness in their linguistic realisations. One example of this arbitrariness is the relation between metaphorical use and grammar.

In this section I use the example of **shoulder** to discuss the apparently unpredictable relation between occurrence and frequency of metaphorical use and part of speech. Low notes that where two words exist which are identical in form and semantically related but of a different grammatical class, one may have a metaphorical use which is not extended to the other; for example, whereas the verb **snake** is a conventional metaphor in "The river snaked (its way) through the jungle" the noun **snake** is not conventionally used to refer to a river (1988: 131). Corpus investigation of a number of words with their derived and inflected forms has shown that this is not an unusual occurrence.

A randomly selected set of 1000 citations of the word forms **shoulder, shouldering, shouldered** and **shoulders** was taken from the Bank of English and examined by word class. Of the sample 1000 citations, 13 appeared in non-metaphorical adjectival combinations such as **broad-shouldered** and **round-shouldered**, and were discounted for this study. 940 citations were of the singular or plural noun, and the remaining 47 citations were various forms of the verb. The noun and verb forms are discussed here in terms of the frequency and distribution of their metaphorical and non-metaphorical uses.

In six of the 47 verbal uses, **shoulder** is used in the expression **cold-shoulder**, a compound verb derived from the canonical forms **give someone the cold shoulder** and **turn a cold shoulder on someone**. In

39 further citations, verbal **shoulder** is metaphorical and is used to connote responsibility, as the following examples illustrate:

4. All over the country, but particularly in London, other hospitals are being required **to shoulder** similar burdens.
5. By **shouldering** a wide variety of risks, an investor reduces the volatility of his portfolio.

This use of **shoulder** seems to suggest an image of a person carrying a heavy load on their shoulders; the load is a metaphor for their responsibility, problem or risk, and the verb **shoulder** is a metaphor for taking on or coping with this responsibility, problem or risk. This image is reinforced by the items **burden** and **load**, both of which frequently appear as the direct object of **shoulder**. Other items which appear frequently in this slot are **responsibility** and **blame**.

There are two non-metaphorical verbal uses of **shoulder** in the sample looked at. It was expected that these would have the meaning 'carry on the shoulders with difficulty', the physical act to which the metaphorical use seems to be an allusion. In fact this turned out not be the case; in both citations the action referred to was 'moving through a crowd by pushing past people with the shoulders', as the following citation shows:

6. Then he **shouldered** his way through the soldiers shouting in five languages.

There is no evidence in the sample looked at for a verb **shoulder** with the meaning of 'carry on the shoulders', although this sense is attested in *SOED*.

Of 940 citations of **shoulder(s)** as a singular or plural noun, 828 refer to part of the human body, or, occasionally, to an upper supporting part of another physical entity. Of the remaining 112, eleven are accounted for by the compound **hard shoulder** (of a motorway), ten by the idiom **have a chip on one's shoulder,** seven by **cold shoulder,** in expressions such as **give someone the cold shoulder,** and six by the expression **be head and shoulders above someone.**

A further 31 uses are metaphorical, and are semantically related to the verbal metaphorical use discussed above, evoking the same image of a person struggling under a load that is a metaphor for responsibility or problems. The following citations are typical:

7. Don't start on Newtie, he's got enough on his **shoulders.**
8. Debt can seem like an unbearable **load** on your **shoulders.**

The collocational pattern of this use of **shoulder(s)** is very close to that for metaphorical verbal **shoulder**, with items such as **load**,

weight, burden and **responsibility** occurring several times in the sample. These nominal and verbal uses of **shoulder** seem to be closely related linguistic expressions of the same conceptual metaphor.

The remaining 47 nominal uses have been classified as metonymic, and in each case **shoulder(s)** is part of a regular and fairly fixed collocation. The most frequent metonymic expression in the sample was **to rub shoulders with someone,** which appeared in 26 citations, including the following:

9. The most learned scholars **rubbed shoulders with** young graduates nervously presenting their first communications.
10. New York has always had great contrasts, wealth **rubbing shoulders with** poverty.

As was seen in the case of the expression **to take a deep breath,** it is sometimes difficult to decide whether the literal sense or the figurative sense is intended, or whether the writer intends to allude to both senses at once.

Other metonyms in which nominal **shoulder(s)** occurs in the sample include **to look over someone's shoulder,** with the meanings of 'supervise' and 'observe warily', in the following examples:

11. And you've got to get on with things without someone **looking over your shoulder.**
12. American retailers in particular **are looking** anxiously **over their shoulders** at a new threat in their own backyard.

Nominal **shoulder** is also used metonymically to suggest comfort, in expressions such as for example **cry on someone's shoulder** and **a shoulder to lean on.**

Table 1 overleaf summarises the senses of **shoulder** found in the sample and gives numbers of each.

I shall now attempt to summarise the main points emerging from this study of metaphorical and non-metaphorical uses of **shoulder/s/ed/ing** by noun and verb uses as follows:

• If all nominal uses of **shoulder** which do not appear to have a concrete referent are grouped together, they total 101 citations, or 10.7 per cent of the total nominal uses.
• There are 45 metaphorical and idiomatic citations for verbal **shoulder;** this represents 95.7 per cent of all verbal uses: i.e. the non-literal use is a great deal more significant for the verb than for the noun.
• Where nominal **shoulder** is used figuratively, it is more likely to occur in one of a number of limited and fairly inflexible metonymic expressions than with independent metaphorical meaning. (*ctd. p. 189*)

Table 1. *Senses of **shoulder** in the sample*

Part of speech/sense	No. of citations	Example
Adjectival	13 *(total)*	
physical appearance of shoulders: non-metaphorical	13	If he is very depressed, he could look **round-shouldered** with his head bowed or pushed forward like a turtle.
Verbal	47 *(total)*	
'push': non-metaphorical	2	Then he **shouldered** his way through the soldiers …
'have responsibility, debt, blame': metaphorical	39	All over the country, but particularly in London, other hospitals are being required **to shoulder** similar risks.
cold-shoulder: idiom*	6	**I'm not being cold-shouldered**, but I'm not exactly being welcomed with open arms either.
Nominal	940 *(total)*	
part of body: non-metaphorical	828	He'd sing with a parrot on his **shoulder.**
'place where responsibility, debt, blame is felt': metaphorical	31	Debt can seem like an unbearable **load** on your **shoulders.**
various metonymic* expressions	47	The most learned scholars **rubbed shoulders with** young graduates … They have been at the end of a phone, or **a shoulder to cry on** when she found the going tough.
have a chip on one's shoulder: idiom*	10	I didn't like it, maybe I had a bit of **a chip on my shoulder.**
cold shoulder: idiom*	7	Her book is chilling in its description of what it feels like **to be given the cold shoulder** by Hollywood.
be head and shoulders above someone: idiom*	6	I think David Lloyd **is head and shoulders above** everyone else that operates in that lifestyle kind of business.
hard shoulder: 'dead' metaphor*	11	A few moments later, the car really does lurch towards the **hard shoulder.**

* Depending on the definitions of the terms 'metaphor', 'idiom', 'metonymy' and 'dead metaphor' used by the individual researcher (see previous section).

- Verbal **shoulder** on the other hand is likely to be used with an independent meaning, albeit within a fairly predictable collocational frame.
- Metaphorical verbal **shoulder** does not appear to have a corresponding non-metaphorical sense; there is no evidence that phrases such as 'He shouldered a sack of potatoes' occur at all frequently in current English.

The pattern described in the last observation, of syntactic divergence, is not uncommon in the concordance data looked at. A similar case is the metaphorical use of **blossom**. **Blossom** is rarely, if ever, used as a noun with its metaphorical meaning of 'develop', although *SOED* gives evidence of a former use in poetry. As a verb, the metaphorical use of **blossom** is slightly more frequent than the non-metaphorical use in the corpus.

The pattern in these and other metaphors looked at is of a shift from nominal to verbal use; examples of this are several animal metaphors, including **squirrel, ape, hare** and **hound**:

13. ... as consumers **squirrel** away huge sums for the downpayment on a home.
14. He **apes** their walk and mannerisms behind their backs with hilarious results.
15. He went **haring** round to her flat.
16. She couldn't bear to return to the house, to the people **hounding** her.

Although a pattern of shift from noun to verb seems to be emerging, a great deal more evidence is needed before it could be argued that this represents a general feature of metaphoric mapping. It needs to be seen whether particular semantic groups tend to shift in particular directions; for example, as animal metaphors are often used to describe ways of behaving, it might be expected that a metaphorical verbal use would develop from the non-metaphorical noun.

This discussion also raises a technical point. The frequency of these syntactic shifts demonstrates the importance of checking every possible inflected and derived form of a word stem when examining concordances. If only the base form is studied, some metaphorical uses may be missed.

Semantic relations

It is argued by many modern writers on metaphor that central and frequent metaphors organise thought by mapping conceptual domains onto a target domain (see for example Lakoff & Johnson, 1980; Gibbs, 1994). In a strong version of this theory, this should result in the generation of sets of linguistic metaphors which have at least some sense relations within two spheres, the target domain and the source domain. Kittay expresses this as follows:

Metaphorical transfers of meaning are transfers from the field of the vehicle to the field of the topic of the relations of affinity and opposition that the vehicle term(s) bears to other terms in its field. More precisely, in metaphor what is transferred are the relations which pertain within one semantic field to a second, distinct context domain.   (Kittay, 1987: 36)

She exemplifies this point with reference to the lexical set **hot, warm, cool, cold**, arguing that as **hot** can be used to describe the good performance of a basketball player, other members of the temperature set can be transferred, the lexical relations existing in the literal domain being preserved. This would mean that **cold** can be used to describe a poor performance, **warm** one which is reasonably good and so on (1987: 37). Corpus data is ideally suited to testing this claim, and extracts from the concordances of these four items are discussed below. I use this evidence to argue that the sense relations between the metaphorical uses of these items are more complex than Kittay's argument would seem to suggest.

Kittay writes of the potential of metaphor to create such sense relations, but she does not claim that they are always created. For the researcher into linguistic metaphors, it is of interest to attempt to establish whether these relations are in fact regularly created: whether lexical relations between non-metaphorical senses of words are maintained when these words are used with metaphorical meanings. The question also has implications for language teaching as, if lexical relations are generally carried over into the target domain, sizeable areas of vocabulary-learning could be facilitated.

At first glance, the answer seems to be that they are. Relations of antonymy between some adjectives in particular seem to be transferred; concordances for **deep** and **shallow** show the words to be antonyms when used to talk about character as well as when used to talk about physical depth:

17. She emerges from the book as a vain **shallow**, greedy tyrant.
18. He was a voracious reader with a sharp intellect and an inner reserve which suggested a **deeper** and more complex personality.

Similarly, **bright** and **dull** are antonymous when used to talk about intellect, as well as when used non-metaphorically to talk about colours:

19. He was particularly impressed by a planned fast-stream curriculum which would allow **bright** children to progress according to ability rather than age.

20. Though Japan is over-indulgent towards its **duller** middle managers, it is also incredibly good at cultivating **brighter** ones.

However, neither of these patterns represents the most frequent metaphorical senses, and closer examination shows these demonstrations of metaphorical antonymy to be selective, even contrived, at least in terms of frequent linguistic patterning. The most frequent metaphorical sense of **deep** is 'severe', collocating with items such as depression and financial problems. This sense is many times more frequent than the sense exemplified above, and **shallow** is not normally used as an antonym of it; **mild** or **slight** are more usual. **Dull** is only very rarely used to talk about intellect; in the majority of citations in the corpus it is a near synonym of 'boring', and the non-metaphorical **lively** or **interesting** are the most usual antonyms. **Dim** is sometimes used as an antonym of **bright** in its metaphorical sense, and this would seem to bear out a strong version of Kittay's argument. However, while **witted** occurs frequently to the right of **dim**, suggesting a metaphorical sense of 'stupid', in antonymy to metaphorical **bright**, **view** (in, for example, 'take a dim view of something') is the item most frequently appearing to the right of a non-literal use of **dim** (dim+view is exactly three times as frequent as **dim+witted** in the data studied). **Dim+memory** is also a frequent collocation, suggesting yet another metaphorical sense. Neither of these last two senses is used in antonymy with a sense of **bright**. In summary, while evidence from senses of some words can be found to support the notion of mapping of sense relations, there often seems to be a larger amount of counter-evidence to be found, through studying the same words.

I now discuss the relations between metaphorical uses of the four central temperature terms (**hot**, **cold**, **cool** and **warm**) in some detail to see whether the potential for developing lexical relations analogous to those between non-metaphorical senses, which Kittay describes, is in fact realised in language in use. The following summarises some of the relations between the metaphorical senses of these words. 1000 citations of each word were taken; and only their uses as adjectives are discussed here. This limited investigation suggests that lexical relations between non-metaphorical uses are not in fact usually maintained when these temperature terms are used metaphorically.

There are two pairs of antonyms between the non-metaphorical senses of these four words: **hot** and **cold**, and **warm** and **cool**. There is evidence that hot is used to talk metaphorically about feelings; citations are divided between anger and sexual feelings.

21. Tempers are **hot** in Buffalo, New York, where activists on both sides of the abortion debate are preparing for massive anti-abortion protests next week.
22. The couple are tipped to steam up the screen with red-**hot** love scenes.

The uses of **cold** to talk about feelings are much more numerous. One use seems to have a relationship of opposition with the second use of **hot**, above:

23. What I adore about her is the fact that sexually she's rather **cold** and remote.

This is not a completely clear-cut opposition; while **hot** used in a sexual sense collocates principally with words used to refer to texts, such as **book** and **film, cold** collocates with words used to refer to people, and there was no evidence in the sample looked at that **cold** with this sense collocates with words for texts. Implicit in most discussions of antonymy is the requirement that each of the pair of lexical items described as antonyms is used to talk about the same entities; for example, the pair **young** and **old** are both used to talk about people (see for example Palmer, 1974: 78–81 and Leech, 1974: 101–102). By this criterion, these uses of **hot** and **cold** are *not* antonyms in the same, strict sense as their literal counterparts are.

Other uses of **cold** have connotations of control, which could be considered as loosely opposed to the two senses of **hot** looked at above. Where **cold** is used to talk about anger or dislike, it seems to imply restraint:

24. Stephen had noticed the expression of **cold** hatred on Fox's white, closed face.

Although intuition suggests that **hot** is a possible antonym of this sense, there was no evidence for it collocating with items such as **hatred** and **anger** in the citations studied, suggesting that it is infrequent, relative to this use of **cold**.

Facts and ways of thinking about them that are not influenced by emotion may be described as **cold**:

25. It's time for investors to take a hard, **cold** look at the stocks they own and consider some careful pruning.

There is no evidence in the concordance of **hot** that it is used as an antonym of either of these uses of **cold**.

Lack of friendly feelings is also expressed metaphorically as **cold**:

26. ... giving me a bright, **cold** stare.

Corpus evidence suggests that **warm,** rather than **hot** is used as the antonym of this sense. This is one of the most frequent metaphorical uses of **warm**. Typical right collocates include **smile** and **welcome**.

While the uses discussed above suggest that although **cold** and **hot** do not maintain antonymy in the sense referred to above, of being available as interchangeable, with opposing meanings, in any context, they seem to express notions that are opposed in very loose terms. **Hot** implies strong, possibly uncontrolled feelings while **cold** implies lack of feelings, or the intellectual control of feelings.

Each lexeme also has senses which do not seem to have any even loosely corresponding opposition in their literal antonyms. A closely related series of uses of **hot** describes topics or people who are of current interest, are considered good (such as Kittay's basketball player) or are competitive. A common feature of these uses seems to be intensity of interest in the person or topic so described:

27. Now the quest for antibacterial drugs and therapies has become **hot** science.
28. My geography's not all that **hot**.
29. ... in a future of **hot** competition for premium programming.

Hot is also used to talk about stolen goods which are being searched for by the police:

30. <He> has signed more T-shirts than you've handled **hot** car stereos.

There is no evidence that **cold** is used as an antonym to any of these uses, although it is (just) conceivable that a speaker might exploit the established antonymy of literal **hot/cold** to use **cold** in this way.

Cold also has a sense for which there is no corresponding antonymic sense of **hot**; it is used to describe fear, in citations which strongly suggest that the motivation for the metaphor is metonymic:

31. I shivered as **cold** chills of fear crept over me.

While it may well be true that the relationship of antonymy holding between the literal senses of **hot** and **cold** can be exploited metaphorically in the way that Kittay suggests, this seems to have remained at the level of innovative metaphor in most, if not all, cases. The corpus evidence examined here does not yield any examples of metaphorical senses of **hot** and **cold** which are antonyms in the strictest sense, of having both opposing meaning and shared collocates.

There is more evidence that the antonymy of non-metaphorical **cool** and **warm** is preserved in their metaphoric uses. The most frequent metaphorical sense of **warm** is to describe friendly feelings; **cool** is used in opposition to this sense:

32. ... her own parents were **warm** and friendly.
33. It may be a **cool** and lonely partnership.

The most frequent metaphorical sense of adjectival **cool** is to describe feelings which are calm and controlled:

34. The timing of his tackles and his **cool** assurance were first class.

Cool here seems to be used with positive evaluation; in other citations of this sense, **cool** collocates with **ingenuous** and **common sense** in structures which suggest approval. This is in contrast to the evaluative slant of **cool** in the **warm/cool** antonymy discussed above, in which **warm** seems to positively evaluate, collocating with items such as **friendly** and **affection**, while **cool** negatively evaluates, collocating with items such as **distancing** and **lonely**. This in itself suggests that there is not one, systematic, metaphorical mapping of **cool**, but several different ones.

Studies of the graded relationship between **hot** and **warm** show even less coherence between their metaphorical uses, with these items often being actually opposed in their evaluative meaning. There is no evidence that they are treated as related items on a scale, although **cool** and **cold** are sometimes used in this way, for example to discuss unfriendly feelings.

One area in which there does seem to be a systematic transfer of meaning is the use of the four central temperature terms to describe colour, scent and taste. Although there are relatively few citations of this type of transfer in each of the samples, it is interesting that there seems to be some consistency of collocational patterns across the terms. However, it is less easy to analyse senses conclusively in terms of antonymy and near synonymy, as it is difficult to say, for example, in what way a **hot light** is related to a **cold light**. This is because these senses of **hot** and **cold** are rarely used contrastively in text, and because they describe subtle, subjective perceptions. Citations include, of colour:

35. **hot** colours ...
36. **cold**, gold light ...
37. a soft **warm** palette of sugar pinks, chalky pale pistachio greens and restful blue tones ...
38. Choose a **cool** colour such as cream.

of taste:

39. a very fine claret, rounded, smooth and deliciously **warm** ...
40. I prefer **cool** fruity red wines to whites.

One writer, who argues that large groups of many semantic fields are mapped from a source to a target domain in metaphor, bases much of her research on the terms used to talk about food and wine (Lehrer, 1978). This brief study suggests that such mappings may be more typical of the lexis of colour, scent, food and wine than of fields such as emotions. This may be because talk of the type illustrated in the above citations (35–39) is done by experts who consciously, or self-consciously, extend the language, leading to more exploitation of metaphor and lexical structure than is usual.

The above summary of lexical relations holding between four central temperature terms suggests that, while some lexical relations between metaphorical uses parallel those between non-metaphorical senses, this is not usually the case. The whole area of emotions is too complex to be represented metaphorically by a scalar set of terms such as those used for talking about temperature. Further, the notion of mapping at an intellectual level seems to neglect the importance of metonymy.

This is not to say that lexical relations between non-metaphorical senses cannot be exploited both to create conventional metaphorical uses and for innovative effect. In the following citation (also quoted above), the antonymy between **dull** and **bright** at two levels is exploited (and contributes to the cohesion of the sentence):

20. Though Japan is over-indulgent towards its **duller** middle managers, it is also incredibly good at cultivating **brighter** ones.

Syntagmatic relations between non-metaphorical uses are also exploited to create extended metaphors, as in the following citation:

41. Since then, designers **have pulled** fashion **apart at the seams**, only to **restitch the shreds** in new ways.

It seems then that lexical relations between non-metaphorical senses of words are available as a way of creating new metaphorical meanings, but that these relations cannot by themselves account completely for lexical relations between metaphorical senses, which are often complex. It should again be emphasised that the examples discussed above are not intended to suggest definitive conclusions about the frequency and syntax of linguistic metaphors, or about the semantic relations holding between them. Rather, they are intended as a guide to some areas which need to be explored further, and as illustrations of the methodology that can be employed in order to undertake such research.

Other directions

There are numerous directions in which corpus-based research into linguistic metaphor could be taken, only a few of which (frequency, syntax and lexical relations) have been discussed here.

Most large, modern corpora are sub-divided by text type, which opens up possibilities for diachronic and genre-based studies. For example, a comparison of metaphor use between historical and contemporary corpora would allow the researcher to trace the development of metaphorical uses from their first appearance as innovative metaphors through to their becoming fully established senses. Within contemporary corpora, a study of metaphors across different text types might span two or more categories such as academic writing, writing about economics, informal speech, women's magazines, children's fiction or political speeches. An initial survey might look at whether the language of certain genres is intrinsically more 'metaphorical' than that of others. Genre studies of metaphor would also provide a useful backdrop to studies such as those by Cortazzi and Jin (this volume), which analyse the metaphors from a very specific type of text. It could be established, for example, whether such metaphors are unique to that text type or whether they are shared by other genres. It would be interesting and suggestive to note, for example, if certain semantic groups of metaphors isolated in the above studies are shared with other, broader genres, such as business, the law or politics.

Limitations of a corpus-based approach

While a corpus-based approach to the study of metaphor shows up syntactic, collocational and semantic patterns which are difficult to access in any other way, this method has limitations, and has received some criticism. Three possible limitations are looked at here:

- the limited usefulness of corpora in the study of innovative metaphor;
- the necessity of working bottom-up rather than top-down in terms of developing models of linguistic patterning;
- the issue of representativeness.

I shall look briefly at each of these three areas, and I shall acknowledge that the first two represent genuine limitations on corpus work, but argue that the third point is not the intractable problem suggested by some critics of corpus-based approaches.

Firstly, concordance data are unlikely to be of great interest to researchers who are interested in innovative metaphors. Corpus linguistics is based on huge samples of language from which typical and frequent patterns are pulled out; corpus studies help to provide ways of determining what is usual, not what is inventive. However, one application of corpus data to the study of literary effect has been described by Louw (1993), who discusses unusual collocations in literature, using concordance data to demonstrate ways in which some collocations found in literature break typical patterns found in the corpus and so create particular stylistic effects. Presumably, on the same principle, literary metaphors could be compared and contrasted with typical patterns found in a corpus.

A second drawback to the use of corpora for any kind of semantic investigation has already been mentioned; the researcher will only uncover what he or she sets out to look for. There is no way of, say, entering a speaker meaning or conceptual metaphor into a computer and being provided with a list of lexical items realising that particular meaning or metaphor. Some metaphorical uses can be quickly isolated from a concordance as they have a different collocational profile from non-metaphorical uses of the same word; however, it is common for more than one item from the same semantic field to be used metaphorically (see for example, Citation 41 above), in which case the collocational profiles of metaphorical and non-metaphorical uses would be similar. This means that, if collocational profiles alone are used to separate uses, a metaphorical use may remain hidden.

However, the investigation of a particular semantic field can be made more systematic with the use of a comprehensive thesaurus. It is conceivable that in the future linguistic metaphor databases based on concordance data might be set up along the lines of on-line thesauri or dictionaries. This would be a huge undertaking, as it is difficult to see how the necessary linguistic research could ever be done automatically. At present, the corpus-based metaphor researcher has little alternative but to scan the concordances of numerous lexical items, looking intuitively for patterns.

A third problem concerns the representativeness of the data used. A common criticism of corpus-based reference texts and studies is that the corpus that they are based on is not truly representative of the language. For example, Summers criticises the Bank of English (the corpus used for the studies reported here) for its "dependence on news media source material" (1996: 266). It is certainly true that newspapers are one of the most readily available sources of machine-readable texts, and predominate in many modern corpora. However, in defence of such corpora it could be argued that journalism probably represents a large proportion of the reading of many users of language, and so deserves to be well-represented in a large general corpus. Further, by including a number of different news titles, the corpus is probably more balanced in its journalistic intake than the average reader of newspapers, who may only read one or two titles on a regular basis.

This raises the question 'a corpus representative of what?', or 'whose corpus?' In the late twentieth century, different people's daily lives span a wide range of specialised occupations and activities, and as a result, each person's daily diet of language will be different. Some language users spend much of their time engaged in spoken interaction, while other people's language input might consist of a great deal of specialist written material. Consequently, the types of vocabulary and structures encountered frequently will vary a good deal from person to person. Because of this variation in language experience, the composition of any corpus will be at odds with most individuals' personal experience of language, and it is to be hoped that a well balanced corpus will be superior to any individual's 'personal corpus' in its range and balance. It should be acknowledged however that many corpora are probably genuinely under-representative of spoken texts; these are difficult to collect because of many people's natural reluctance to allow their private conversations to be recorded, and such data are also time-consuming, and therefore expensive, to key into a database.

Knowles answers the common criticism that corpus linguistics relies on unrepresentative samples of texts by pointing out, somewhat wryly, that although current corpora may be limited, they at least provide authentic evidence:

[Another] objection raised against the corpus approach is that corpus linguists collect a restricted sample of an arbitrary subset of the language and then pontificate about the language as a whole. If only they could be persuaded to invent their own data, then they would not have any such problem.   (Knowles, 1996: 52)

Statements made about language by linguists who do not consult external, naturally occurring data must presumably be based on their own experience of language use at some level. The 'personal corpus' of an academic may well be highly skewed compared with the language experience of the general population. Furthermore, as has already been argued, it seems that such 'personal corpora' are not easily and reliably accessible in the way that a computerised corpus is, and the observations made by consulting a personal corpus are not replicable or falsifiable.

Researchers can, in any case, allow for the possibility that a corpus in its entirety may be misrepresentative of the language as a whole by examining and comparing sections of it. The composition of most modern corpora allows users to examine sub-corpora and to compare frequencies of different usages in different genres. Information about the frequency of lexical items (presented in the form of average number of citations per million words) is automatically broken down by the different sub-corpora, enabling the user to see instantly if a use is over- or under-represented in, say, news media in comparison to, say, the spoken or fiction corpora.

Conclusion

Kövecses, in his discussion of the conceptual metaphors of happiness, summarises his methodology as follows:

> ... in order to be able to arrive at [the] metaphors, metonymies, and inherent concepts, and, eventually, [the] prototypical cognitive models, one needs to study the conventionalized linguistic expressions that are related to a given notion.   (Kövecses, 1991: 30)

In this paper I have attempted to demonstrate one type of study of conventionalised linguistic expressions which takes authentic data as its starting point.

PART IV

ANALYSING METAPHOR
IN ELICITED DATA

10 "Captain of my own ship"
Metaphor and the discourse of chronic illness

Richard Gwyn

Metaphor and serious illness

The writer most commonly associated with metaphor and illness is
Sontag, whose two essays (collected in one volume, 1991) examined
the metaphors associated with, firstly, tuberculosis and cancer, and
several years later, with AIDS. It is an irony of Sontag's endeavour
that in arguing for a metaphor-free view of illness, she finds herself
constantly seduced by and reverting to, the rich and potent supply of
metaphoric devices that she herself employs to put forward her
argument. Thus, at the start of *Illness as Metaphor* we are told:
"Illness is the night-side of life, a more onerous citizenship. Everyone
who is born holds dual citizenship, in the kingdom of the well and in
the kingdom of the sick" (1991: 3). And throughout Sontag's
articulate and elegant work we are reminded of the difference
between the things she wants to say and the means by which she
must say them. She wishes to "demythicize" disease and over and
over again reiterates that "my point is that illness is *not* a metaphor,
and that the most truthful way of regarding illness ... is one most
purified of, most resistant to, metaphoric thinking" (*ibid.*).

Sontag collates an abundant supply of metaphoric representations
from various sources: cancer is a "demonic pregnancy" (1991: 14),
and a "degeneration". "In cancer the patient is 'invaded' by alien
cells, which multiply, causing an atrophy or blockage of bodily
functions" (*ibid.*). Further descriptions of cancer inform us that "it
crawls and creeps like a crab" (p. 11); that it is "unholy granite
substance" (p. 14); that it represents "repression of passion" (p. 22),
"frustration", "emotional resignation", "giving up", "to resign", "to
shrink" (p. 24); that the personality of the cancer sufferer is "un-
emotional, inhibited, repressed" (p. 40); and that the disease is "an
outlet for ... foiled creative fire" (p. 50). We hear of a "fight" or
"crusade against cancer" (p. 59); of the "killer disease" (*ibid.*); of a
"scourge" (p. 63) that is "invasive" (p. 65); one that will "colonise"

(p. 66), "setting up outposts" (p. 66), a veritable "tumor invasion" (*ibid.*), whose *treatment is* to be "bombarded with toxic rays, chemical warfare" in order to "kill the cancer" (*ibid.*). Cancer is the "disease of the Other" (p. 69); it is "an invasion of 'alien' or 'mutant' cells, stronger than normal cells" (*Invasion of the Body Snatchers, The Incredible Shrinking Man, The Blob, The Thing*); it is a "triumphant mutation" (p. 69).

If we can accept that metaphor is a central tool of our cognitive apparatus (e.g. Lakoff, 1993; Gibbs, 1994, and Chapter 2), it seems difficult if not impossible to conceive of illnesses – especially those, like cancer, that have become established in our cultural mythology as metaphors for other things (e.g. a 'cancer in society') – as not themselves being described metaphorically in everyday discourse. We might recall Vico's aphorism that 'metaphors are myths in miniature'. Sontag herself admits to once writing "in the heat of despair over America's war on Vietnam, that 'the white race is the cancer of human history'" (1991: 85).

However, Sontag tells us, it is hard for a society to be obsessed with more than one illness at a time, and much of the metaphoric demonising that not so long ago pertained to cancer (and before cancer, to TB) has now been re-allocated to AIDS. Again, the metaphors are predominantly those of invasion and war, but this time there is a fiercer moral dimension, and rather than being accused, as were cancer victims, of 'repression' and 'frustration', AIDS victims are the harbingers of a new moral degradation, itself emanating from the Other, from Elsewhere (more specifically from Africa, traditional seat of the white race's primordial terror). AIDS is, then, an "invasion" (p. 102); a "pollution" (p. 103). The virus, we are told, with its alien cunning, "hides in cells", "can lurk for years in microphages" (p. 105) before blooming into "full-blown" or "fully-fledged" (p. 114) AIDS. It is a "plague" (p. 130), "God's judgement on a society that does not live by his rules" (p. 147), a "consequence of moral decadence" (p. 147); a "gay plague" (p. 148).

The metaphoric representation of AIDS as invader, of the war with AIDS, is one that Helman (1984: 101) sees as being linked to identifiable groups of foreigners (Africans, Haitians etc.), as well as invoking the science fiction interest of an alien body lodging itself in the normally healthy body of the host. It is not difficult to associate the one with the other and to create xenophobia from a bacterium. AIDS as *war* is, similarly, an image in which normal society can be seen to defend itself against the degenerate lifestyles of a sexually promiscuous and deviant drug-abusing nucleus of 'carriers'. But the metaphoric resonance of the war against an invasive disease is central to an understanding of illness as something *external* to the individual, an *exogenous* entity to be battled with, and in this respect corresponds to Herzlich's (1973) account of the intrinsically healthy individual pitted against a health-threatening society. However, there are times, it seems, when that society is itself under threat, and these are the occasions which prompt a spirit of resistance (*viz.* the 'war against cancer', 'the battle with AIDS'), and, in an example from May 1994, the passionate responses provoked by the mass media to the apparent proliferation in cases of streptococcus A infection, reported in the popular press as 'The Killer Bug Disease'.

The power of the military metaphor lies in its ability to arouse people into a state of fear and preventive activity, to mobilise against an emergency. In the reification of the 'Germ', and more so the 'Bug', the 'enemy' is one that can be pictorially imaged: Helman (1984: 113) claims that some bugs are thought of as tiny insects – which, since that is precisely what a 'bug' is in English, is unsurprising. It is known that certain bugs visible to the naked eye (the louse, the flea, the nit) can cause illness, and so it is a short step to imagine a 'stomach bug' in similar terms.

Texts abound from the Edwardian period onward (Lupton, 1994: 62) in which the 'war against germs' is promoted as though it were like any other war, with children especially being targeted as at risk from "bacteria ... anthropomorphized into wily aggressors, deliberately changing themselves to elude detection and attack from their human foes" (Lupton, 1994: 63). The 'war on cancer' perfectly encapsulates the sense of total war, with civilians both the victims and the stalwarts of the home guard in their support for campaigns to 'wipe out' the 'threat' of cancer. The war is fought on several fronts, with surges in public optimism followed by periods of decline and deadlock:

> The bromides of the American cancer establishment, tirelessly hailing the imminent victory over cancer; the professional pessimism of a large number of cancer specialists, talking like battle-weary officers mired down in an interminable colonial war – these are twin distortions in this military rhetoric about cancer.   (Sontag, 1991: 68)

And like all the most terrifying enemies, cancer is faceless: it is "understood as the overwhelming or obliterating of consciousness (by a mindless IT)" (*ibid.*). It stands for all that de-personalises, renders non-human, non-creative, sterile, dead:

> In cancer, non-intelligent ('primitive', 'embryonic', 'atavistic') cells are multiplying, and you are being replaced by the nonyou. Immunologists class the body's cancer cells as 'nonself'.   (*ibid.*)

Doctors of medicine are especially prone to employing the metaphors of war in describing their activities. Stein (1990) found that doctors working in hospitals frequently spoke of "being on the front line", of the need to "get aggressive" with certain patients, as well as of "shotgun therapy" and "magic bullets" (cited in Lupton, 1994: 63). Such metaphors were common in "informal and formal discussions between doctors, talk between doctors and patients, at medical seminars and conferences, in drug advertisements and articles in medical journals and in representations of medicine and disease in the popular media" (Lupton, 1994: 63). AIDS has provided a new arena for the exchange of military metaphors, one that is particularly poignant given the life-and-death character of the struggle that sufferers have to endure:

My personal war began two years ago when I was mobilised by AIDS. All the pleasures of peacetime and my carefree life were suddenly banished, as if an orchestra had stopped playing to let the theatre manager announce that war had just been declared, that Pearl Harbour had been bombed.
                                        (Dreuihle, 1988, cited in Lupton, 1994: 63).

The particular way in which the HIV virus lodges itself in its human host secures for science writers a free pass into the domain of science fiction. Sontag (1991: 104) refers us to a *Time* magazine article from 1986, which captures the flavour of an invasion from outer space as well as well as its contemporaneous movies or space invader games:

On the surface of that cell, it finds a receptor into which one of its envelope proteins fits perfectly, like a key into a lock.

Here the invading disease is seen as a diabolically clever agent of destruction: *it* knows the secret ways to the body's weaknesses. Moreover, it takes over the body's own cells in familiar science fiction fashion, so that the victim's cells *themselves* become the invader:

The naked AIDS virus converts its RNA ... into DNA, the master molecule of life. The molecule then penetrates the cell nucleus, inserts itself into a chromosome and takes over part of the cellular machinery, directing it to produce more AIDS viruses. Eventually, overcome by its alien product, the cell swells and dies, releasing a flood of new viruses to attack other cells.   (Sontag, 1991: 104)

The military metaphor is dangerous, argues Sontag (and I would agree), because it implicitly provides the argument for widespread oppression in the guise of protecting civilian lives. Already we are familiar with the representation of heterosexuals as 'innocent bystanders' felled by the crossfire in the triangular war waged between the medical establishment, the AIDS virus and the cohorts of homosexuals, blacks and junkies who, we are informed, constitute the greater part of its victims (and this is to ignore, of course, the continent of Africa, where AIDS is transmitted overwhelmingly through hetero-sexual contact). The representation of the AIDS virus, or any other disease, as an invasive, alien and murderous entity can only impart upon its sufferers, by proxy, the stigma of alien and destructive intent. To defend oneself against such a monstrous enemy is not only *just*, it is *obligatory*. The military metaphor thus provokes the cry for institutionalised marginalisation and repression, even, Sontag sug-gests, of violence, "the equivalent of surgical removal or chemical control of the offending or 'unhealthy' parts of the body politic" (1991: 180). In its wrongful overstatement, the military metaphor provides us all (and the mass media in particular thrive on this) with an identifiable evil that is all too easily transferred onto the persons who are subject to the illnesses themselves. As Sontag writes: "We are not being invaded. The body is not a battlefield. The ill are neither unavoidable casualties nor the enemy" (*ibid.*). In sum, the military metaphor "overmobilizes, it overdescribes, and it powerfully contri-butes to the excommunicating and stigmatising of the ill" (1991: 180).

Now, one of the strongest criticisms of Sontag's argument is that illness is never simply illness, but is the focus of a culturally experienced phenomenon. As Fox puts it:

Illness cannot be just illness, for the simple reason that human culture is constituted in language, that *there is nothing knowable outside language*, and that health and illness, being things which fundamentally concern humans, and hence need to be 'explained', enter into language and are constituted in language, regardless of whether or not they have some independent reality in nature.   (Fox, 1993: 6)

Scheper-Hughes and Lock (1986) claim that Sontag's conclusions only support the notion of the reification of disease, and do not empower those patients who employ such metaphors. DiGiacomo agrees, commenting:

No-one ever experiences cancer as the uncontrolled proliferation of abnormal cells. Indeed, we can experience anything at all only through and by means of culturally constructed and socially reproduced structures of metaphor and meaning.   (DiGiacomo, 1992: 117)

Most convincingly, Montgomery (1991) argues that we should no longer even consider the military metaphor to be a metaphor at all in the biomedical arena. Taking his lead from Nietzsche's statement that the metaphors of yesterday become the truths of today, he claims that the military metaphor is static, or *dead* (*cf.* Lakoff & Johnson, 1980) in relation to medical discourse. Although the origin of the metaphor of invasion began with scientific/medical writing, it is now fully popularised and accepted and no longer metaphoric:

> In speaking of 'metaphoric systems' I do not wish to imply that such systems still function on a (purely) figurative level, only that they began as such. On the contrary, their operation today is almost entirely on the literal plane: disease is not *like* these systems and their related terms, it is them, inasmuch as it is a concept whose existence depends on expression.
>
> (Montgomery, 1991: 345)

Montgomery argues that the invasion metaphor and its accompanying bio-militarism all began around the time of Pasteur and the emergence of germ theory. This theory "gave medicine its first real claim to the 'scientific', and was thereafter rapidly expanded far beyond its original limits by the medical community as the *prima facie* model for *all* disease" (1991: 367). But, Montgomery continues, "the language of war in Pasteur's day held another ground. It dovetailed neatly with the late nineteenth-century view of the nation state as a living body (the 'body politic'), an organism subject to varied forms of assault from foreign powers" (1991: 367). In his paper Montgomery concludes that bio-militarism combines with "information technology" in the most modern writing on medicine, thus correlating with a more modern view of computerised warfare.

At this point it is necessary to consider that, if the metaphors of invasion/war are no longer truly metaphors in relation to illness, then are there other strategies that may be termed metaphoric, which individuals *do* use in order to come to an understanding of, or to find an explanatory model for (Kleinman, 1988), their own chronic illnesses or the illnesses of those around them? How is a command of metaphor employed in people's accounts of illness? Is metaphor transferable into action; that is to say, quite apart from thinking and speaking metaphorically, do people 'act metaphorically'? How can research into 'metaphorical behaviours', both linguistic and non-linguistic, add to the work being done in cognitive psychology, anthropology and linguistics?

The study

My ethnographic research involved the tape-recording of informal, semi-structured interviews with 28 people who had experience of chronic illness themselves, or had looked after a family member who suffered chronic illness. Although there were a series of questions that I asked later on in each session, the larger part of our talk involved the interviewee's response to the question *What is your experience of illness?* Much of the talk that ensued fell into the category defined by Wolfson (1976) as "conversational narrative", in which the role of the researcher is to encourage the interviewee to speak freely, to introduce his or her own topics, and to tell stories (1976: 196). By having myself introduced, or introducing myself, as somebody engaged in research who was "making audio-tape recordings with individuals relating to their experience of illness and health care", as the consent form reads, I avoided the term 'interview'. Moreover, by verbally assuring my informants that I had sought out their 'help' in my project, I was, to a degree, assigning to them the role of collaborator, which, according to Mishler (1986: 126) is a way of reducing the power differential in interviews.

With regard to the actual content of the interviews, I selected the same broad spectrum of question topics as those used in the now classic study by Herzlich (1973). Since I had been so intrigued by Herzlich's work and was particularly interested in the question of the social representation of health and illness, it seemed felicitous to follow her example. However, Herzlich provides the minimum of information concerning her own methodology (1973: 13–16). Indeed, she observes that, given the lack of any "fully rigorous and satisfactory method" available to social psychology, "strict methodological unity seems neither possible nor desirable" (1973: 16). "Strict methodological unity" suggested to me an inflexibility that was not in focus with my own aims anyhow. My major concern was that by having a fixed strategy, I would inevitably begin to organise and dominate the interview in an unsuitable manner. I wanted the respondents to take control of the interview as far as possible, and speak about things that were of interest to them. My questions served, in an important sense, as something to 'fall back on' should the flow of talk cease. My list of questions, which has close parallels with that of Herzlich's in the 1960s, was as follows:

Q1 What experience do you have of illness?
Q2 How do you decide when an illness is serious?
Q3 What do you consider to be your 'normal' state of health?
Q4 What are the causes of illness?
Q5 Is there a difference between 'illness' and 'disease'?
Q6 Can you have a disease but not be ill?
Q7 How does your behaviour differ when you are ill?
Q8 Can a person's attitude change illness?
Q9 What illnesses do you most fear? What illnesses are most feared in society?

Q10 What factors are most important for maintaining good health?

Q11 What is a doctor? How are doctors perceived in our society?

Q12 Should doctors tell you what to do or advise you on the best course of action?

Q13 Do you think doctors should have a wide knowledge of your non-medical life in order to treat you effectively?

Q14 Have you ever had a disagreement with a doctor?

Q15 Is it possible to imagine a world free of illness? Can illness be eradicated?

As it turned out, not all the questions were always asked in the same order; sometimes the interviewee would provide an answer to a specific question listed at a later stage in my 'fall back' question schedule, making that question redundant. On one occasion I did not get beyond the first question, *What is your experience of illness?*, since the respondent spent two and a half hours answering that single question. I had access to a list of questions during the interview, but made a point of not referring to it frequently, and certainly never held it in front of me in a reading position. In some interviews, I did not use the list at all, not wishing to upset the open or spontaneous drift of conversation. The transcribed interviews were eventually subjected to a process of discourse analysis, with the aim of drawing attention to the ways people formulate their illness experiences discursively, and the meanings they attach to illness in their lives (Gwyn, 1996).

Studying the transcripts, my interest focused not so much upon the 'conventional' types of metaphor associated with illness (those of *invasion, struggle, battle*), but on those appearances in the text where reality is viewed through a distinct domain of experience, and a metaphoric transfer (if that is not a pleonasm) takes place as a means of explaining or coming to terms with the lived experience of illness. The idea that metaphor is not simply an 'as if' phenomenon, but suggests a transference of 'domains of experience', corresponded well with another thread of my investigation, namely the belief that storytelling is a longstanding human resource for understanding experiences (see e.g. Churchill & Churchill, 1982; Hillman, 1983; Kleinman, 1988). The resulting synthesis of narrative laced with metaphoric detail provides the basis for my analysis, and is close to that described by Radley:

> Adjustment to illness, if it is to be self-legitimating, needs to have a certain communicative structure. This structure is most readily seen as metaphor, or rather as one kind of metaphor among several that are used by patients to give expressive form to their condition.   (Radley, 1993: 110)

Radley cites as an example the case of a male cardiac patient who "always insisted on digging his garden even though he knew it upset his wife". It is worth quoting the relevant passage from Radley in its entirety:

The act of digging can be seen as important because it signified to those around him the attitude that he took to his illness. It was not the only act of this kind, but it was readily specifiable as such. What might it be meant to convey? That he was active? Certainly. That he was healthy? Only in part. For the digging was only salient in the context of his heart disease, something known to his family and friends. Therefore, this action can be seen to stand for a relationship of the man to his illness and to the world of health. It said – perhaps more powerfully than words – that he refused the sick role in spite of the doctor having diagnosed him as having a serious illness. It becomes understandable in terms of his relationships to his wife and to his work ... in the way he could signify with bodily potentialities of sexuality and maleness. In this example, the digging can be read as standing for the man's relationship to other areas of life, including his role as husband in the home and as someone still capable of doing a day's work if need be (he was a retired manual worker). This is a metonymic relationship in that the physical actions involved are also constituent 'parts' of other areas of life, which (were they to be put into words) might be described as benefiting from 'putting one's back into it' or 'getting stuck in'.

(Radley, 1993: 117)

When Radley's account is added to those considered thus far, it seems to me that the most appropriate position to take, when analysing reactions to illness, is not to even try and separate metonymy from metaphor (though Cameron, in Chapter 1, and Gibbs, in Chapter 2, both suggest that separation is desirable in many research situations), but rather, to adopt something close to the 'treatment' definition described by Low (in Chapter 11). In this, the metaphoric process relates to a situation where 'X is treated as if it were partially, but not completely Y'. The definition does not predetermine how distinct or incongruous X and Y need to be; where they are very distinct, the expression will be metaphoric, but where they can be said to belong to the same domain, the expression will be metonymic. Employing a 'treatment' definition will thus allow me to take a broad view and to consider metaphor and metonymy together, as two aspects of the metaphoric process.

It is also evident from the Radley passage that metaphor and metonymy need not be restricted to the medium of language, to what can be said in words:

The idea of reflecting one domain of experience through another is a way of intending a meaning, engaging the world.   (Radley, 1993: 116)

Another way of describing this might be to say that perceptions and actions are recorded in language that lends shape to the speakers' relationship to illness, quite apart from the 'conventional' metaphors that populate my recorded accounts. I consider these perceptions and actions to be as 'metaphoric' as any of the linguistic tropes which we are accustomed to thinking of as being metaphors proper. Such a belief finds support in the work of Richards (1936). Richards included as "metaphoric, those processes in which we perceive or think or feel about one thing in terms of another". For Richards a command of metaphor could "go deeper still into the control of the world that we make for ourselves to live in" (1936: 135–136, cited in Mair, 1976: 249). He further suggested that what psychoanalysts term 'transference' is another name for metaphor: "how constantly modes of regarding, of loving, of acting, that have developed with one set of things or people, are shifted to another" (*ibid.*). Again, Radley states (1993: 113) that metaphor need not be restricted to the medium of language, to what can be said in words, but that it is a way of "reflecting one reality through another". A first example from my interviews will serve to illustrate this proposition.

Nerys Williams is describing the nine years she spent nursing her youngest son, who had cancer.[1] A brain tumor was first diagnosed when Joey was ten; he died at the age of nineteen, seven weeks before the interview took place. Nerys, a fifty-year old social worker, frequently employs the metaphors of war in the course of her interview, along with references to the speed of growth of the malignant tumor:

because if it had been a very fast growing tumor then it had come back then he would have died probably within the year whereas *what it bought us was lots of time* (.) um (.) so (.) at the time obviously your your child's life is so precious that even if you're being told well you know *he's got a fighting chance* and um it's a slow growing tumor and you think well that's great you know we're not looking at a crisis this month next month *the frontier's been pushed back*

The conventional metaphorisation of time as being a buyable commodity (*cf*. Lakoff & Johnson, 1980; Gibbs, 1994: 441) might seem to ring hollow in the context, where what is being 'purchased' is a temporary reprieve from early death. However, we are sharply reminded that this struggle is a fight to the end ("he's got a fighting chance"), that on the battle-front of cancer, some ground has been won ("the frontier's been pushed back"). These metaphors no longer *sound* like metaphors to our ears, but more like commonsense

---

[1] The names of the people in my study have all been changed, and those quoted are pseudonyms.

representations (*cf.* Moscovici, 1984). Elsewhere Nerys speaks of the "more aggressive surgery" that had to be employed in the later operations to counteract the faster-growing tumor, of a "great big thing swelling up inside your head". Of her first meeting with the consultant who informs her of Joey's condition, she says:

I've I've never experienced a shock quite like it I felt as if I'd been physically *hit* (.) I really felt (.) my stomach turn over

These reactions and the descriptions of the fight against Joey's cancer correspond to the first category of metaphor described by Radley, that is "the way that individuals use figures of speech in how they represent their illness to themselves and to others"(1993: 110). Radley's second category, "the way that certain adjustments involve a re-figuration of the subject in his or her dealings with other people" (1993: 110), aligns with the objectives of this paper, and can perhaps be illustrated by a passage immediately following the breaking of the news to Nerys, when Joey, aged ten, is invited into the consultant's room to be told that:

your headaches are caused by (.) pressure inside your head and we're going to have to get you in to hospital to have an operation to remove the pressure (.) true (.) and he sat there and he said oh and she said we'll have you in on Monday and we'll shave your head and do the operation and then you won't have any more headaches

For some cancer patients, hair loss through chemotherapy seems to act as a poignant metaphor for all that the illness entails (Lanceley, personal correspondence, 1995). It symbolises the dehumanising and de-sexualising effects of cancer, a visible stigma, a marking and humiliation of the surface of the body that corresponds to the internal ravages of the tumor. In Nerys Williams' interview, it is a theme that is taken up later, when, throughout Joey's teenage years, he suffers hair loss because of radiotherapy. However, that is to pre-empt the narrative, because at this point in time Joey knows nothing of his cancer. He reacts to the news as follows:

so we came out of the room and Joey then promptly had a tantrum as we walked down down the corridor saying *he* was not having his head shaved there was no way he wanted his head shaved and rather he'd have the headaches he'd rather have the headaches thank you very much

Over the years that follow, Joey undergoes brain surgery six times, experiences extended bouts of chemotherapy and radiotherapy, continues going to school, taking GCSEs and later, when very ill, his A levels. At eighteen he is told that the tumor is back and growing faster, and that a new course of radiotherapy may be his only hope.

Nerys, Joey and a visiting nurse sit down together to formulate a plan of action:

> so we had to get a big piece of paper out and put for and against and it was things like (.) against having it was that you'd lose your hair you'd be ill um (.) and the for was (.) you're going to live longer

The prominence attached to this side-effect of his illness seems to add significance, retrospectively, to the episode of Joey, aged ten, throwing a tantrum because he doesn't want his head shaved. It is possible to read into Nerys' account precisely that "backward action of self-understanding" that is central to the process of narrative reconstruction (Churchill & Churchill, 1982: 73). It might even be suggested that Joey's violent rejection of having his head shaved provides an anticipatory rejection of the tumor and of all that it entailed. What can be stated with certainty is that the associations of hair loss (depersonalising, de-sexing and degrading) that the older Joey so disliked, were anticipated by the obligatory shaving of his head for the preliminary operation, one that was repeated at intervals thereafter; and that the loss of hair, either through shaving or through radiation treatment, came to represent the same thing to Joey, namely his "re-figuration" through illness. Now "metonymy", to quote Gibbs (1994: 358), is frequently envisaged as "a widely-used figure of thought, whereby we take one well-understood or easily perceived aspect of something to represent or stand for the thing as a whole". This re-figuration, then, would appear to be constituted in a metonymic relationship, one in which a part of the body comes to represent the body subject to illness. The hair, or at least the head, is the most "easily-perceived aspect" of any individual, and a shaved head would therefore stand in clear relation to the illness as something quite specific and meaningful.

On 2nd December, 1995, a story appeared in the Welsh newspaper *The Western Mail*, which confirmed to me the salience of hair loss in relation to young cancer sufferers. Under the headline **Kindest cut is a real snip**, it told the story of a thirteen-year-old girl, Andrea Matthews, who had "all her hair shaved off as a touching gesture of support to her sister, who has lost hers through chemotherapy". The article continued:

> On Thursday, we reported how 13-year-old Andrea planned to lose her shoulder-length locks in sympathy with sister Amanda, 16, whose treatment for leukaemia has meant the loss of her own long blonde hair. ... Before an assembly of 100 classmates, Andrea took the stage at Tredegar Comprehensive and spoke about the meaning of her sister's illness, before family friend and hairdresser Lorraine Rees shaved off her crowning glory.

We are then told how Andrea decided on the public haircut in order to raise awareness of the problems raised by her sister's illness, particularly with regard to the hair loss: "Amanda ... was rejected by some of her friends when she became ill and felt even worse when her hair fell out as a result of the treatment".

Here is an example of what we might conveniently term symbolic action – and one involving a *conceptual transfer from one domain to another*: the healthy younger sister shows her support and solidarity by transferring the perceived sufferings of her sick sister, through symbolic sacrifice, onto herself. It is precisely this kind of action which merits the description *metaphoric*, and if we are to follow Gibbs (1994: 1) into an acceptance of metaphor as constituting the "basic schemes by which people conceptualise their experience and the external world", then we must be prepared to make this leap from the social semiotic of language into the domain of symbolic social action.

There is, of course, a traditional cultural stereotyping of long hair with unrestrained sexuality and cropped hair with celibacy, though it is one which is open to question (*cf.* Hallpike, 1969). Whatever associations are appropriate in this case (and there is no doubt of the ritual import of the ceremony because of the public nature of its execution), in the story of Andrea Matthews we can again refer to the explicit relationship between the shaved hair and the suffering individual as *metonymic*, in that the part (the hair) stands for another feature of the body (its illness), or for the body itself.

Symbolic action is significant in the account given by another speaker. Bill Morgan, 55, describes his coronary condition in exquisite detail. As a successful young construction engineer in the Far East, Bill led a hedonistic lifestyle, ate and drank excessively, and weighed over nineteen stone. At the age of thirty-four he suffered two heart attacks in quick succession, and a third one seven years later. Back in Wales, and at the age of fifty, he suffered a fourth heart attack. On being discharged from hospital, Bill found he had great difficulty in walking and breathing. He began an exercise programme to combat this, despite a long-standing dislike of walking anywhere ("walking was something I hated doing in my life"). Within a month however, he had begun mountain walking and within six months his first long-distance walk:

what happened in the twelve months twelve months I continued that programme was an awful lot of long-distance walking (.) walking about seventy miles a week plus doing four long distance back packs

Bill had to go in for a four-way bypass operation at the end of the year he refers to here, but by this time he was walking everywhere. I would argue that, like Radley's digger, walking had become the metaphor (or the metonym, or possibly both) of his opposition to heart disease. Bill's own account would appear to support the positive aspects of such a stance: "I felt that what I was doing was doing me good". Just as digging can be seen as a process of discovery (digging for something), walking is the simplest means for an able-bodied person of getting from one place to the next. The metaphor of the journey is a fundamental one. Moreover, Western culture is steeped in the mythological tradition of the journey, from the *Odyssey* onwards (see Gibbs, 1994: 188–192, for a discussion of journey myths). Specifically, we walk 'the road to recovery', we get 'back on the right track' we 'get better one step at a time'. Bill lived out the ambulatory metaphor to its full:

> I had the operation I *walked* to the hospital nineteen miles to have the operation (.) I *felt* I could walk home but they insisted on me going by taxi (.) and (.) within a week I was back I was back out walking and (.) six weeks after I walked the Pennine Way (.) with a back pack I felt this was the right way I'm a bit of an obsessive personality

For some heart attack victims (Helman, 1987; Radley, 1993), the adjustment to a new regime can be seen as a means of renouncing that lifestyle which led to the heart attack in the first place. If, as Helman argues, Western societies regard the heart attack victim as a figure of moral ambiguity, then such a renunciation might be seen as a metaphoric departure, hence the appropriateness of the kind of physical response involved in digging and long-distance backpacking. In fact Helman refers to recovering cardiac patients engaging in narrative reconstruction of their life-stories with the specific end of imaging the heart attack as a kind of nemesis – the only one appropriate to the accepted mythology of their predetermined careers as heart attack victims (see also Cassell, 1976; Cowie, 1976). More-over, writing of coronary bypass surgery, Scheper-Hughes and Lock refer to the "powerfully metaphoric effects of the [bypass] operation as a cosmic drama of death and rebirth" (1987: 30).

The third example from my interviews is that of Yumiko Thomas, an assistant manager with a Japanese electronics company based in South Wales. Yumiko grew up in Japan but came to Britain after marrying a British merchant seaman. Yumiko begins her account, atypically, by categorising herself as chronically ill. Her own comments locate her more eloquently than any third-person description would be able to do:

> I was ill all my life (.) because as you know I was born in Hiroshima in 1948 three years after (.) that horrific incident had occurred and now we

know uh we have knowledge about nuclear (4.0) effect but then [they] didn't know you see so people who ate vegetables from contaminated areas and ate fish from contaminated water so I was actually um (.) wasn't there I wasn't born then because [the] atomic bomb was dropped in 1945 still my body was to a certain degree contaminated

Yumiko's Buddhist faith sustains her in what she regards as a lifelong struggle with illness. The 'conventional' metaphors decorate her account, but throughout the interview there is another agenda, an underlying epic beneath the surface description of 'battle being done' with illness, and that is one which depends upon acceptance of the Buddhist notion of *karma*. To employ her own terms, the challenge to 'change her karma', lies at the very heart of Yumiko's story, and the location of her birth, her illnesses and hardships are presented as illustrations of, or better still as metaphors for, her capacity for victory in that other, greater task:

usually when I become ill I almost if you like prepare (.) that is I psyche up myself and chant a lot and make conscious effort from corner to corner do everything that I have to do in order to overcome this illness and I become so if you like fighting machine mental physical that's how I approach that but this time it is very solid but very relaxed and I'm going to fight and I'm going to win I know that and keep saying that but not like uh standing on the cliff or edge of cliff not that sort of desperate just I know I can do it but I've got to do it in a short time

For a Buddhist, illness might be represented as a metaphor for an underlying spiritual struggle, that is, the external manifestation of an 'internalised' condition (and this connects with dominant themes in Oriental and holistic medicines). It is, too, a well documented feature of folk-beliefs about illness, one which might be indicated by a patient stating that "I'm not feeling good in myself", which suggests a kind of internal disharmony or displacement that is integral to 'objective' illness (*cf.* Macleod, 1993). In fact, the sort of Cartesian body/mind dichotomy that preoccupies the Western scientific tradition and the biomedical description of illness seems to be far from happily installed in folk beliefs (Helman, 1978) and is overtly rejected in Yumiko's representation as well as others in my data. The anthropological literature provides a wealth of examples for the making of metaphors in illness and body imagery that break down or ignore biomedical dualism, the distinction between mind and body (as well as the distinction between 'self' and the 'other'). One example will suffice here, reflecting on how an 'inner' disease can produce a transference onto the physical production of human milk: Scheper-Hughes reports that impoverished Brazilian mothers perceive their breast milk as "sour, curdled, bitter, and diseased, a metaphorical projection of their inability to pass anything untainted to their children" (Scheper-Hughes, 1984, cited in Scheper-Hughes & Lock, 1987: 17).

If we consider the holistic notion that illness may occur because there is something amiss in another area of one's life (emotional, psychological), we are again faced with the question of transfer from one domain of experience to another. What holistic and Oriental medicine systems seem to hold in common is the belief that an imbalance in one's emotional or psychological state predisposes one towards a physical illness. Whereas the Oriental and holistic traditions regard the mental and the physical as two facets of a single integrated system, and therefore treat interaction and transfer from one 'domain' to another as the norm, Western medicine prefers to term this phenomenon 'psychosomatic'. Or, as one account summarises: "while modern medicine tends to view the ailing part of the body in isolation from the rest, treating it alone as if one were fixing a malfunctioning part of a machine, Buddhist medicine views disease as a reflection of the total body system, or life itself, and seeks to cure it not only through medical treatment but also through adjustments in the person's lifestyle and outlook" (Ikeda, 1988: 69).

Conclusion

The three speakers I have discussed here present distinct metaphoric perspectives on their experience of illness. Nerys Williams, through identifying an episode in her son's illness that carried continued valency for him (and her) until the end, provides an emotionally charged and *visual* representation of *one* aspect of what it meant for Joey to have cancer. To say that his hair loss 'symbolised' his cancer is to say that he was *marked* by cancer, that his illness was visible for all to see. I have suggested that in Joey's case, his hair held a *metonymic* relationship to his illness. The newspaper story about Andrea and Amanda Matthews seems to add credence to this perspective. A teenager is able to support her sister through symbolic action which succinctly marks her out as *more alike*, acting at the same time as a reprimand to those in her school who had stigmatised her sister on account of her illness.

Bill Morgan adopted a position towards his heart condition that seemed to involve a rejection of the lifestyle that led to his coronary. He left behind him his (on his own admission) gluttonous and bibulous lifestyle, to become a vegan and a long-distance walker. Some might say that this is not metaphoric at all, but simply a survival strategy. However, seen in the light of Helman's writings on heart disease and the cultural construction of time, the heart attack can be conceptualised by the victim as a kind of nemesis, and the only suitable response would be the adoption of a new 'metaphor for living' (Mair, 1976). This is particularly interesting when compared with Radley's digger, whose digging seems to stand for a re-statement of his 'old self' rather than the radical re-figuring of himself as a consequence of his cardiac condition. Both are metaphoric responses, perhaps diametrically opposed ones, but no less metaphoric for that.

Yumiko Thomas sees her lifelong physical illness (along with the time and place of her birth) as the metaphoric correlative of her karmic state. She believes that her life's mission is to challenge that condition through her religious practice, so that not only can she triumph over her illnesses, but she might use those struggles to develop herself personally into a "fighting machine" against whatever "destiny" brings to her. She refuses to be like a "puppet", or like somebody "standing on the edge of the cliff". She is the "captain of [her] own ship". The metaphor is apt, certainly with respect to this particular speaker, a woman of apparently indefatigable certitude:

I'm glad I'm quite strong enough to take it and I may get [laughs] graceful possibly [laughs] (.) and if there are pains the pain's absolutely minimal (3.0) and I feel that I always wanted I don't want to be manipulated by the environment I don't want to be like a puppet like my (.) upbringing in Hiroshima those hoi. ndous experiences or karma or whatever des destiny manipulating your life (.) because of that in your life you don't know what's next what happens next year or even next month some people have that sort of life (.) I don't want to be like that my life is my own I want to be uh captain of my *own* ship that ship called Yumiko that's always what I wanted

In their critique of a bio-medicine still in the clutches of a Cartesian dichotomy, Scheper-Hughes and Lock (1987: 30) alert us to the dangers of thinking in a reductionist way about the mind-body split. According to this model, most sickness can be viewed mechanistically, as an isolated event. But "to do otherwise", they suggest, "using a radically different metaphysics, *would* imply the 'unmaking' of our own assumptive world and its culture-bound definitions of reality".

The study or pursuit of metaphor is a means of questioning the assumptions, descriptions and definitions of a literalistic and constricting outlook on reality. The ability of ethnography to present alien cultures as *not-so-strange* and our own as *strange* might therefore be a metaphor itself for the distinction between 'literal' and 'metaphoric' thought. Research that uses ethnographic and reflexive perspectives in order to establish conceptual structures of metaphor in talk is one way in which researchers can approach questions of representation and meaning in language. The body and its illnesses serve as a perfect locus for the investigation of our most involved and expressive emotions and language. "Sickness", as Scheper-Hughes and Lock remind us, "is a form of communication ... through which nature, society and culture speak simultaneously". It is in that simultaneity that metaphor thrives.

11 "This paper thinks …"
Investigating the acceptability of the metaphor AN ESSAY IS A PERSON

Graham Low

Introduction

The following passage comes from a book of edited research papers on language programme evaluation and formed the starting point for the present study.[1]

... assessment is not only a difficult area but dangerous and sensitive too. And if it's difficult and dangerous to assess other people, is it more or less difficult and dangerous to assess ourselves? **This paper doesn't know the answer** to that question. ... Can learners really begin to diagnose themselves with regard to their own educational attainments as these must have some bearing on their future requirements?

This paper thinks that they might, and more to the point **thinks in addition that** in certain situations there is no valid educational alternative.

[Paragraph concluding that tests resemble teaching materials in that they are educationally unsound if they 'fail to further, or even detract from' learning]

It is for this reason that **this paper, accepting** that educational systems are at present dependent on an amount of assessment activities, **has been arguing** for self-assessment as an improvement over testing.

(Kenny & Hall, 1987: 462–463)

I have to teach university students how to improve their academic writing in English as a foreign language and thus need to provide them with guidelines on acceptability. To me, the first four bolded expressions in the extract above are totally unacceptable English, whether in a research paper or anywhere else; papers cannot **think, know** or **accept**. The fifth (**arguing**) is a grey area; I am not sure whether it sounds acceptable or not. On the other hand, all five expressions were presumably perfectly acceptable to the authors of the paper and the editors of the book. Faced with a mismatch

---

[1] My thanks to the staff in Language and in Social Policy at York, to Alice Deignan for searching the Cobuild database, to Margaret Ferguson for piloting the procedure and to Peter Master, Derek Rodger and Peter Bull for helpful discussions and comments.

between published texts and my own instinct, I am at a loss to know what to recommend to students.

The Kenny and Hall passage highlights the fact that the relationship between prescription and description in language teaching is rarely straightforward. One cannot assume that, simply because an utterance is published, it would be found acceptable in a student assignment, which will *not* be published and where the relationship between reader and writer inevitably differs from that in either a journal article or a textbook. Indeed, the fact of appearing in print does not even guarantee that an utterance is generally acceptable, or recommendable, within the domain of journal articles and textbooks. The implication is therefore that guidelines for teaching should not be based solely on the description of published texts.

It is sometimes argued (e.g. Deignan, *personal communication*) that, if a corpus of relevant texts is large enough, the problems discussed above can be resolved in a straightforward way by corpus analysis, since acceptability will be reliably indicated by a relatively high frequency of occurrence. However, even if one were to accept the idea that there is a clear link between frequency and acceptability, in this particular case corpus analysis could *not* be applied, since university teachers do not normally *write* assessed student essays. It is true that they create secondary documentation, in the form of grades and feedback reports, but assessment procedures tend, for obvious reasons, to focus on detailed reactions to the content of assignments, rather than on reactions to specific linguistic points. Thus, however one looks at the situation, there is strictly speaking, no valid corpus to examine.

In this paper I shall examine how a number of markers react to personification in university assignments and consider how far they agree on what is acceptable and unacceptable. The primary object is to see whether it is possible to develop a set of straightforward guidelines for students.

Treating personification as metaphor

Most researchers appear to agree that personification is a type of figurative language, but what is not entirely clear is the extent to which specific instances of personification can be unambiguously classified as examples of metaphor. The classification problem seems to be particularly acute precisely for the context being examined here, namely that of formal written documents. The analyst effectively has a choice and can interpret expressions like **This essay thinks that** X either as metaphor or metonymy, depending on whether the writer's starting point for a decision is seen as the noun or the verb.

For example, if the writer wants to write the noun phrase **This essay**, and conceives of the primary task as that of *finding an appropriate verb* to accompany it, then the decision to use any of a series of verbs like **believes, thinks** or **intends** represents the humanisation of the essay, that is to say the use of the *metaphor* AN ESSAY IS A PERSON.

The opposite situation is where the writer wants to use the verb **think**, but is worried about *which noun phrase subjects* might be acceptable. If s/he is afraid that self-reference, in the form of **I** (**think**), would lead to an inappropriately 'subjective' or 'personal' style, then s/he might well prefer to mention the resulting product (**the essay**), rather than the author (**I**). In this case, the production of expressions like **This essay thinks** is not so much the creation of animacy, but rather part of a strategy for avoiding or reducing subjectivity. This use of a less subjective noun phrase to stand for a more subjective one could be classed as *metonymy*, inasmuch as one item is standing for another without significantly altering the meaning, and the RESULT FOR ACTOR, or PRODUCT FOR PRODUCER, substitution can be seen as the selection of one salient feature (the essay) from the broader concept of 'the person writing the essay'.

Two questions arise for the researcher. The first is whether any principled way exists to determine whether one is, in any given case, dealing with metaphor or metonymy. I know of no empirical methods for answering this question in the present context of Noun Subject + Verb, but it might be possible to establish from a Think–Aloud protocol, or a transcript of spoken comments, whether an essay marker is reacting more to the verb or the noun.

The second question is whether anything much is gained by choosing to restrict the focus to either metaphor or metonymy, and by implication ignoring the other. In a research project designed to improve the teaching of writing, the evaluation of written texts requires us to recognise the roles of both writer and reader. Thus, even if one of the two people operates purely in terms of, say, metaphor, there is no guarantee that the other will; just as an author and his/her text are intimately related, so the topics of *a subjective style* and *the animacy of the text* are always going to be closely intertwined.

At this point, a working definition of metaphor is needed. For the purposes of this study, I shall adopt the 'treatment' definition of metaphor used in Low (1988), namely that a metaphor is where 'X is treated as if it was to some extent (but not completely) Y'. This is a broad definition, and as a result, has several advantages for this sort of investigation. Perhaps the two most important features are that nothing is said about whether X and Y both need to be mentioned explicitly, or about the precise form required to depict the metaphor. This freedom allows us to recognise that, while some personifications might have both the Topic (**The essay**) and the Vehicle (**a person**) present in the surface utterance, it is likely that many (possibly most) will not, and the actual lexical items in an utterance will be more easily explained as deriving from an underlying metaphor. The labels Topic and Vehicle will accordingly be taken to refer to the major terms of this conceptual, or underlying, metaphor. The terms of the underlying metaphor can only be hypothesised in many cases, but verbal propositional forms such as AN ESSAY IS A PERSON, or A RESEARCH PAPER IS A PERSON, ought to prove adequate in the present instance. An expression such as **This essay thinks** will thus be considered to be *metaphoric*, but not itself *a metaphor*. Although conceptual features and connotations will be transferred from the (underlying) metaphor Vehicle (A PERSON), part of the appropriateness, or 'meaning' of the metaphoric expression will also derive from the semantic associations and contrasts relating to the precise lexical item involved (here, **thinks**). Thus the general position is taken that both conceptual and linguistic factors are important, as are both surface and underlying ones.

Can essays think? A non-metaphoric explanation

Although personification can be described fairly naturally in terms of metaphor and metonymy, there is at least one account in the literature which makes no use of figurative explanations at all. This is contained in Master (1991), one of very few corpus-based analyses of active verbs and inanimate subjects in scientific prose. Master (p. 18) came to the conclusion that collocations like **the graph showed X, the law states Y**, or **the theory suggests Z** are acceptable when "the verb represents an inherent aspect or function of that subject". Thus **a research study** can, he suggested (pp. 29–30), **affect a reputation, find a cause** or **generate funds**, but cannot **steal funds**, or **invent hypotheses**. While Master's thesis is attractive and may indeed account for why thermometers can **measure temperature**, but not **assess it**, it fails to account for the very expressions cited as examples. In what way are reputations 'inherent' parts of studies, or how is generating money any more a necessary part of a research study than stealing it? And surely thinking of hypotheses *is* an essential part of all experimental studies? Master also suggested a second constraint.

Active verbs are not 'usually' permitted if the writer is hedging. Thus a graph can **appear to show X**, but not **hope to show it**. Master's explanation (p. 31) is simply that hedging is 'a very human enter-prise', but this does not by itself explain anything.

The importance of Master's argument in the context of the present study is that it suggests we might be able to provide a general guideline for teaching that does not require learners to ask questions about metaphoric 'propositions' or metaphoric transfer, but requires them rather to ask the question *What are the inherent aspects or features of an essay?*

Can essays think? The structure of the metaphor

Assuming that it *can* be valid to identify A TEXT IS AN OR-GANISM and AN ACADEMIC ESSAY/PAPER IS A PERSON as the metaphors underlying expressions such as **This paper thinks,** we need to ask what aspects of humans might be (and are) transferred to essays and which of these are sufficiently problematic to be worth researching?

Lakoff and Turner (1989) proposed that the question can be answered in terms of coherent personality or job types; that is to say, abstract concepts are conventionally personified as specific types of person. Lakoff and Turner envisaged a personification as something ultimately describing an event (such as death) and of being structured in terms of the key conceptual metaphor AN EVENT IS AN ACTION. The Vehicle AN ACTION serves essentially to introduce notions of time, causality and an agent, while characteristics of the event, such as changing or preserving shape, or our feelings about it, serve to constrain the type of action selected and the nature of the actor. Thus DEATH, frequently occurring when one is old and being 'final', is not just *any* person, but specifically AN OLD ADVER-SARY who cannot be overcome. It is this psychological coherence, they felt, that gives a metaphor its intellectual point.

In the present case, we might start with ARGUMENT IS WAR and see whether ESSAYS/PAPERS ARE WARRIORS generates all or most of the 'seemingly acceptable' reflexes. Thus we might ask whether essays can acceptably 'fight a battle', 'issue a challenge', 'attack a position' or 'employ irony as a weapon'. It is intuitively harder to think of a personality type that encompasses the verbs in the Kenny and Hall extract, but one might perhaps propose ESSAYS/PAPERS ARE ARGUERS, or perhaps ESSAYS/PAPERS ARE INTELLECTUALS, based on the events of 'constructing an essay' or 'presenting an argument' and the action of 'arguing' or 'thinking'.

An alternative approach to identifying researchable items is to note things that real people, in this case writers, can acceptably say about themselves (as writers) in essays. So if people either say of themselves **I intend to argue X** or **The present author hopes to show that Y**, or else they report on other people's texts using **The author thinks Z**, then we might examine whether **essay** can be substituted for **I** or **the author**. If there is reason to believe that the expression is unacceptable, then it is worth researching. This was in fact the approach adopted here, as it reflected my reactions to the verbs in the Kenny and Hall extract. The result of my preliminary analysis was four conceptual groupings in which the reflexes (1) were likely to relate to what writers needed to do and (2) were not 'obviously' acceptable. The present study concentrates on the third, *Having a belief*, but the others are included to suggest potential directions for future research:

- *Activities connected with the ability to speak and to participate in linguistic interactions*, e.g. saying, understanding, shouting, hinting, asking, answering, responding;
- *Activities (or states) connected with the stages of presenting and reacting to rational argument*, e.g. stating an intention to argue (definitely, as in **I intend**, or tentatively, as in **I hope**), selecting/ adopting an approach, putting forward or reviewing evidence, coming to a conclusion;
- *Having a belief or opinion*, e.g. thinking, believing, feeling, being of the opinion, taking the view that, being convinced;
- *Having emotional states relatable to writing and arguing*, e.g. (dis)liking, hoping, wanting, intending, being interested, feeling irritated, happy, surprised, thankful or regretful.

Which factors might be expected to affect acceptability?

This is an interesting question. I know of no empirical work concerning factors affecting acceptability judgements about metaphor in academic texts, let alone with respect to the specific metaphor AN ESSAY IS A PERSON. It is therefore worth trying to predict in some detail likely linguistic factors, even though this particular study was not able to take account of more than a few of them. The value of drawing up such a detailed list is, again, to aid future research projects. In the list below I have isolated seven basic groups of factors, which are labelled (i) to (vii).

(i) The syntactic role of the expression involved

The expressions cited in the previous sections show that noun subject + verb, and nouns (in a prepositional phrase) are definitely involved in personification, and it is not hard to imagine reflexes involving adjectives and adverbials. Unless a reference is given, the examples in this section are invented.

- N+V (+AGENTIVE)
  This paper *deliberately chose* not to use such an approach. [DPhil draft 1995]
  This essay *discusses* whether there is a case for bureaucracy... and *concludes that* there is ... The essay first of all *sets out* to define the term 'bureaucracy' and *traces its development* from the late 16th ... century. [MA Politics essay n.d.]

- N+V (-AGENTIVE)
  There is some significance in the fact that *an article* [= this one] dealing with SLA *finds itself dealing* ... with errors in productive language skills. [MA proposal, 1989]
  This paper *is of the opinion* that Smith was mistaken.
  Master (1991) said that his corpus data indicated that stativity *per se* does not seem to determine acceptability, but it is perfectly possible that the *type* (Cruse, 1973) or else the *degree* (Lakoff, 1977) of agentivity of the verb might affect acceptability – even if it does not determine it.

- NOMINAL GROUP
  This paper, with *its interest in* positivist approaches, focuses on Matza's work.
  The views of this paper have not been communicated to the subjects involved.
  Where the noun is a nominalisation, or part of a prepositional phrase, one might hypothesise that features like humanity are being assumed rather than asserted, and thus that the information communicated by the phrase is being backgrounded in the discourse (Hopper & Thompson, 1984).

- ADJECTIVE
  A *happy* paper. An *optimistic* paper. A *worrying* paper. An *aggressive* paper.
  Instinctively, my feeling is that there is a clear divide between adjectives describing states that people experience (**a happy paper**), which are not acceptable, and effects that people have on others (**a disappointing, worrying** or **depressing paper**), which are much

more acceptable, at least in certain conditions. The 'effect adjectives' do not seem to imply anything about the humanity of the paper. The status of words like **aggressive** seems to me intermediate between **happy** and **depressing**.

- ADVERBIAL
  The paper *happily*, if *selectively*, examines the opposite argument, however.
  I would assume that it is mainly adjuncts that are likely to affect acceptability, since disjuncts in particular tend to be interpreted as the voice of the writer.

(ii) The surrounding textual context

At least three types of context effect appear at first sight to be likely to influence acceptability.

- POSITION WITHIN THE TEXT
  It would not be surprising to find personifications clustering at particular places in essays. For example, I have been told informally by a Fine Art undergraduate at York that she tended to put more personifications in those sections of her essays that involved personal evaluations or opinions.
  At sentence rather than text level, I would assume that sentence-initial expressions like **This paper thinks** ... would be rather more salient than mid-sentence ones (Low, 1995; Steen, in Chapter 5, on Topic and Comment).

- REPETITION + REINFORCEMENT EFFECTS
  A term that was slightly unacceptable might well be perceived as much more unacceptable if it was repeated, particularly within the same sentence, as with the two **thinks** in the Kenny and Hall sentence at the start of the paper.
  Repetition could, on the other hand, *in*crease not decrease acceptability; the development of a network of related details within a text could be felt to justify an expression which on its own might be felt to be odd or innovative.

- TEXT INTERVENING BETWEEN *THIS PAPER* AND THE VERB
  One might hypothesise that intervening text (e.g. **This paper,** ***despite the arguments of the two earlier studies (Smith 1975, 1978), thinks that** ...) might well reduce any dissonance between the noun phrase and the verb in inverse proportion to the distance (in words) between them.

(iii) The type and purpose of the text

It is highly likely that the purpose of the text will constrain the terms which may appropriately be applied to it. Book reviews in journals like *Nature*, for example, are frequently very different linguistically from research papers in the same volume. In a review, an academic can, it appears, be lyrical, make jokes, tell anecdotes, create innovative metaphors and extend them at great length, as well as have a high density of evaluative and opinion terms unsupported by data or even (at times) references.[2] If some 'rules' are relaxed in reviews, then perhaps so are conventions about personification.

There is in fact a surprisingly large number of words describing types or units of academic text (e.g. **book, brochure, volume, monograph, working paper, chapter, assignment, essay, paper, thesis, dissertation, report, review, introduction, section, note**). There is no necessary reason why readers should have identical reactions to each of them, if humanised.

(iv) The function of the statement: assertion vs report

Statements of the type cited in the Kenny and Hall extract frequently have an assertive or constitutive function and are accordingly put in the present tense and accompanied by 'close' deictic markers. **This paper thinks that X** is hence making a salient claim to rational ability. Statements like **The earlier paper thought that Y** do not employ such foregrounding markers and the animacy thus tends to be backgrounded. It would therefore not be surprising to discover that academics find reports (or more generally, descriptions of other texts) less objectionable than direct assertions.

This sort of reasoning suggests that other types of foregrounding and/or backgrounding device might also affect acceptability, and examination of the Kenny and Hall extract immediately suggests two possibilities. The first is whether the expression concerned occurs in the main clause rather than in a dependent clause or, using Mann and Thompson's (1988) more discourse-based terms, whether it occurs in the nuclear rather than a peripheral part of an utterance. The last sentence of the Kenny and Hall extract provides a good illustration of both positions: **This paper,** *accepting* **X,** *has been arguing* **Y.** The second possible factor is whether the expression concerned functions

---

[2] An example of extended metaphor in an academic review would be Braddick's (1986: 223) description (in *Nature*) of the book *Functions of the Brain* as a "scientific pot-luck supper to which a set of enthusiastic cooks each brings his own dish, be it spicy or subtle, a filling casserole or a fluffy confection."

as the first, rather than the second, part of an adjacency pair such as: (rhetorical) question and answer. The opening seven lines of the extract contain two examples of answers: **This paper doesn't know the answer** and **This paper thinks they might.**

(v) The precise wording of the metaphor Topic

There seem to me to be at least three problems connected with the wording of the metaphor Topic (i.e. **essay** or **paper**). The first is that a writer can refer to research in a variety of ways; thus **Smith, Smith (1967), Smith's paper, Smith's (1967) paper,** and **the paper** might all refer to (more or less) the same thing. The terms do, however, appear to vary in the distance from the essential being, or animacy, of the person involved, so it may be that readers are prepared to let some be more human than others.

The second problem relates to collective or group nouns. These can refer to institutions explicitly by name, like **The University of York,** or **The Times,** or implicitly by function, as in **the (news)paper.** The way group nouns are treated may vary regionally (or in terms of language variety). Quirk *et al.* (1985: 19) suggested that in American English, many speakers have no real choice between **The government think** and **The government thinks;** only **The government thinks** is correct. It is not inconceivable that the existence of such choice constrains the acceptability of **The university thinks** or **This paper thinks.** Where choice exists and one *can* say **The government think,** one might expect collective nouns for institutions to be perceived as more human than, say, essays, where there is no such choice.

Lastly, it is also possible that the degree of abstraction of the Topic affects acceptability; thus **This paper argues** might be felt to be different from, say, **Criticism argues.** Although some readers might wonder if expressions like **Criticism argues** would ever occur in print, the following from just one page of a well known paper by John Bayley on Jane Austen make it clear that they do:

The *idea* of that tradition *takes for granted* ... a complete knowledge of the minds of the authors who represent it.

... the same freedom with which *criticism* had *treated* Shakespeare's plays ...

Criticism can *see* her [Jane Austen] now as satisfying our literary appetite even for the strongest emotions.   (Bayley, 1968: 2)

(vi) Local constraints

A *local constraint* is one that operates for a small group of speakers, but is not the case for other groups, who may be completely unaware of it. It is thus hard to predict specific local constraints, but one can at least be prepared to find them operating. One might perhaps expect to find particular academic subject areas, such as pure science, having agreed conventions, or alternatively one might find individual university departments being unduly for or against the expression of particular concepts.

(vii) Age and experience

Since many students do have problems with academic writing, and since universities have accordingly developed formal procedures so that staff can help them via feedback, it follows that age and experience must be associated, even if very roughly, with writing expertise. It is hence quite possible that older or more senior university staff might have given more thought to AN ESSAY IS A PERSON – either as a result of accommodating perceived norms of the 'academic community', or simply by virtue of having written more papers – and that this thought might have affected their judgements of acceptability.

The present study

AN ESSAY IS A PERSON may be a very limited metaphor, but as the previous section has shown, the scope of what one might investigate empirically is extremely broad. This, plus the large number of factors likely to affect acceptability, means that the investigation of even a small fragment (here *Having a belief*) implies presenting informants with a large number of items.

Personification of the text can occur at any point in an essay or paper, but two locations stand out: the Introduction and the Conclusion. As my students' problems centred particularly on Introductions, I decided to limit the research to statements in Introductions where the writer 'takes a position' on the purpose or structure of what is to come. This limitation meant that the verbs in the statements to be rated could be restricted to present tense forms. Eight opinion verbs were selected, to include both weak and strong belief. **Argue (that)** was added to the set to represent 'minimal or zero belief'.

It is of some importance to know whether staff who claimed to find **This paper thinks** unacceptable really would comment on the expression in practice – what Leech (1974) called *actual* as apart from *potential acceptability*. Unfortunately, systematic observation of actual one-to-one, staff–student essay feedback sessions was not possible for ethical and administrative reasons. A degree of simulation was however possible, so the research exercise could begin with a 'naturalistic' phase, where subjects reacted spontaneously to genuine essay introductions. The naturalistic phase could be followed with a more structured test of reactions to opinion statements.

It was decided that a 'pile sort' would be preferable to a standardised questionnaire for the second phase. A pile sort is an exercise where the subject sits in front of a rating scale and is given a set of cards, each containing a statement of some sort. The task is to react to each card in turn and to place it on the appropriate category of the rating scale. The result is a series of 'piles' of cards. The reasons for preferring a pile sort were, (1) it was likely to be more motivating than a questionnaire, (2) the order of presentation of items to each subject could be more easily controlled, and (3) the categorisation procedure could be manipulated. This last point raises the thorny question of how many rating categories to use. Pile sorts often involve 11 categories, presented concurrently on an equal-interval, bipolar scale from -5 to $+5$ (Brown, 1986: 59; McKeown & Thomas, 1988: 31–33). I am not, however, convinced that even highly literate subjects are able to weigh up in their mind this number of meaningful classifications, when the dimension being rated is 'semantic or pragmatic acceptability'. It was accordingly decided to use four categories, as is commonly done in studies investigating grammatical acceptability. As the sample size was going to be small, a multi-stage sort was considered to be preferable; this would allow subjects a chance to rethink and revise their choices, and would thus be likely to increase stability (Weller & Romney, 1988: 25). It was accordingly decided to ask subjects to begin by dividing the statements into two piles, then to re-sort each of the two into two further piles.

Method

Subjects

Two departments at the University of York were selected: *Language & Linguistic Science* and *Social Policy & Social Work*. Both required argumentative essays from students, but were, I predicted, likely to differ markedly in the degree to which linguistic detail formed a central part of teachers' professional endeavour. Fourteen staff were contacted. The criteria for selection were (1) that each subject should be a native speaker of English with recent experience of marking assignments by non-native speakers, and (2) that each departmental group should contain a similar mixture of seniority grades. All but one person contacted agreed to participate. The final sample is set out in Table 1 opposite.

Table 1. *The subjects*

Language & Linguistic Science			Social Policy & Social Work		
Person	*Rank*	*Sex*	*Person*	*Rank*	*Sex*
L1	Lecturer	M	S1	Lecturer	F
L2	Senior lecturer	M	S2	Lecturer	M
L3	Head of department	M	S3	Senior lecturer	M
L4	Senior lecturer	M	S4	Head of department	M
L5	Lecturer	F	S5	Lecturer	M
L6	Lecturer	F	S6	Senior lecturer	F
L7	Lecturer	F			

Instrumentation

STAGE ONE: EXTENDED TEXTS

Introductions to two essays by overseas students were used as the basis for Stage One (the simulated marking and feedback exercise): one from Social Policy and one from Language. The formats were initially very similar. Both texts were manipulated, however, to make them converge slightly more. The result was that both texts:

- set up a problem in the opening lines;
- had an irrelevant 'error' added to the second or third line;
- involved a quotation within 3 or 4 lines with a highly agentive verb + human subject;
- went on to outline the structure of the paper in a second paragraph;
- linked the structural outline with a **This paper thinks** type sentence.[3]

---

[3] The sections of the introductions containing the personifications were as follows:

Language & Linguistic Science essay
"This paper thinks that many of the published findings do appear to converge. The paper begins (Part A) by reviewing and synthesising five relevant studies and then (Part B) discusses 'levelling off in language performance' in the light of the 'critical period'."

Social Policy & Social Work essay
"In order to assess the contributions of Matza's *Delinquency and Drift*, the paper will start with an examination of the assumptions of both classical and positive schools, in order to identify which problems Matza's criticisms address. The discussion will focus particularly on Matza's criticisms of subculture theory. There will then be a description of Matza's alternative theory of delinquency, and finally an overall assessment of Matza's work. In essence, this paper believes that *Delinquency and Drift* does indeed represent a significant change in thought, as it breaks the domination of subculture theory."

STAGE TWO: SENTENCES FOR PILE SORTING

Only a very limited number of variables could be involved, if the pile sort were to be kept to manageable proportions. Each verb needed to be rated in more than one context, so one linguistics sentence frame was selected and one health-problem frame. The sources were the Kenny and Hall (1987) extract for the linguistics sentence(s) and the Cobuild magazines subcorpus for the social policy sentence. Two context effects were built in. Firstly, three noun phrases were used as subject (**This essay**, **This paper** and **The Guardian**), to explore the hypothesis that the nine verbs concerned would be more acceptable with a newspaper than a research paper or essay (see the discussion on collective nouns, above). Secondly, the linguistics sentence had a more interactive context than the social policy sentence, as it formed the answer to a preceding question. The sentence frames thus differed functionally; one was an answer, the other an independent assertion. The result was 54 statements (see Table 2).

Table 2. *Pile sort statements*

Subject NP	Verb	Sentence frame
1. This essay	1. wonders whether	ANSWER TO QUESTION
	2. feels that	1. Can learners really diagnose their own language performance? ....
	3. thinks that	they might, and that (whether/
	4. believes that	since) in certain circumstances there
2. This paper	5. argues that	may be no valid alternative.
	6. is of the opinion that	ASSERTION
	7. takes the view that	2. .... doctors should be obliged in
3. The Guardian		their contracts to inform their
	8. is convinced that	employer if they have the HIV virus.
	9. is certain that	

Pilot

The text and procedure were piloted on a York university teacher who was both a linguist and taught a course for Social Policy. Interestingly, while sorting the cards she spontaneously reworded the first two category labels as *Don't mind* and *Don't like* and the second four as *Perfectly OK, Sort of OK, Don't like much* and *Really don't like*; since these labels appeared intuitively to be reasonably equidistant and not to involve any obvious bias, it was decided to retain them. The 54 statements did not demonstrate any untoward problems, except that those with **is certain** and **is convinced** were rated as unacceptable on the grounds that there was a 'logical' inconsistency with the indefiniteness conveyed by **might; might** in those sentences was accordingly changed to the more definite **can**. Interestingly, and contrary to my expectations, the subject strongly disliked **This essay/paper argues**.

Administration

THE TWO ESSAY INTRODUCTIONS

The package was administered in October 1995, to one subject at a time, and all sessions were tape-recorded. Subjects were given the situation of an overseas student who had handed in an essay and wanted feedback on his/her English. They were asked to look first at the Introduction relating to their own department. A time limit of roughly five minutes per text was given. Subjects were asked to read the texts, ring anything they wanted to mention and then discuss their points orally with me. My role was limited to providing positive support, to making occasional probes and to commenting on the source of the texts (e.g. that the writers had not known each other). Subjects were periodically asked to expand on their reactions, but care was taken not to focus unduly on **thinks** or **believes**.

THE PILE SORT

Subjects were told that task two would involve a pile sort and would focus on one of the points in the introductions. Each of the 54 statements was laser printed onto a small card and the order of presentation re-randomised for each subject. Subjects were told explicitly that the sequence had been randomised and asked not to change it. They were asked initially to divide the cards into broad *Don't mind* and *Don't like* categories and told that they could make changes at any point. They were also told that there was no forced (i.e. imposed) distribution; they could place all the cards in one category, if that was how they felt. When the two piles were complete, subjects were asked whether they were happy with the result. If they were, they were asked to take each pile in turn, shuffle it (as full re-randomisation was impossible at this point) and then subdivide it into two, using the four labels given above. Two subjects rephrased *Sort of OK* as **Iffy**, one preferred **Squiffy** and one opted for **Problematic.**

DEBRIEFING SESSION

After the pile sort, subjects were asked to comment on the way they had categorised the statements. They were also asked questions relating to the validity and reliability of the study:

Q1. Was your judgement impaired by fatigue (and/or by a feeling of being mentally swamped) by being faced with so many similar statements?

Four subjects said that they felt some fatigue. L5 consciously developed a procedure to cope, which involved creating what she called "marker cards", placing them at right angles to the rest and categorising them at the end. Person L1 claimed to feel fatigued about halfway through, S2 felt "a bit confused" at the two-thirds point and L7 said four cards from the end that the statements were beginning to sound the same. While the fatigue felt by L5 and L7 is unlikely to have affected their pile sort results to any marked degree, it is just possible that the results for L1 and S2 *were* affected, though both people claimed to be happy with their final sort patterns.

Q2. Did you create a 'search algorithm'?

Six people reported that they had created a 'short-cut' search procedure to aid decision-making. The short cut tended to be that of making an acceptability decision the moment they found the 'belief verb'. It is accordingly possible that some of the six might have reacted less to the form and more to the function of the sentence (i.e. answer vs assertion), had the environment been less repetitive.

Q3. Could you have sorted the cards if you had been given four or more categories concurrently?

All subjects said that the '2 stage – 2 choice' format worked well, except for Person S6, who reported that she had mentally worked to three categories rather than two. Two subjects (L5 and S6) said that four concurrent categories would have been impossible. Five said that four categories would have been much harder and/or time-consuming. No-one reacted positively to the thought of more than four categories. In fact, the only subject who thought that even four concurrent categories was a good idea was person S3, and he remarked that this might be because he had himself just finished a questionnaire-based research project involving Likert-type scales. Subjectively at least, the subjects' reactions appear to justify the decision to use a 2 + 2 format for acceptability judgements and to stop at four categories.

I argued earlier that it was not crystal-clear how far instances of personification should be classified as relating to metaphor, rather than to metonymy, and that it would be sensible to examine subjects' reactions to the research tasks as a check. In the pile sort, subjects had to react to three noun phrase subjects but nine verbs, so the task was heavily biased towards a focus on the choice of verb. Offering feedback on the two essay introductions in Phase 1, however, contained no such bias, as nothing forced subjects to react to either the noun or the verb, and the instructions made no reference to the importance of the sentences concerned. As some subjects did not object to the personifications, only 17 of the 26 possible reactions are examinable. Of these, 14 focused on the verb, not the noun – by proposing alternative verbs and (in two cases) adding evaluative comments. The reactions that were validly analysable therefore suggested a clear primary focus on the appropriateness of the verb, which was the intended focus of the research. This is highly likely, I would contend, to correspond to a focus by most of the subjects on the personifications as metaphor.

Three of the reactions showed some evidence of a focus on the noun phrase **This paper**. Person L3 focused on the noun in the first essay and the verb in the second, while Person L5 did the opposite. In contrast, Person L7 shifted focus within her discussion of a single text. The fact that all three represent shifts of focus (between or within texts) seems to support the initial claim that, in reactions to formal written texts, metaphor and metonymy are in practice likely to be closely intertwined.

Results and discussion

The reactions to **think** and **believe** in the Introductions and the pile sort are summarised in Table 3 (overleaf).

Looking at Table 3, five subjects showed consistent adverse reactions (L1, L2, L3, S3 and S6); they objected to the verbs in both of the two Introductions and rated them as *Really don't like* all four

Table 3. *Reactions to* **think** *and* **believe**

The columns comprise both the 'introduction-reading' and the pile-sort exercises

Key: Intro: ✓ = Objected to the verb; x = Did not comment on the verb
Pile: OK = 1, *Sort of OK* = 2, *Don't like much* = 3, *Really don't like* = 4.
The figure in the Pile columns is the mean of the 6 ratings.

	Think	*Think*	*Believe*	*Believe*		*Think*	*Think*	*Believe*	*Believe*
L1	✓	4	✓	4	S1	x	4	x	3.7
L2	✓	4	✓	4	S2	x	3.5	x	3.7
L3	✓	4	✓	4	S3	✓	4	✓	4
L4	x	2.5	x	2.5	S4	✓	2.5	x	4
L5	✓	1.5	x	1.5	S5	✓	3.7	✓	3.7
L6	✓	3.7	✓	3.5	S6	✓	4	✓	4
L7	✓	3	✓	3					

times in the pile sort. Conversely, two subjects (L4 and L5) seem to have had relatively consistent tolerant reactions – though L4 remarked during debriefing that he did not personally like **This paper thinks** or **believes**. Three subjects, all from Social Policy (S1, S2 and S4), showed inconsistent reactions. Of these, S1 and S2 both failed to 'feed back' **think** or **believe** to the hypothetical student, but rated both verbs as *un*acceptable in the pile sort. Person S4 was unique in showing a cross-over pattern. On the one hand, he objected to **think** in the Introductions, but rated it twice as *Sort of OK* in the pile sort. At the same time, he did not object to **believe**, yet rated all occurrences of it as *Really don't like*.

From the teaching point of view, it looks as though students are likely to receive very different indications about their English from different markers, and that the advice does not always depend on the marker's actual linguistic opinions.

The reactions of the thirteen subjects to the pile sort are summarised in Table 4 opposite.

The results show a preponderance of clear, definite reactions; overall, only 34% of ratings are 'grey' (i.e. *Sort of OK* or *Don't much like*) and only one person (L4) rated over 50% of the statements as 'grey'. As might be expected, Social Policy was a little less definite in its reactions than Language & Linguistics (39% 'grey' versus 30%). It was also marginally less tolerant (41% OK or *Sort of OK*, versus 54%). In addition, the pattern was slightly different between the two departments as regards *Perfectly OK* decisions;

Table 4. *Pile sort decisions by subject (%)*

Each row represents the 54 categorisations (as a percentage) of one subject

Subject	Perfectly OK	Sort of OK	Don't like much	Really don't like
L1	41	0	7	52
L2	48	2	6	44
L3	28	7	19	46
L4	28	33	39	0
L5	59	39	0	2
L6	24	20	15	41
L7	46	4	19	31
Language & *Linguistic Science*	39	15	15	31
S1	24	13	15	48
S2	15	22	26	37
S3	22	13	24	41
S4	37	30	11	22
S5	22	26	19	33
S6	11	11	24	54
Social Policy & *Social Work*	22	19	20	39
Overall	31	17	17	35

Language & Linguistics generally had a higher proportion (39%, to Social Policy's 22%).

In sum, the combination of lower tolerance and less consistency might indicate that the Social Policy teachers were marginally more worried about linguistic problems than the Language Department teachers, and that a number of the Social Policy teachers were less confident about dealing with them. Though there is some evidence on tape to support this, the differences are not large and the data do *not* show two distinct and well defined departmental response patterns.

The reactions to the 54 individual statements are summarised in Table 5 overleaf.

The simplest approach to analysis would be to take the modal values. In the case of the nine verbs, this locates all but **wonder** very clearly into *Perfectly OK* or *Really don't like* piles respectively (Table 6; see p. 240).

Table 5. *Pile sort results by verb (%)*

Each row derives from 52 categorisations for **Essay/paper** and 26 for **The Guardian**.
The modal value (per row) is bolded.

		Perfectly OK	Sort of OK	Don't like much	Really don't like
Wonders	Essay/paper	6	17	**38**	**38**
	Guardian	23	**35**	31	12
Feels	Essay/paper	4	12	10	**75**
	Guardian	**31**	27	23	19
Thinks	Essay/paper	4	13	15	**67**
	Guardian	**42**	8	19	0
Believes	Essay/paper	4	8	17	**71**
	Guardian	**58**	31	12	0
Argues	Essay/paper	**85**	4	10	0
	Guardian	**85**	8	8	0
Is of the opinion	Essay/paper	4	15	23	**58**
	Guardian	**69**	8	23	0
Takes the view	Essay/paper	**62**	17	21	0
	Guardian	**69**	23	8	0
Is convinced	Essay/paper	12	15	10	**65**
	Guardian	**54**	27	15	4
Is certain	Essay/paper	6	21	0	**73**
	Guardian	**46**	19	31	4

Table 6. *Acceptability of verbs (using modal values)*

	Perfectly OK		*Grey area*	Really Don't like	
Essay/paper	Argues		(Wonders)	Feels	Is of the opinion
	Takes the view			Thinks	Is convinced
				Believes	Is certain
The Guardian	Feels	Is of the opinion	Wonders		
	Thinks	Takes the view			
	Argues	Is convinced			
	Believes	Is certain			

Table 7. *Acceptability of verbs with* The Guardian *(using mean values)*

1.2	1.3	1.5	1.7	1.9	2.3	3
argue	view	opinion.believe	think.convinced	certain	feel	wonder

The mode imposes a clearly defined solution in terms of the original categories, and this gives it a certain attractiveness when it comes to deriving guidelines for teaching purposes. The disadvantage is of course that it fails to reflect situations where there is considerable variation. In the present case, the data are fairly clearly defined at an overall level and in only one case of **This essay/paper** does the mode account for less than 55% of the category decisions. However, the situation is not as clear-cut with respect to **The Guardian**, and the 26 decisions for **The Guardian feels**, for example, are distributed (from *Perfectly OK* to *Really don't like*): 8 – 7 – 6 – 5. Using the mean (and making an assumption of equal intervals) for **The Guardian** gives a better idea of the spread of reactions (Table 7; see left).

The result is similar to Table 6, except that **feel** and **wonder** are shown to be generally unacceptable.

Tables 5 to 7 have treated all the data as if it is of equal importance to the creation of teaching guidelines. However, it is clear from Table 4, as well as from the verbal comments made during the interviews, that Persons L4 and L5 organised the pile-sort statements somewhat differently from the other teachers; Person L4 rated none of the statements as *Really don't like* and Person L5 went even further, by rating nothing as either *Don't like much* or *Really don't like*, except for statement 43 (which was rated as *Really don't like*). A simple, if drastic, solution would be to remove both teachers completely from the analysis (Table 8 overleaf).

The result is to make **wonders** definitely unacceptable and thus to divide the set of verbs, when paired with **This essay** and **This paper**, into two clear piles; only **argues** and **takes the view** are *OK*. To the extent that the research interest of this study lies in the writing of academic essays, this increased dichotomisation is clearly a good result. The downside is that without L4 and L5, verbs with **The Guardian** are less sharply divided; both **feels** and **thinks** are now slightly less OK.

Much useful information can be gained from plotting distributions of rating scores in an extremely straightforward way, and for many purposes, no more complex exploration is required than that in Tables 5 to 8 (above and overleaf). It would, however, be useful to have a rather more principled way of establishing just how much consensus there was between the teachers. It would also be useful to have a more sophisticated approach to handling differences between teachers' pile sorts than simply eliminating from the analysis anyone who seemed different.

If one has reason to believe that the different reactions to the 54 sentences might be the effect of a smaller number of underlying

Table 8. *Pile sort results by verb, with L4 and L5 removed (%)*

Each row derives from 44 categorisations for **Essay/paper** and 22 for
The Guardian.
Modal values are bolded.

		Perfectly OK	Sort of OK	Don't like much	Really don't like
Wonders	Essay/paper	0	14	**41**	**45**
	Guardian	18	**36**	32	14
Feels	Essay/paper	0	0	7	**89**
	Guardian	**27**	**27**	23	23
Thinks	Essay/paper	0	7	14	**80**
	Guardian	**41**	**41**	18	0
Believes	Essay/paper	0	0	16	**84**
	Guardian	**59**	32	9	0
Argues	Essay/paper	**91**	0	7	0
	Guardian	**91**	5	5	0
Is of the opinion	Essay/paper	0	9	23	**68**
	Guardian	**73**	5	23	0
Takes the view	Essay/paper	**64**	16	20	0
	Guardian	**73**	23	5	0
Is convinced	Essay/paper	5	9	11	**77**
	Guardian	**45**	32	18	5
Is certain	Essay/paper	0	14	0	**86**
	Guardian	**50**	18	36	0

clusters of reactions (which we may call 'attitudes'), a data reduction technique can often prove helpful. If the data is continuous and roughly normally distributed, then some form of factor analysis is normally used; if not, then a technique such as metric scaling can be employed – although, if a choice exists, factor analytic techniques are preferable. In this particular case, the data comprised four ordinal categories and showed a marked tendency to cluster at the ends of the 'scale'. However, factor analysis is a remarkably robust procedure, and since this is just an exploratory study and the method of Unweighted Least Squares demonstrated an excellent fit with the original data, it was decided to use it. Data for the first four factors are given in Table 9 (opposite). The variables being factored are the 13 pile sorts (i.e. the teachers).

Table 9 suggests that the variation in the teachers' reactions can best be represented by two factors (using the Kaiser criterion) or three (by the Scree test). The two-factor model gave an acceptable fit with the original data, while the three-factor model fitted extremely

Table 9. *Initial factor analysis statistics*

Factor	Eigenvalue	% of Variance	Cumulative %
1	8.3	63.9	63.9
2	1.7	13.1	77.1
3	.8	6.0	83.1
4	.5	4.2	87.3

Table 10. *Rotated 2- and 3- factor solutions*

Person	Factor 1	Factor 2		Factor 1	Factor 2	Factor 3
L1	.98	.04		.70	.68	.05
L2	.93	.02		.83	.49	-.00
L3	.91	.07		.72	.55	.07
L4	.29	.96		.27	.11	.96
L5	-.13	.58		-.11	-.08	.59
L6	.82	.01		.51	.65	.03
L7	.87	.02		.73	.50	-.03
S1	.80	-.06		.33	.83	.01
S2	.69	-.40		.33	.65	-.36
S3	.75	-.04		.84	.23	-.01
S4	.80	.11		.58	.54	.13
S5	.89	-.09		.67	.59	-.08
S6	.88	-.06		.42	.86	.01

Loadings above F1 = .42, F2 = .44, F3 = .50 are bolded
(using Burt & Banks correction for p ≤ .01)

well.[4] The extent to which the variables (here teachers/pile sorts) 'load' onto the factors is given in Table 10 (overleaf). The rotation used is Varimax, as this is designed to make the factors as clear cut as possible.

The main thing that stands out about the two-factor solution is that it groups the teachers in much the same way that Table 4 (p. 239) suggested: Persons L4 and L5 against the rest. The three-factor

---

[4] One way to measure goodness of fit is to look at the difference between the *observed* correlations between the variables and those *estimated* from the fitted model. The differences (or 'residuals') should be fairly small. In the present case, the 2-factor solution was acceptable, with 20 residuals (25%) larger than .05. However, the 3-factor solution was a very good fit, with just 6 residuals (7%) larger than .05 (and five of those were below .065).

Table 11. *Acceptability of verbs (using factor scores)*

The factor scores are (standardised) regression scores.
Cut-off point for Table 10 = $\pm$ .09

	OK		NOT OK
Essay/paper	Argues		Is certain
	Takes the view		Essay feels, thinks, is convinced
			Paper believes
The Guardian	Argues	Takes the view	
	Believes	Is of the opinion	
	Is convinced		

solution retains the close L4, L5 grouping, but additionally suggests that S1, S2 and S3 showed highly polarised reactions.

It is possible to discover which statements are strongly associated (positively or negatively) with each factor, by calculating the 'factor scores'. Despite a certain scepticism about the value of factor scores on the part of some statisticians (see Manly, 1986: 84), they can prove useful in cases like the present, where the results can easily be cross-checked against, for example, the subjects' verbal comments. Using factor scores to establish the 'attitude' represented by Factor 1 of the two-factor solution will provide the clearest possible indication of which verbs were acceptable and unacceptable. Table 11 (above) shows verbs which are OK or NOT OK across *both* the assertion and answer conditions. The result, unsurprisingly, resembles the effect of removing L4 and L5 from Table 6.

Turning to the three-factor solution, the factors have a reasonable conceptual coherence and may be summarised as follows:

Factor 1 *Genre* (or document-type) reactions
A strong **The Guardian** = OK reaction, plus a less coherent **This essay/paper** = NOT OK reaction.
Factor 2 *Verb* reactions
Argues and (**paper/essay**) **takes the view** = OK; **feel** and **wonder** (as an answer) are NOT OK.
Factor 3 *Context/function* reaction
Functioning as an independent assertion = OK; functioning as an answer = NOT OK.
[Factor 3 also has **The Guardian is convinced / is certain** = OK]

Simply noting that the thirteen teachers manifested three different 'attitudes' does not go very far towards explaining how the people concerned actually felt. However, linking the factor analysis with verbal comments made during the (recorded) discussions takes us rather further.

Person S3, for example, was a particularly strong adherent to the Factor 1 view that newspapers can do most things, but essays and academic papers cannot. His reasoning was based around two types of expectation: *the make-up of the noun* and *the degree of bias in the text*. Firstly, he considered that "The Guardian is an entity which can have a view ... a body that *could* think" and was opposed to essays and papers which "can't actually advance an argument in the way the Guardian can". He even proposed an operational test: *Can you attribute authorship to it?* His answer was Yes in this case, as one can reference quotations to **The Guardian** in the same way as to 'Smith, 1989'. An essay was, he thought, different, as "you are the one who's doing the arguing". The second dimension was S3's expectations about the type of argument involved; essays and papers are matched (by their markers) against written criteria, they are evaluated for rigour and should "look at the evidence from a variety of sources across different positions, and they're weighed up at the end", whereas "you wouldn't necessarily *expect* a balanced argument" from a newspaper.

Person L3 also had a genre reaction (Factor 1), but it was less marked and was combined with a verb reaction (Factor 2). This 'spread' reflected the fact that Person L3 was motivated by a rather different pair of expectations, this time involving *formality* and *definiteness*. L3 was unhappy about **The Guardian thinks** and **The Guardian feels**, not "because [either activity] is totally impossible", but rather because they are too informal for a quality paper. Moreover, while essays are expected to hedge, newspapers are not, since "editors don't **feel things might,** or **wonder; they know.**"

Subjects differed about just how human a newspaper was. S3, who showed only a genre reaction (F1), considered that The Guardian was very human and could take any of the eight verbs. L1, with less of a genre reaction, felt differently: "an institution can't **feel**". L3, on the other hand, had less of a verb reaction than L1, and viewed the situation as "the editor writing on behalf of the newspaper". He accordingly rated it midway between S3 and L1's ratings.

Most subjects reacted strongly against **This essay thinks** ("Essays don't think; *people* think" (L1); "No native speaker would say **thinks**" (L7)), but often had difficulty saying what essays *could* do and why. Person S6 thought, not unreasonably, that it was "the role of a paper to present an argument", but even this did not stop L4, L5,

S3 and the pilot subject from finding the expression **This essay/paper argues** less than acceptable. L6 regarded **takes the view** as less subjective and more related to open arguing than **be of the opinion**. L3 did not; to L3, **adopt a view** represented a position from which one argued, but **taking a view** implied thinking. Curiously, L3 himself proposed **suggests**. The only explanation I can find why he should accept **suggests**, relates to the belief (v. above) that newspapers should be definite, but essays hedged. Thus to L3, the hedging in **suggest** was more salient than the subjectivity. **Reviews** is another term which can be interpreted in at least two different ways, either as bringing in and synthesising evidence from many sources, or as offering a (subjective) evaluation of them. Thus L6 proposed **This paper reviews** for the Introduction texts, but S3 rejected it. It is a question, not of 'inherent meaning', but of which aspects of meaning are more salient to the individuals in that context.

Conclusion

The results provide a fairly clear answer to the teaching problem of *Can essays think?* The answer is no. The majority of the teachers in the study reacted negatively to a student writing **This essay thinks** or **believes** in a 'position statement', but considered **This essay argues** or **takes the view** to be acceptable.

Despite these majority views, there were nevertheless marked differences in teachers' reactions towards animacy in essays. Some reacted to whether or not the metaphor was an answer to a question, while others reacted more to whether the (grammatical) subject was an **essay**, a (research) **paper** or **The Guardian.**

Master (1991) offered the non-metaphoric proposal that active verbs are *unacceptable* in academic text if a sentence is hedged, but *acceptable* if they describe inherent features of (here) documents. The present study did not consider hedging, but it does provide evidence on the question of inherence. In essence, the verbal comments lent little support to the idea that the academics concerned were operating in terms of inherent features. The nearest the data came to inherence was S6's remark that "the role of a paper is to present an argument", but even here four people did not find its linguistic expression, **This essay/paper argues**, perfectly acceptable. I conclude that, for all except possibly S6, essays that do not argue may be bad essays, but they are still essays, just as newspapers that do not take a view are perhaps boring, but are nonetheless newspapers. We are thus dealing with *typical* or *expected characteristics* of texts. Though there was not universal agreement, a quality newspaper was in general expected

(1) to evaluate, but not give a balanced argument, and (2) to use slightly more colloquial language to do so, while an essay was expected to do the opposite. The non-metaphorical account is therefore not supported, and there seems to be little reason for not treating the active verbs in this study as reflexes of an underlying personification metaphor.

Turning to Lakoff and Turner's idea of personification involving coherent types of people, virtually all the subjects' verbal comments related to what newspapers, essays and papers do and almost none were couched in terms of what 'arguers', 'intellectuals' or 'warriors' do. Admittedly, one or two comments about The Guardian referred to tasks that editors carry out and some of the essay/paper comments could conceivably be classified as relating to 'desirable professional characteristics of academics' (e.g. "open arguing" and thinking). But for the most part, the subjects' reactions and comments did not support the idea of PAPERS ARE ARGUERS.

Why this should be is an interesting point and worth briefly pursuing. The personification involved in **This paper thinks** or **This essay takes the view** seems to be different in at least two ways from those discussed by Lakoff and Turner, such as Time as a healer, or Death as a grim reaper. Firstly, important aspects of events such as time, causality and agency are not very relevant to utterances about essays or papers; for example, personifications involving the active and highly agentive verb **think** met with some of the most negative reactions. Secondly, the 'actions' concerned are not necessarily structured in terms of feelings about the events of constructing a paper or presenting an argument; arguing, for example, is a central component of both events and highly valued by academics, yet the personification **This essay argues** was rejected as unacceptable by some of the subjects. I discussed at the start of the paper how essay and (research) paper personification metaphor was closely bound to the metonymy of the essay standing for the person who wrote it. The major concern of virtually all the university teachers interviewed for this study was to keep the writer and what s/he wrote together, and to limit the possibility of the essay becoming an independent agent, which would be tantamount to its becoming a second person and thus the rival of the author. I therefore propose that personifications where (a) there is metonymy, and (b) the metonymy could prove undesirable or counterproductive, tend to be treated by speakers as restricted or 'weak' personification; either they are not structured in terms of AN EVENT IS AN ACTION, or there is an added constraint that the agent of the action should not be (very) mentally independent of the agent of the event.

Finally, there were two methodological findings of some interest. Firstly, several of the subjects indicated a strong preference for highly colloquial category labels such as **iffy** or **squiffy**. Bearing in mind that the subjects are practising researchers and spend much of their time working with formal texts, the dislike of the formal labels that questionnaire design manuals tend to suggest is highly significant. A second preference was for a small number (two, possibly three) of concurrently presented rating categories. This evidence may be subjective, but it should, I think, be taken very seriously by researchers wanting to adopt the +5 to -5 scales used by many social scientists, or even the 4-category scales used by some linguists. The moral is that extended Likert-type scales may not be ideal for the study of linguistic acceptability.

One of the implicit purposes of conducting this study was to uncover directions for future research, and I would like to end by indicating what I think are the main ones. The present study examined the reactions of staff but not EFL students/learners; it would be extremely useful, though difficult, to develop a method of data gathering which could be applied equally to both groups. Secondly, much of the interest of reactions to metaphor in real texts lies in the extent to which acceptability relates to contextual factors; while pile sorts are good at eliciting reactions to fairly large numbers of 'stimuli', the fact remains that they are not very context sensitive. Future research would benefit enormously from the development of more context-sensitive methods for gathering reactions to metaphor. This study has also raised serious questions about the common research assumption that speakers can mentally juggle up to eleven meaningful semantic evaluations concerning any given word or statement; what is needed is the development of practical techniques for avoiding multiple categorisation and for obtaining acceptability judgements on continuous scales. Bard *et al.* (1996) recommend the revival of Magnitude Estimation, whereby subjects manipulate non-verbal scales such as the length of a line, but the technique is still extremely time-consuming and cumbersome. Lastly, it would be useful to broaden research beyond 'belief', to other human states and actions, and not just with respect to English. There is a marked lack of cross-cultural and cross-linguistic studies on the use and acceptability of personification metaphor.

12 When is a dead rainbow not like a dead rainbow?

A context-sensitive method for investigating differences between metaphor and simile

Zazie Todd and David D. Clarke

Nous avons supprimé le mot *comme*   Surrealist slogan

Introduction

The use of the experimental method in metaphor research is beset with a number of problems. Traditionally, experimental stimuli consist of a set of phrases containing some kind of metaphor, which are presented in isolation. Participants are then asked to make some kind of judgement, such as how apt they find the metaphors to be. Although this method has yielded useful information, it has two key faults. Firstly, divorcing metaphor from its context may have important implications for comprehension. This point was made by Black (1990), who argued that context was not only important for the comprehension of metaphor, but that in many cases it was absolutely necessary in order to distinguish whether a phrase was literal or metaphorical in the first place. Context may also be a crucial factor in studies investigating the differential features of different types of figurative language. For example, a simile can be considered to be more explicit than a metaphor (Glucksberg & Keysar, 1990) and so the extent to which the context permits an implicit statement may affect production of metaphor over simile. A second problem is that the examples of metaphor typically used in these experiments are created by the researchers. Although this allows for some manipulation of the kind of metaphor used, it leaves a very real possibility that the results are not typical either of the kind of metaphor used in real speech, or of metaphor used in poetic writing and literature, whichever is the topic of investigation.

Qualitative studies of naturally occurring tropes have typically come under the study of rhetoric (e.g. Billig, 1987), where the interest lies more in how the tropes are used to shape the discourse and to construct a persuasive argument, than in the cognitive or linguistic schemata invoked. These approaches use naturally occurring data

249

from speeches or passages of text and so are very rich in terms of detail. Their main advantage lies in the fact that the metaphors are 'real' (as opposed to being created by the researcher) and are studied in the context in which they appear. The disadvantage, however, is that it is difficult to generalise, either from one text to another, or across speakers/writers or styles of genre. It also prevents a systematic analysis of differences between the tropes.

The False Transcript Method

The False Transcript Method was designed specifically to allow for the manipulation of a target phrase, whilst keeping the discourse context around that phrase constant. Basically, it consists of taking transcripts of passages of dialogue containing a particular phrase which is of interest (say, because it is metaphorical). This target phrase can then be re-written in several forms, for example as a simile, and presented without changing any other aspects of the transcript. In this way, a false transcript is created, which can then be used in various experimental procedures.

The method allows a direct comparison between different types of figurative language, whilst retaining some element of ecological validity. The passages used are of real speech, so the target phrase is embedded in a naturally occurring context; and whilst two out of every three target phrases are artificially produced, checks can be made to ensure they are appropriate. The False Transcript Method therefore represents a compromise between, on the one hand, maintaining rich, natural stimuli and, on the other, of controlling for extraneous factors. For example, it has been asserted (Black, 1990) that to reduce a metaphor to its corresponding simile would result in a loss of cognitive power; this kind of research question can be answered directly with the False Transcript Method. The method seems particularly suited to written stimuli and this is what has been used in our work to date; while it would be theoretically possible to use it with spoken stimuli, great care would be needed to ensure that factors like prosody, tone of voice and rate of speaking were equivalent across the different versions. However, given the difficulty of segmenting running speech, this would be extremely difficult to carry out in practice.

In the following studies, a set of twelve basic transcripts was used. Three versions of each were produced, involving a target phrase that was either a metaphor, simile or literal phrase. The twelve basic transcripts were created by taking samples of dialogue between a child (or children) and an adult from a number of sources. Some were reported to us as part of an ongoing study into children's use of metaphor, while others were taken from transcripts of conversation in the CHILDES database (MacWhinney, 1991; Brown, 1973; MacWhinney & Snow, 1985 and 1990). The children concerned varied in age from just over two to nearly five years old. The transcripts were chosen because they contained either a metaphor or a simile, produced by the child without prompting from the adult. This expression was called the *target phrase*, and different versions of it were then constructed, in keeping with the rest of the passage. Where the target phrase was a simile, the words **like** or **as** were generally removed to convert it to a metaphor, and a corresponding literal version was written. The transcripts originally containing a metaphorical target phrase tended to create more problems, in terms of producing a literal version. Several versions were often produced before a choice was made as to which versions would be used in the study. The validity of these choices will be discussed later. Another possibility, which has not yet been tested, would be to use the False Transcript Method to vary aspects of the context, and see how that affected features of the target phrases.

An example transcript is given below. In this case, the transcript is given in its original metaphorical form, with the target phrase in italics. The two alternative phrases which would be substituted into the passage are also listed.

Mother: Wave goodbye to daddy then
Usha: Bye bye
Mother: Let's hope he has a good day at work today, eh?
Usha: What's that?
Mother: What?
Usha: There! (pointing)
Mother: oh … it's oil from the car
Usha: *It's a dead rainbow*
Mother: We need to get that fixed.

Alternatives

Simile   It's like a dead rainbow
Literal   It's oil

The False Transcript Method is especially suitable for between-subjects designs, or within-subjects designs in which the particular transcripts associated with each condition are varied. The point is that for a within-subjects design, it is highly likely that participants would remember transcripts from one session (or condition) to another, and so either not notice the change in the target phrase, or, more likely, become aware of the changes and alter their responses accordingly. As can be seen from the example on p. 251, it is also generally impossible to control fully for the length of the target phrases; different versions will be of different lengths. This is unavoidable, particularly where the method of converting simile to metaphor involves deletion of the word **like** or **as**. In general, the simile versions of the target phrases were longer than either the metaphor or literal versions, although this was not always the case. However, whilst it is not possible to control for length of target phrase (in terms of the number of words), it *can* be taken into account in subsequent statistical analysis, for example by treating it as a covariate in an analysis of covariance.

In the two experiments described here, twelve transcripts were used in order to ensure that the results would not be due to a feature of any one text, but could be generalised to metaphor and simile in general. The statistical analysis used, analysis of variance (ANOVA), is widely used in psychology because it is a particularly robust parametric technique. Following significant ANOVA results, what are called 'planned comparisons' can be carried out to ascertain whether hypothesised differences between pairs of stimuli have indeed been found.

The False Transcript Method has now been used for several studies with some success and could be adapted to a number of research questions. We shall give details here of two such experiments, including an assessment of the validity of the approach itself, before returning to a further discussion of the method.

Experiment One

The aim of Experiment One was to explore the use of the False Transcript Method to investigate certain aspects of young children's use of metaphor and simile. Collecting spontaneous examples of metaphor and simile is a time-consuming process; in a study by Winner (1988) of one child, Adam, it was found that he produced on average one metaphor per hour. The rate of one an hour includes so-called 'symbolic play' metaphor, where the utterance is produced during pretend play, but this definition is problematic if we take metaphor to be a statement about the world (Marjanovic-Shane, 1989b). However, if this type of metaphor were not counted, the figure would be even lower. The False Transcript Method can therefore be used as a way of studying children's figurative utterances on a more limited timescale.

One question which this study set out to address was whether apparent differences which have been shown to exist between metaphor and simile in adult use (Verbrugge, 1980; Gibb & Wales, 1990) can also be found in children. Although traditional Aristotelian approaches to metaphor have taken it to be an elliptical simile (McKeon Ed., 1941; Fogelin, 1988), more recent approaches, particularly interaction theories, have suggested that there are important differences between metaphor and simile (e.g. Black, 1990). Ricoeur (1978), for example, argued that metaphor had more force than a simile, and work by Verbrugge (1980), showing greater 'fusion' between the tenor and vehicle of a metaphor than of a simile, suggests an empirical reason why this might be the case. In a study of the sentential determinants of metaphor and simile, Gibb and Wales (1990) concluded that " ... the differential purpose of a metaphor might be to draw out a resemblance that is strongly evocative, or to highlight generalised qualities ... of the tenor ... Similes might then be ... more suited to the depiction of a figurative relation that is highly specific in terms of its focus in the tenor and the way in which it is depicted in the predicate". Gibbs (1994) points out that metaphors are not always based on similarity, and that similarity itself can have different dimensions; therefore converting them into similes does not always make them easily understood. Waggoner (1990), in his review of the literature concerning interaction theories of metaphor, concluded that the evidence for differences between metaphor and simile is now compelling. The question for this study is whether these differences also apply to metaphor and simile as used by children.

In a study of children's comprehension, Vosniadou (1987) reported that children could interpret similes describing a given situation better than they could interpret a metaphor about the same situation. Observational studies have shown that children produce figurative language from an early age, largely in a symbolic play situation; by five years, they are more like the kind of phrase an adult might produce (Billow, 1981). Interestingly, comprehension seems to lag behind production (Vosniadou, 1987); in other words, children are producing what appear to be metaphorical statements before they can understand those produced by others. To some extent, this may reflect both the nature of the child's utterances (which may require further explanation) and the types of stimuli used in experiments, which are not typical of those they might come across in real life (Broderick, 1992).

This particular study set out simply to investigate whether children who used metaphor were thought to be older or cleverer than those who used simile or literal phrases in the same situation. If we take metaphor to be a means of describing the 'inchoate' (Fernandez, 1986), it could be seen as a clever way of talking about something; alternatively, children who use metaphor could be seen as less bright or younger, either because they 'had' to use a metaphor, or because the metaphor is a play on words and therefore seen as more playful and more childish.

Method

PARTICIPANTS

A sample of convenience of forty undergraduates from the University of Nottingham was employed for the study. All participants were native speakers of English.

APPARATUS

The apparatus consisted of a questionnaire in which participants were presented with twelve passages. Each passage was the transcript of a conversation between a child and someone else, usually a parent. Each transcript contained either a metaphor, a simile or a corresponding literal statement uttered by the child (the target phrase). There were three different versions of each target phrase (one metaphor, one simile and one literal phrase) which were checked for appropriateness by two independent raters. Participants, of course, saw only one version of each passage; and each questionnaire contained four of each type of passage. All the passages were based on a real utterance from a child, although the dialogue had often been altered to allow for the substitution of metaphor, simile or literal versions as required. The names of all the speakers, and any people or animals referred to in the passages, were changed. Examples of the passages used can be found in Appendices 1 and 2 (p. 265ff.).

DESIGN

This was a within-subjects design. Each participant saw four passages containing each type of target phrase; however, they saw twelve different passages in total (i.e. they only saw each passage in one form). Passages were blocked (grouped) by the type of language contained, but there were six versions of the questionnaire so as to counterbalance for any order effects. The dependent variables were the *perceived age* and *perceived intelligence* of the child. A further dependent variable was *what the participants said the child meant* by the target phrase.

PROCEDURE

Participants were approached on campus and asked if they would mind taking part in a study to do with children's language. No mention was made of metaphor or simile. The instructions were standardised and appeared on the front of the questionnaire as follows:

On each of the following pages, you will find a short passage of dialogue. Usually, it is a conversation between a mother and her child.

After reading each dialogue, rate the child to say how old s/he is, and how intelligent you think they are. Do this by putting a ring round the number that you think corresponds to their age/intelligence. Don't worry if you have to guess.

Age and intelligence had to be noted on a numerical seven-point scale (from 2 to 5 *years old* in six-month steps, and from *below* to *above average intelligence*).

In order to increase the salience of the target phrase, a second stage was added. After completing all the ratings, subjects were shown a list of the target phrases. They were asked to look back at each transcript and to say what the target phrase meant in each case. They were given the opportunity at this point to change any of the ratings, but the wording of the instructions was such that there was no demand upon them to make any changes. Participants were finally asked whether they had any children of their own; if so, what their ages were, and if not, how much regular contact they had with pre-school children (again on a seven-point scale).

Results

The ratings for age and intelligence for each type of transcript were collated, in order to perform an analysis of variance. The mean age was highest for the passages containing simile, and lowest for the passages containing metaphor (Figure 1). An analysis of variance (Figure 2) showed a main effect of *passage type* (F 2,20 = 4.08,

Apparent Age (in years)

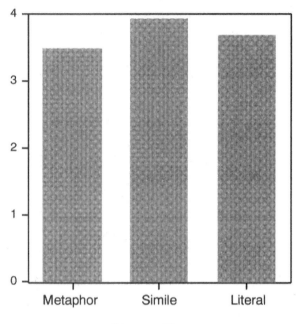

Phrase Type

Figure 1   Experiment One: Apparent age by type of phrase

$p < 0.05$). Planned comparisons showed that only the difference between metaphor and simile was significant (F 1,20 = 8.129, $p < 0.01$), with children being rated as older when the passage contained a simile rather than a metaphor. There were no significant differences between simile and literal phrases, or between literal phrases and metaphor.

The data for intelligence were also analysed and the means are as shown in Figure 3 (p. 258). An analysis of variance was conducted on these data, but the results were not significant. A possible explanation for the failure to reach significance is that people were responding with a ranking of average intelligence in all cases: in other words, although they were varying the rankings for age, they were holding intelligence constant. One possibility is that it was too difficult for participants to vary both rankings together, and that it was easier to estimate the age of a child who, with average intelligence, might have produced that utterance, than to think about the boundaries at which say a particularly intelligent but younger child might have said the same thing. One way of dealing with this might have been to ask

ANOVA

Source	SS	df	MS	F	p
Subjects	22.5000	10	2.25		
Phrase	16.470	2	8.235	4.08	0.0326
Error	40.364	20	2.018		

Planned Comparison

Source	SS	df	MS	F	p
M Vs S	16.404	1	16.404	8.129	<0.01
M Vs L	3.28	1	3.28	1.628	ns
S Vs L	5.006	1	5.006	2.481	ns
Error	40.364	20	2.018		

Figure 2   Analysis of variance and planned comparisons for age

participants to rate not just the age at which they thought an average child might have produced the utterance, but the youngest at which an intelligent child and the oldest at which a not so intelligent child might have been likely to say it. An additional factor may have been that it is difficult for participants who are not parents to estimate intelligence with any particular accuracy.

Discussion

The results show that, when the passages contained similes, participants rated the child speakers as older (but not more intelligent for their age) than when the passages contained metaphors. There were no differences between metaphor and literal phrases, or between literal and simile utterances. This may seem surprising at first; however, it is worth noting that it does *not* mean there were no differences between those passages, just that differences were not perceived as being due to the age of the children. There were no differences found for intelligence, but this is thought to be because participants assumed that the children were all of average intelligence for their age, and they only varied the age ranking.

The responses to what the children meant generally agreed with

Intelligence Rating

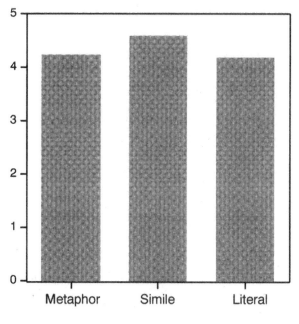

Type of Phrase

Figure 3   Experiment One: Intelligence ratings by type of phrase

what the researchers had assumed the children to mean (and in some cases the children themselves had explained), with one exception. This was Passage 10 (see Appendix 1, p. 267) which involved a father trying to show another adult (who was present but does not speak in this extract) something which the child always found difficult; perhaps there was not enough background information for all participants to decipher what was going on, so that many of them also found it hard to understand. Although the target phrase represents a slight change in topic from the concept the child was finding hard to grasp, some participants still appeared to be confused. Since this passage was presented to different subjects in different forms, this has not affected the overall findings.

Experiment Two

The False Transcript Method can also be used to tell us something about the processes which drive the production of figurative language, and this is one of the aims of Experiment Two. It also provides some validation of the different versions of the target phrases used.

Method

PARTICIPANTS

The participants in this experiment were a sample of convenience of 40 undergraduates and postgraduates at Nottingham University.

APPARATUS

The apparatus consisted of a questionnaire in which subjects were asked to rewrite phrases from a series of twelve transcripts. The same transcripts were used as in Experiment One.

DESIGN

This was again a within-subjects design, with each participant seeing four transcripts containing each type of target phrase. The independent variable was the *type of target phrase* that participants were asked to rewrite, and had three levels: metaphor, simile and literal. The dependent variables were the *ease of rewriting*, and *the extent to which the meaning changed* for each answer given (both rated on a seven-point scale). In addition, further dependent variables were the *type of phrase used by participants*, the *best answer given* in each case (as chosen by the subject) and the *reason given for its choice*. The transcripts were blocked (e.g. all examples of metaphor were put together) and the order of presentation of blocks was counter-balanced (to reduce bias arising from sequencing effects).

PROCEDURE

Participants were recruited by posters on campus and were paid for their time. The instructions appeared on the first page of the questionnaire, and asked the participant to think of different ways of saying one phrase (the target phrase) from each of the transcripts which followed. Participants were informed that the passages were examples of dialogue between a child and an adult, and that they had to think about what the child had said and try to produce phrases which the child might have said (rather than something they themselves would have said). After each transcript, there were spaces for up to four answers. Beneath each answer, participants had to rate both the ease of rewriting and the extent by which the meaning was changed, on a seven-point scale (from *very easy* to *very difficult*, and from *not at all* to *changed a lot*). Participants then had to put an asterisk next to the answer they thought the best, and say why they had chosen it by ticking either *elegant, concise, same meaning, clever* or *other (please specify)*. *Elegant, concise* and *clever* were chosen as possibly representing perceived functions of metaphor, whereas *same meaning* was intended to represent choices which were closest to the original.

Results

Examination of participants' responses showed that in some cases they failed to produce four alternative ways of rewriting the target phrase. The responses that participants had elected as the 'best' of the four responses in each case were collated, and classified according to whether they were metaphorical, literal or simile. A graph of these results is shown in Figure 4 opposite. Across all three types of target phrase, literal phrases were produced the most frequently, with similes forming the next most frequent response. However, the types of language produced did vary according to the target phrase. Although the number of metaphors is low throughout, the highest proportion was produced in response to a metaphor target. Simile responses are broadly equivalent in number with literal ones for both the metaphor and simile target phrases; however, with a literal target phrase, an overwhelming number of literal responses was given.

The numbers of responses given to each type of target phrase were analysed. The data were transformed (square root) due to a lack of homogeneity of variance and a within-subjects ANOVA was performed. No significant differences were found. There was a ceiling effect, with most participants producing four responses to most of the target phrases. A within-subjects ANOVA was also performed on participants' ratings for *change in meaning* and again no differences were found. This may in part be due to the difficulties of participants rating their own productions (see Discussion below). A follow-up experiment which asked a different set of thirty people (recruited on the University of Nottingham campus) to rate the phrases produced by participants in this experiment *did* find significant differences in meaning change (see Figure 5 p. 262 for a summary of the results). In this case participants were comparing the phrases back to either metaphor, simile or literal phrases, and so the analysis was in terms of both *what the phrase had originally been produced in response to*, and in terms of *what the participant was comparing the phrase to*.

No. of phrases produced

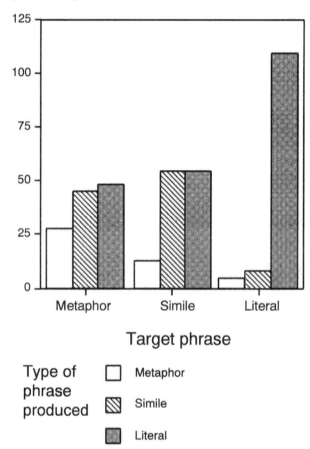

Figure 4   Experiment Two: Types of phrase produced

Since there were three levels (metaphor, simile, literal) in each case, we might have expected that ratings for *meaning change* would be lowest when the basis for comparison by the new participants was the same as the basis for production by the original participants. This was indeed the case for comparisons with metaphor and literal phrases. However, when the basis for comparison was a simile, there was no difference between ratings for phrases produced in response to metaphor or simile. This suggests that, while metaphor can encompass simile, the reverse is not the case.

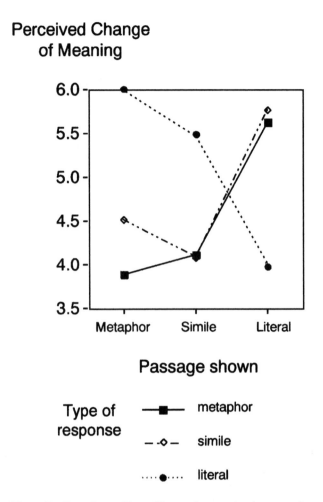

Figure 5   Experiment Two: Change in meaning by type of passage shown

In order to assess the validity of the target phrases chosen as stimuli in this experiment, participants' responses were analysed to see how often they produced the alternative versions of the target phrases. In other words, because participants had only been presented with one of the three forms of the target phrase, it was possible to study their responses and see whether they had produced either of the other two versions of the same target phrase, which were used as stimuli in other conditions. In this case, all the responses were studied, as opposed to just the one they had picked out as the 'best'. Participants' responses were generally quite close to the target phrase they had been presented with (e.g. "it's a pretty rainbow", in response to the passage given on p. 251), and in a number of cases they also gave responses similar to the alternative versions of the target phrase (e.g. the original metaphor from the simile version of the transcript). This gives us some confidence that the alternative versions of the phrases chosen as stimuli represented a valid choice as target phrases. This confidence is tempered by the experimental findings; as an overwhelming number of literal responses were given to literal target phrases, in these cases very few participants produced the alternative versions used. However, this has little to say about the validity of the metaphor/simile phrases that were taken from naturally occurring speech; in these cases, validity can be assumed. None of the target phrases were originally literal.

Discussion

The first experiment showed that children who apparently used metaphor were seen by the adult (undergraduate) subjects as younger – but not less intelligent for their age – than those who used simile; no differences were found between literal language and either metaphor or simile. This finding is not due to metaphors being perceived as incorrect, as participants were able to state what they thought the child meant in each case. It would seem therefore that the 'childish' nature of the metaphor is responsible for differences in perceived age. This could also be due in part to differences in discourse function. In the second experiment, it was shown that the type of language produced when rewriting a phrase was highly dependent on the type of target phrase itself. Overall, more literal phrases were produced than simile, and more simile than metaphor; when the target phrase was literal, the number of literal responses was overwhelming, and most metaphors were produced in response to a metaphorical target phrase. This provides a measure of experimental evidence that production of metaphor is in response to some idea that cannot easily be coded in literal language. In this experiment (i.e. Experiment Two), it seems that the transformation is generally one-way. In other words, once something has been rewritten as a literal statement, it is not so likely to be rewritten (again) in its original (metaphorical/simile) form. While one of the advantages of the False Transcript Method is its ability to highlight the effects of differences in function of discourse, the experiment should be repeated with a different set of transcripts, some of which were *originally* literal (as opposed to just metaphor or simile), in order to confirm that the results are due to differences in types of language use *per se*, as opposed to simply being a feature of literal rewritings of metaphor/simile.

Although no differences were found in ratings of difficulty or change in meaning, this could be due to a number of factors. The fact that almost all participants were able to produce four alternative versions of each target phrase, suggests that a ceiling effect was involved. If participants were asked to produce more (say, ten) target phrases, differences might become apparent; alternatively, if they were simply asked to produce as many different versions as possible, there might be more variation in the overall numbers produced. Difficulty of production and overall numbers produced are probably linked; at the point at which production reaches a certain level of difficulty, it seems plausible that people would give up and move on to the next question. Ratings of the amount of change in meaning from one phrase to another are probably unreliable when given by the person producing the phrases – their involvement in the production and knowledge of the particular chain of thought involved may bias the results. Confirmation of this was found in the results of other people's ratings of these responses, which *did* show significant differences. While responses to metaphor were rated closest in meaning to the metaphorical passages, and responses to literal phrases closest to the literal passage, this was not the case for simile, where there were no differences between the metaphor and simile conditions. This would seem to show that, while metaphor can encompass simile, the reverse is not the case, accounting for the asymmetry between conditions. These results also suggest that the False Transcript Method is indeed capable of yielding rich data, and further work to explicate these results is under way. In addition, although qualitative analyses of the responses have not been discussed here, there is no reason why qualitative data could not be collected of people's responses to the passages.

There are a number of problems with these experiments. It is possible, as noted above, that the results are slightly biased by the fact that no target phrases were used which were originally literal; however, this would be relatively easy to remedy in future experiments. A further suggestion to ensure the validity of target phrases used would be to use the methodology of Experiment Two: ask people to rewrite the original target phrases, and select alternative phrases from those produced, according to relevant criteria (such as *most frequently produced* or *preferred by the participant*). Of course, it is also quite possible that production of metaphor or simile is partly a reflection of the context, in which case holding the context constant across all three conditions could be a source of bias in itself (see the discussion by Low, in Chapter 3). In order to investigate this, further experiments could be conducted in which the context could be changed.

The differences between the versions of the transcripts are also worth considering in terms of the functions of the utterances. For example, in the sample transcript given on p. 251, the literal version might be said to be redundant (repeating information) whereas the metaphor and simile versions are commenting on appearance. The different versions of other transcripts can be found in the Appendices, and the same criticism could be made of the literal versions of several other transcripts. The statistical analyses, of course, apply to the set of twelve transcripts in aggregate rather than to individual passages, and a number of transcripts were used precisely so that peculiarities of any individual transcripts would not affect the generalisability of results. However, for this set of transcripts it is possible that the literal versions do not fit with the dialogue in the same way as the metaphorical and simile versions. Even if this is the case, though, it should be noted that it does not affect the differences found between metaphor and simile.

Conclusion

The findings from the two experiments reported here demonstrate the usefulness of the False Transcript Method for investigating differences between different types of trope. The possibility of manipulating both the target phrase and the context enable a wide range of research questions to be considered. The False Transcript Method was developed in response to the low rates of metaphor production amongst children, but it could also be used to investigate aspects of adults' production or indeed comprehension. The main strength of the approach lies in the relative richness and validity of the stimuli, whilst allowing for the manipulation of a range of experimental factors.

Appendix 1: Passages used as stimuli

For economy of space, all passages are shown in the metaphoric format; the target phrase is in italics. See Appendix 2 for a table of the alternative versions used.

Passage 1

MOTHER: We got two cats from the cat rescue. One of them only had three legs, do you remember, Ruth?

RUTH: Yeah, Felix

MOTHER: His leg fell off just after he was born; the oxygen had been cut off. But the funny thing was, the stump still had those soft pads like on the paws

RUTH: What? oh yeah, *the beans* ... he still had *the beans*

Passage 2

MOTHER: How's your arm? Does it still hurt where you banged yourself yesterday?

JOE: Mmmm. Look

MOTHER: Oh dear, that's a big bruise, isn't it?

JOE: *It's a tower bruise*

MOTHER: You poor thing!

Passage 3

MOTHER: We've got to clean the room

SARAH: Clean room

MOTHER: Will you help me with the dusting?

(Sarah nods)

MOTHER: Look, there's a cobweb, it's all dusty

SARAH: *It's hair* ... how come it's up there?

MOTHER: I don't know

Passage 4

MOTHER: Look at the cat in the garden

PAUL: Where? ... oh yeah

MOTHER: He's hunting

PAUL: *A tiger!*

MOTHER: He wants to catch the bird

PAUL: Oh!

MOTHER: Oh it's flown away

Passage 5

MOTHER: Would you like an ice-cream Liz?

LIZ: Yes!

MOTHER: Yes, what?

JOHN: She's already had one

LIZ: Yes please

JOHN: *She's a pig!*

MOTHER: That's not a nice thing to say, John

JOHN: I want one!

Passage 6

FATHER: Would you like a balloon?
TOM: Yes, please
FATHER: Okay, what colour would you like?
TOM: Red one!!!
FATHER: There you go . . . a red balloon . . .
TOM: *It's a tomato!!*
FATHER: What do you say?
TOM: Thank you Daddy

Passage 7

FATHER: Eat your tea, Louise
LOUISE: But I don't like stew!!
FATHER: Never mind, eat up
LOUISE: *But it's sick!!*
FATHER: Well you can't have any ice cream afterwards if you don't eat it
LOUISE: Oh but Dad!!

Passage 8

MOTHER: No don't pull his tail he won't like that
HENRY: Want to stroke him!
MOTHER: Yes, you can stroke him . . . there, he likes that, listen!
HENRY: *He's an engine!*
MOTHER: Yes, he's purring because he's a happy cat
HENRY: (makes purring noise)

Passage 9

FATHER: Let's find out all about the baby rabbits . . .
JAMES: They hop . . . *they're kangaroos*
FATHER: What colour were the rabbits?
JAMES: um . . . black and white
FATHER: Yeah . . . and any grey and white?
JAMES: Yep . . . grey and black and orange

Passage 10

FATHER: Who's bigger, Little Ernie or Big Ernie?
LUCY: No Big Ernie and Little Ernie
FATHER: Who's bigger, Little Ernie or his dad?
LUCY: Little Ernie
FATHER: Little Ernie is bigger . . .
LUCY: Yeah

FATHER: than Big Ernie, that's right. Big Ernie is smaller
LUCY: *He's an old funny bird*

Passage 11

FATHER: Not far to go now, we're nearly there
NICOLA: Can you carry me?
FATHER: What for?
NICOLA: *Because my legs have run out of petrol*
FATHER: Oh, okay then, up you get
NICOLA: Don't like long walks

Passage 12

MOTHER: Wave goodbye to daddy then
USHA: Bye bye
MOTHER: Let's hope he has a good day at work today, eh?
USHA: What's that?
MOTHER: What?
USHA: There! (pointing)
MOTHER: Oh . . . it's oil from the car
USHA: *It's a dead rainbow*
MOTHER: We need to get that fixed

Appendix 2: Table of target phrases

Passage	Metaphor	Simile	Literal phrase
1	Oh yeah, the beans	Oh yeah, they're like beans	Oh yeah, the pads
2	It's a tower bruise	It's as big as a tower	It's a big bruise
3	It's hair	It's like hair	It's a cobweb
4	A tiger	Like a tiger	Cat!
5	She's a pig	She's like a pig	She's greedy
6	It's a tomato	It's like a tomato	It's a red balloon
7	But it's sick	But it's like sick	But it's disgusting
8	He's an engine	He's like an engine	He's purring
9	They're kangaroos	They're like kangaroos	They hop
10	He's an old funny bird	He's like an old funny bird	He's an old man
11	Because my legs have run out of petrol	Because my legs are like a car	Because my legs are tired
12	It's a dead rainbow	It's like a dead rainbow	It's oil

References

Ahlers, J. 1997. Metaphors in second language teaching/acquisition. Paper presented at the Researching and Applying Metaphor II conference, University of Copenhagen.

Aitchison, J. 1987. *Words in the Mind: An Introduction to the Mental Lexicon*. Oxford: Blackwell.

Altmann, G. (Ed.) 1990. *Cognitive Models of Speech Processing: Psycholinguistic and Computational Perspectives*. Cambridge, MA: MIT Press.

Aristotle. 1991. *Rhetoric*. Translated by H. Lawson-Tancred. London: Penguin.

Bard, E. G., D. Robertson, and A. Sorace. 1996. Magnitude estimation of linguistic acceptability. *Language*, 75 (1): 32–68.

Barsalou, L. W. 1987. The instability of graded structure: Implications for the nature of concepts. In *Concepts and Conceptual Development: Ecological and Intellectual Factors*, U. Neisser (Ed.). Cambridge: Cambridge University Press.

Barsalou, L. W. 1989. Intraconcept similarity and its implications for interconcept similarity. In *Similarity and Analogical Reasoning*, S. Vosniadou, and A. Ortony (Eds.). Cambridge: Cambridge University Press.

Bayley, J. 1968. The 'Irresponsibility' of Jane Austen. In B. C. Southam (Ed.), *Critical Essays on Jane Austen*. London: Routledge and Kegan Paul.

Berendt, E., and Y. Mori. 1995. Convergent and divergent conceptualization patterns on learning in English and Japanese. Paper presented at the 5th international conference on Cross-Cultural Communication, Harbin, China.

Beretta, A. 1991. Theory construction in SLA: Complementarity and opposition. *Studies in Second Language Acquisition*, 13 (4): 493–511.

Billig, M. 1987. *Arguing and Thinking: A Rhetorical Approach to Social Psychology*. Cambridge: Cambridge University Press.

Billow, R. M. 1981. Observing spontaneous metaphor in children. *Journal of Experimental Child Psychology*, 31: 430–435.

Black, M. 1962. *Models and Metaphors*. New York: Cornell University Press.
    1979. More about metaphor. In *Metaphor and Thought*, A. Ortony (Ed.). New York: Cambridge University Press.

1990. *Perplexities: Rational Choice, the Prisoner's Dilemma, Metaphor, Poetic Ambiguity and Other Puzzles*. London: Cornell University Press.

Blakemore, D. 1991. *Understanding Utterances*. Oxford: Blackwell.

Block, D. 1992. Metaphors we teach and learn by. *Prospect*, 7 (3): 42–55.

1996. Not so fast: Some thoughts on theory culling, relativism, accepted findings and the heart and soul of SLA. *Applied Linguistics*, 17 (1): 63–83.

Bond, M. H. 1991. *Beyond the Chinese Face*. Oxford: Oxford University Press.

Booth, W. 1979. Metaphor as rhetoric: The problem of evaluation. In *On Metaphor*, S. Sacks (Ed.). Chicago, IL: University of Chicago Press.

Bovair, S., and D. Kieras. 1985. A guide to propositional analysis for research on technical prose. In *Understanding Expository Text: A Theoretical and Practical Handbook for Analyzing Explanatory Text*, B. Britton, and J. Black (Eds.). Hillsdale, NJ: Erlbaum.

Boyle, O. F., and S. F. Peregoy. 1990. Literacy scaffolds: Strategies for first- and second-language readers and writers. *The Reading Teacher*, 44 (3): 194–200.

Braddick, O. 1986. Inside the working of the brain. A review of C. W. Coen (Ed.), 'Functions of the Brain'. *Nature*, 320 (20): 223.

Breton, A. 1931/1974. L'Union libre. Translated as 'Free Union' by David Antin. In *Poetry of Surrealism*, M. Benedikt (Ed.). 1974. Boston, MA: Little, Brown.

Brett-Smith, H. F. (Ed.). 1921. *Peacock's Four Ages of Poetry, Shelley's Defence of Poetry, and Browning's Essay on Shelley*. New York: Houghton Mifflin.

Bright, M. 1991. *The Ozone Layer*. London: Gloucester Press.

Britton, B., and J. Black (Eds.) 1985. *Understanding Expository Text: A Theoretical and Practical Handbook for Analyzing Explanatory Text*. Hillsdale, NJ: Erlbaum.

Broderick, V. 1992. Incidence of verbal comparisons in beginners' books and in metaphor comprehension: A search for ecological validity. *Journal of Child Language*, 19: 183–193.

Brooke-Rose, C. 1958. *A Grammar of Metaphor*. London: Secker and Warburg.

Brown, R. 1973. *A First Language – The Early Stages*. London: Allen and Unwin.

Brown, S. R. 1986. Q technique and method: Principles and procedures. In *New Tools for Social Scientists*, W. D. Berry, and M. S. Lewis-Beck (Eds.). London: Sage.

Bruner, J. S. 1978. The role of dialogue in language acquisition. In *The Child's Conception of Language*, A. Sinclair, R. Jaovella, and W. Levelt (Eds.). New York: Springer Verlag.

Buley-Meissner, M. L. 1991. Teachers and teacher education: A view from the People's Republic of China. *International Journal of Educational Development*, 11 (1): 41–53.

Bullough, R. V. 1991. Exploring personal teaching metaphors in pre-service teacher education. *Journal of Teacher Education*, 42 (1): 43–51.

1992. Beginning teacher curriculum decision making, personal teaching metaphors, and teacher education. *Teaching and Teacher Education*, 8 (3): 239–252.

Burke, K. 1945. *A Grammar of Motives*. New York: Prentice Hall.

Cambridge International English Dictionary. 1995. P. Proctor, J. Ayto, A. Stenton, and P. Stock (Eds.). Cambridge: Cambridge University Press.

Cameron, L. 1996. Discourse context and the development of metaphor in children. *Current Issues in Language and Society*, 3 (1/2): 49–64.

1997a. Working with the complexity of language in use: The case of metaphor. Paper presented at the 1997 Annual Meeting of the British Association for Applied Linguistics, University of Birmingham.

1997b. *Metaphorical Use of Language in Educational Discourse: A Theoretical and Empirical Investigation*. University of London, Institute of Education: Unpublished PhD thesis.

(*Submitted for publication*) Researching prosaic metaphor in talk.

Carey, S. 1985. *Conceptual Change in Childhood*. Cambridge, MA: MIT Press.

Cassell, E. 1976. *The Healer's Art*. Harmondsworth: Penguin.

Central Advisory Council for Education. 1967. *Children and their Primary Schools: A Report of the Central Advisory Council for Education* (Chair: Baroness Plowden). London: HMSO.

Chandler, S. 1991. Metaphor comprehension: A connectionist approach to implications for the mental lexicon. *Metaphor and Symbolic Activity*, 6 (2): 227–258.

Channell, J. 1994. *Vague Language*. Describing English Language series. Oxford: Oxford University Press.

Chomsky, N. 1978. The ideas of Chomsky. In *Men of Ideas, Some Creators of Contemporary Philosophy*, B. Magee (Ed.). London: British Broadcasting Corporation.

Churchill, L., and S. Churchill. 1982. Storytelling in medical arenas: The art of self-determination. *Literature and Medicine*, 1: 73–79.

Clandinin, D. J. 1985. Personal practical knowledge: A study of teachers' practical knowledge. *Curriculum Enquiry*, 15: 361–385.

Clark, H. 1996. *Using Language*. Cambridge: Cambridge University Press.

Clay, M. M., and C. B. Cazden. 1990. A Vygotskian interpretation of reading recovery. In *Vygotsky and Education*, L. Moll (Ed.). Cambridge: Cambridge University Press.

Cleverley, J. 1985/91. *The Schooling of China: Tradition and Modernity in Chinese Education*. Sydney: Allen and Unwin.

Cohen, L. J. 1977. Can the conversationalist hypothesis be defended? *Philosophical Studies*, 31: 81–90.

Cohen, J., and I. Stewart. 1994. *The Collapse of Chaos*. London: Viking.

Cole, A. (Ed.) 1980. *Perception and Production of Fluent Speech*. Hillsdale, NJ: Erlbaum.

Collins Cobuild English Dictionary. 1995. (2nd edition). J. Sinclair, G. Fox, and S. Bullon (Eds.). London: Harper Collins.

Connelly, E. M., and D. J. Clandinin. 1988. *Teachers as Curriculum Planners: Narratives of Experience.* New York: Teachers College Press.

Cook-Gumperz, J. (Ed.). 1986. *The Social Construction of Literacy.* Cambridge: Cambridge University Press.

Cooper, D. 1986. *Metaphor.* Oxford: Blackwell.

Cortazzi, M. 1991. *Primary Teaching, How It Is: A Narrative Account.* London: David Fulton.

    1993. *Narrative Analysis.* London: Falmer.

Cortazzi, M., and L. Jin. 1994. Narrative analysis: Applying linguistics to cultural models of learning. In *Evaluating Language*, D. Graddol, and J. Swann (Eds.). Clevedon: Multilingual Matters.

    1996. Cultures of Learning: Language classrooms in China. In *Society and the Language Classroom*, H. Coleman (Ed.). Cambridge: Cambridge University Press.

    1997. Communication for learning across cultures. In *Overseas Students in Higher Education*, D. McNamara (Ed.). London: Routledge.

Cowie, B. 1976. The cardiac patient's perception of his heart attack. *Social Science and Medicine*, 10: 87–96.

Croft, W. 1993. The role of domains in the interpretation of metaphors and metonymies. *Cognitive Linguistics*, 4 (4): 335–370.

Cruse, D. A. 1973. Some thoughts on agentivity. *Journal of Linguistics*, 9: 11–23.

Davidson, D. 1979. What metaphors mean. In *On Metaphor*, S. Sacks (Ed.). Chicago, IL: University of Chicago Press.

Dearden, R. F. 1968. *The Philosophy of Primary Education.* London: Routledge and Kegan Paul.

Debatin, B., T. Jackson, and D. Steuer (Eds.). 1997. *Metaphor and Rational Discourse.* Tübingen: Max Niemeyer Verlag.

De Castell, S. 1988. Metaphors into models. In *Becoming a Teacher*, P. Holborn, M. Widean, and I. Andarewski (Eds.). Toronto: Kagan.

Dennett, D. 1991. *Consciousness Explained.* Harmondsworth: Penguin.

DiGiacomo, S. 1992. Metaphor as illness: Postmodern dilemmas in the representation of body, mind and disorder. *Medical Anthropology*, 14: 109–137.

Dreuihle, E. 1988. *Mortal Embrace: Living With AIDS.* New York: Hill and Wang.

Drew, P., and E. Holt. 1988. Complainable matters: The use of idiomatic expressions in making complaints. *Social Problems*, 35 (4): 398–417.

    1995. Idiomatic expressions and their role in the organisation of topic transition in conversation. In *Idioms: Structural and Psychological Perspectives*, M. Everaert, E.-J. van der Linden, A. Schenk, and R. Schreuder (Eds.). Hillsdale, NJ: Erlbaum.

Dubin, F., and E. Olshtain. 1986. *Course Design: Developing Materials for Language Learning.* Cambridge: Cambridge University Press.

Dzau, Y. F. (Ed.). 1990. *English in China*. Hong Kong: API Press.

Eco, U. 1984. *Semiotics and the Philosophy of Language*. London: Macmillan.

Editors of *Applied Linguistics*. 1994. The editors' comment. *Applied Linguistics*, 15 (3): 347.

Editors of *Studies in Second Language Acquisition*. 1993. Replication study. *Studies in Second Language Acquisition*, 15 (4): 505.

Edwards, D. 1997. *Discourse and Cognition*. London: Sage.

Edwards, D., and N. Mercer. 1987. *Common Knowledge: The Development of Understanding in the Classroom*. London: Methuen.

Elbaz, F. 1983. *Teacher Thinking: A Study of Practical Knowledge*. London: Croom Helm.

Ellis, R. 1994. *The Study of Second Language Acquisition*. Oxford: Oxford University Press.

Ericsson, K. A. 1988. Concurrent verbal reports on text comprehension: A review. *Text*, 8 (4): 295–325.

Ericsson, K. A., and H. A. Simon. 1984. *Protocol Analysis: Verbal Reports as Data*. Cambridge, MA: MIT Press.

Evans, M. A., and D. Gamble. 1988. Attribute saliency and metaphor interpretation in school-age children. *Journal of Child Language*, 15: 435–449.

Eysenck, M., and M. Keane. 1995. *Cognitive Psychology* (3rd edition). Hove: Erlbaum.

Fairclough, N. 1995. *Critical Discourse Analysis: The Critical Study of Language*. Harlow: Longman.

Fernandez, J. W. 1986. *Persuasions and Performances: The Play of Tropes in Culture*. Chicago, IL: University of Chicago Press.

Fogelin, R. J. 1988. *Figuratively Speaking*. New Haven, NJ: Yale University Press.

Fox, N. 1993. *Postmodernism, Sociology and Health*. Buckingham: Open University Press.

Francis, G., S. Hunston, and E. Manning (Eds.). 1996. *Collins Cobuild Grammar Patterns 1: Verbs*. London: Harper Collins.

Gentner, D. 1982. Are scientific analogies metaphors? In *Metaphor: Problems and Perspectives*, D. Miall (Ed.). Brighton: Harvester.

    1983. Structure-mapping: A theoretical framework for analogy. *Cognitive Science*, 7: 155–170.

    1989. The mechanisms of analogical learning. In *Similarity and Analogical Reasoning*, S. Vosniadou, and A. Ortony (Eds.). Cambridge: Cambridge University Press.

Gentner, D., and C. Clements. 1988. Evidence for relational selectivity in the interpretation of analogy and metaphor. In *The Psychology of Learning and Motivation*, Vol. 22, G. Bower (Ed.). Orlando, FL: Academic Press.

Gentner, D., B. Falkenhainer, B. and J. Skorstad. 1988. Viewing metaphor as analogy. In *Analogical Reasoning: Perspectives of Artificial Intelligence,*

Cognitive Science and Philosophy, D. H. Helman (Ed.). Dordrecht: Kluwer.

Gentner, D., and J. Grudin. 1985. The evolution of mental metaphors in psychology: A 90-year retrospective. *American Psychologist*, 40: 181–192.

Gernsbacher, M. (Ed.) 1994. *Handbook of Psycholinguistics*. New York: Academic Press.

Gerrig, R. J. 1993. *Experiencing Narrative Worlds*. New Haven, CT: Yale University Press.

Gerrig, R. J., and A. Healey. 1983. Dual processes in metaphor understanding: Comprehension and appreciation. *Journal of Experimental Psychology: Learning, Memory, and Cognition*, 9: 667–675.

Gibb, H., and R. Wales. 1990. Metaphor or simile: Psychological determinants of the differential use of each sentence form. *Metaphor and Symbolic Activity*, 5 (4): 119–213.

Gibbs, R. W. 1982. A critical examination of the contribution of literal meaning to understanding nonliteral discourse. *Text*, 2 (1–3): 9–27.

1990. Comprehending figurative referential expressions. *Journal of Experimental Psychology: Learning, Memory and Cognition*, 16: 56–66.

1992. When is metaphor: The idea of understanding in theories of metaphor. *Poetics Today*, 13: 575–606.

1993. Process and products in making sense of tropes. In *Metaphor and Thought*, A. Ortony (Ed.). New York: Cambridge University Press.

1994. *The Poetics of Mind: Figurative Thought, Language and Understanding*. New York: Cambridge University Press.

Gibbs, R. W., D. Beitel, M. Harrington, and D. Sanders. 1995. Taking a stand on the meanings of stand: Bodily experience as motivation for polysemy. *Journal of Semantics*, 11: 231–251.

Gibbs, R. W., and J. Bogdonovich (*Submitted for publication*). Mental imagery in interpreting poetic metaphor.

Gibbs, R. W., J. Bogdonovich, J. Sykes, and D. Barr (*Submitted for publication*). Metaphor in idiom comprehension.

Gibbs, R. W., D. Buchalter, J. Moise, and W. Farrar. 1993. Literal meaning and figurative language. *Discourse Processes*, 16: 387–403.

Gibbs, R. W., and H. Colston. 1995. The cognitive psychological reality of image schemas and their transformations. *Cognitive Linguistics*, 6: 347–378.

Gibbs, R. W., and L. Daughters (*In preparation*). Proverbs are the children of experience: Interpreting XYZ metaphors.

Giora, R., and O. Fein. 1996. On understanding familiar and less familiar figurative language. Paper presented at the 5th International Pragmatics Conference, Mexico City.

Glucksberg, S. 1995. Commentary on nonliteral language: Processing and use. *Metaphor and Symbolic Activity*, 10 (1): 47–57.

Glucksberg, S., and B. Keysar. 1990. Understanding metaphorical comparisons: Beyond similarity. *Psychological Review*, 97 (1): 3–18.

1993. How metaphors work. In *Metaphor and Thought*, A. Ortony (Ed.). New York: Cambridge University Press.

Glucksberg, S., and M. S. McGlone. 1992. When love is not a journey: What metaphors mean. Paper presented at the Metaphor and Cognition Conference, Tel Aviv, Israel.

Goatly, A. 1997. *The Language of Metaphors*. London: Routledge.

Goossens, L. 1990. Metaphtonymy: The interaction of metaphor and metonymy in expressions for linguistic action. *Cognitive Linguistics*, 1: 323–340.

Gordon, W. J. J. 1966. *The Metaphorical Way of Knowing*. Cambridge, MA: Porpoise.

Gould, S. J. 1995. Ladders and Cones: Constraining Evolution by Canonical Icons. In *Hidden Histories of Science*, R. B. Silvers (Ed.). London: Granta.

Grant, G. E. 1992. The sources of structural metaphors in teacher knowledge: three cases. *Teaching & Teacher Education*, 8 (5/6): 433–440.

Graumann, C. 1990. Perspective structure and dynamics in dialogues. In *The Dynamics of Dialogue*, I. Markova, and K. Foppa (Eds.). London: Harvester Wheatsheaf.

Grotjahn, R. 1991. The research programme subjective theories. *Studies in Second Language Acquisition*, 13: 187–214.

Grube, G. M. A. 1958. *Aristotle on Poetry and Style*. New York: Liberal Arts Press.

Gwyn, R. 1996. *The Voicing of Illness*. University of Wales: Unpublished PhD thesis.

Halliday, M. A. K. 1978. *Language as Social Semiotic*. London: Arnold.

1985. *An Introduction to Functional Grammar*. London: Arnold.

Hallpike, C. 1969. Social hair. *MAN*, 4 (2): 256–264.

Hamilton, E., and H. Cairns (Eds.). 1963. *The Collected Dialogues of Plato*. Princeton, NJ: Princeton University Press.

Harman, H. H. 1976. *Modern Factor Analysis*. Chicago, IL: Chicago University Press.

Harris, R., M. Lahey, and F. Marsalek. 1980. Metaphors and images: Rating, reporting and remembering. In *Cognition and Figurative Language*, R. Honeck, and R. Hoffmann (Eds.). Hillsdale, NJ: Erlbaum.

Harrison, A. G., and D. F. Treagust. 1996. Secondary students' mental models of atoms and molecules: Implications for teaching chemistry. *Science Education*, 80 (5): 509–534.

Harvey, P. 1985. A Lesson to be learned: Chinese approaches to language learning. *ELT Journal*, 39 (3): 183–186.

Hawkes, T. 1984. *Metaphor* (2nd edition). London: Routledge.

Helman, C. 1978. 'Feed a Cold, Starve a Fever': Folk models of infection in an English suburban community, and their relation to medical treatment. *Culture, Medicine and Psychiatry*, 2: 107–137.

1984. *Culture, Health and Illness*. Oxford: Butterworth-Heinemann.

1987. Heart disease and the cultural construction of time: The Type A behaviour pattern as a Western culture-bound syndrome. *Social Science and Medicine*, 25 (9): 969–979.

Heritage, J. 1996. Conversational Analysis and institutional analysis: Analysing data. Manuscript.

Herzlich, C. 1973. *Health and Illness*. London: Academic Press.

Hillman, J. 1981. Psychology: Monotheistic or polytheistic? In *The New Polytheism*, D. L. Miller (Ed.). Dallas: Spring Publications.

—— 1983. *Healing Fiction*. Woodstock, CT: Spring Publications.

Hiraga, M. K. 1995. Japanese metaphors for learning. Paper presented at the 5th international conference on Cross-Cultural Communication, Harbin, China.

Hoffman, R., and S. Kemper. 1987. What could reaction time studies be telling us about metaphor comprehension? *Metaphor and Symbolic Activity*, 2: 149–186.

Hofstede, G. 1991. *Cultures and Organizations*. London: Harper Collins.

Holton, G. 1984. Metaphors in science and education. In *Metaphors of Education*, W. Taylor (Ed.). London: Heinemann.

Holyoak, K., and P. Thagard. 1989. Analogical mapping by constraint satisfaction. *Cognitive Science*, 13: 295–355.

Honeck, R. 1980. Historical notes on figurative language. In *Cognition and Figurative Language*, R. Honeck, and R. Hoffman (Eds.). Hillsdale, NJ: Erlbaum.

Honeck, R., and R. Hoffman (Eds.). 1980. *Cognition and Figurative Language*. Hillsdale, NJ: Erlbaum.

Hopper, P. J., and S. A. Thompson, 1984. The discourse basis for lexical categories in universal grammar. *Language*, 60: 703–783.

Hymes, D. 1972. Models of the Interaction of language and social life. In *Directions in Sociolinguistics: The Ethnography of Communication*, J. Gumperz, and D. Hymes (Eds.). New York: Holt Reinhart and Winston.

Ikeda, D. 1988. *Unlocking the Mysteries of Birth and Death: Buddhism in the Contemporary World*. London: Macdonald.

Indurkhaya, B. 1992. Metaphor and cognition: An interactionist approach. Dordrecht: Kluwer.

Jackendoff, R. 1983. *Semantics and Cognition*. Cambridge, MA: MIT Press.

—— 1992. *Languages of the Mind*. Cambridge, MA: MIT Press.

Janus, R., and T. Bever. 1985. Processing metaphoric language: An investigation of the three-stage model of metaphor comprehension. *Journal of Psycholinguistic Research*, 14: 473–487.

Jin, L., and M. Cortazzi. 1993. Cultural orientation and academic language use. In *Language and Culture*, D. Graddol, L. Thompson, and M. Byram (Eds.). Clevedon: Multilingual Matters.

—— 1995. A Cultural Synergy Model for academic language use. In *Explorations in English for Professional Communication*, P. Bruthiaux, T. Boswood, B. Du-Babcock (Eds.). Hong Kong: City University of Hong Kong Press.

Johnson, M. 1987. *The Body in the Mind: The Bodily Basis of Meaning, Imagination and Reason*. Chicago, IL: University of Chicago Press.
Johnston, S. 1992. Images: A way of understanding the practical knowledge of student teachers. *Teaching and Teacher Education*, 8 (2): 123–136.
Jones, R. 1983. *Physics as Metaphor*. London: Abacus Books.
Kallen, H. 1915. Democracy versus the melting pot. *Nation*, 25 February 1915.
Keil, F. C. 1979. *Semantic and Conceptual Development: an Ontological Perspective*. Cambridge, MA: Harvard University Press.
     1983. On the emergence of semantic and conceptual distinctions. *Journal of Experimental Psychology: General*, 112: 357–389.
Kenny, B., and D. Hall, 1987. Self-assessment as an alternative to testing. In *Trends in Language Programme Evaluation*, A. Wangsotorn, K. Prapphal, A. Maurice, and B. Kenny (Eds.). Bangkok: Chulalongkorn University Language Institute.
King, A., and M. Bond. 1985. The Confucian paradigm of Man: A sociological view. In *Chinese Culture and Mental Health*, W. S. Tseng, and D. Y. H. Wu (Eds.). Orlando: Academic Press.
Kittay, E. 1987. *Metaphor: Its Cognitive Force and Linguistic Structure*. Oxford: Oxford University Press.
Kleinman, A. 1988. *The Illness Narratives*. New York: Basic Books.
Kline, P. 1991. *Intelligence: The Psychometric View*. London: Routledge.
Knowles, G. 1996. Corpora, databases and the organization of linguistic data. In *Using Corpora for Language Research*, J. Thomas, and M. Short (Eds.). London: Longman.
Knudsen, S. 1996. *By the Grace of Gods – and Years and Years of Evolution. Analysis of the Development of Metaphors in Scientific Discourse*. University of Roskilde. PhD thesis.
Kövecses, Z. 1991. Happiness, a definitional effort. *Metaphor and Symbolic Activity*, 6 (1): 29– 46.
Kövecses, Z. and P. Szabó. 1996. Idioms: A view from cognitive semantics. *Applied Linguistics*, 17 (3): 326–355.
Kozulin, A. 1990. *Vygotsky's Psychology*. Hemel Hempstead: Harvester Wheatsheaf.
Kreuz, R. S., and M. S. MacNealy (Eds.). 1996. *Empirical Approaches to Literature and Aesthetics*. Norwood, NJ: Ablex.
Kuhn, T. 1970. *The Structure of Scientific Revolutions* (2nd edition). Chicago, IL: Chicago University Press.
Labov, W. 1972. The transformation of experience in narrative syntax. In *Language in the Inner City*, W. Labov (Ed.). Philadelphia, PA: University of Pennsylvania Press.
Lakoff, G. 1977. Linguistic Gestalts. In *Proceedings of the Thirteenth Regional Meeting of the Chicago Linguistics Society*. Chicago, IL: CLS.
     1986. The meanings of literal. *Metaphor and Symbolic Activity*, 1: 291–296.

1987a. *Women, Fire, and Dangerous Things*. Chicago, IL: Chicago University Press.

1987b. The death of dead metaphor. *Metaphor and Symbolic Activity*, 2 (2): 143–147.

1990. The invariance hypothesis: Is abstract reasoning based on image-schemas? *Cognitive Linguistics*, 1 (1): 39–74.

1993. The contemporary theory of metaphor. In *Metaphor and Thought*, A. Ortony (Ed.) 2nd edition. New York: Cambridge University Press.

Lakoff, G., and M. Johnson. 1980. *Metaphors We Live By*. Chicago, IL: Chicago University Press.

Lakoff, G., and M. Turner. 1989. *More Than Cool Reason: A Field Guide to Poetic Metaphor*. Chicago, IL: University of Chicago Press.

Langacker, R. 1986. *Foundations of Cognitive Grammar* (Vol. 1). Stanford, CA: Stanford University Press.

Lantolf, J. 1996. Second language acquisition theory building? In *Language and Education*, G. Blue, and R. Mitchell (Eds.). Clevedon: BAAL and Multilingual Matters.

Leary, D. E. 1990. Psyche's muse: The role of metaphor in the history of psychology. In *Metaphors in the History of Psychology*, D. E. Leary (Ed.). Cambridge: Cambridge University Press.

(Ed.). 1990. *Metaphors in the History of Psychology*. Cambridge: Cambridge University Press.

Leech, G. 1969. *A Linguistic Guide to English Poetry*. London: Longman.

1974. *Semantics*. Harmondsworth: Penguin.

Leech, G., and M. Short. 1981. *Style in Fiction: A Linguistic Introduction to English Fictional Prose*. London: Longman.

Lehrer, A. 1978. Structures of the lexicon and the transfer of meaning. *Lingua*, 45: 95–123.

Lerman, C. L. 1984. The functions of metaphor in discourse: Masking metaphor in the Nixon conversations. Expanded version of paper in *Whimsy 2. Proceedings of the 1983 Whim Conference 'Metaphors be With You: Humour and Metaphor'*, D. L. F. Nilsen (Ed.). Arizona State University, English Department. Manuscript.

Levin, S. R. 1977. *The Semantics of Metaphor*. Baltimore, PA: John Hopkins University Press.

Lewin, K., A. Little, H. Xu, and J. Zheng. 1994. *Educational Innovation in China: Tracing the Impact of the 1985 Reforms*. Harlow: Longman.

Lin, J. 1993. *Education in post-Mao China*. Westport, CT: Praeger.

Lindstromberg, S. 1996. Prepositional denotation and metaphor: Case studies of **against** and **with**. Paper presented at the BAAL/CUP Seminar on Researching and Applying Metaphor, University of York.

Lodge, D. 1977. *The Modes of Modern Writing*. London: Arnold.

Long, M. 1990. The least a second language acquisition theory needs to explain. *TESOL Quarterly*, 24 (4): 649–666.

Long, M. 1993. Assessment strategies for SLA theories. *Applied Linguistics*, 14 (3): 225–249.

Longman Dictionary of Contemporary English. 1995. (3rd edition). D. Summers, and M. Rundell (Eds.). London: Longman.

Louw, W. 1993. Irony in the text or insincerity in the writer? The diagnostic potential of semantic prosodies. In *Text and Technology: In Honour of John Sinclair*, M. Baker, G. Francis, and E. Tognini-Bonelli (Eds.). Amsterdam: John Benjamins.

Low, G. D. 1988. On teaching metaphor. *Applied Linguistics*, 9 (2): 125–147.

1991. Talking to questionnaires: Pragmatic models in questionnaire design. In *Sociocultural Aspects of English for Academic Purposes*, J. B. Heaton, P. Adams, and P. Howarth (Eds.). London: Macmillan and The British Council.

1995. *Answerability in Attitude Measurement Questionnaires: An Applied Linguistic Study of Reactions to 'Statement+Rating' Pairs.* University of York. Unpublished DPhil thesis.

1996a. Intensifiers and hedges in questionnaire items and the lexical invisibility hypothesis. *Applied Linguistics*, 17 (1): 1–37.

1996b. Validating research questionnaires: The value of common sense. *Research News*, 9: 1–8.

1997. Celebrations and squid sandwiches: Figurative language and the management of academic text. University of York, Department of Educational Studies, Project report.

Lowe, E. J. 1996. *Subjects of Experience.* Oxford: Oxford University Press.

Lupton, D. 1994. *Medicine as Culture.* London: Sage.

MacCormac, E. R. 1985. *A Cognitive Theory of Metaphor.* Cambridge, MA: MIT Press.

Macleod, M. 1993. On knowing the patient: Experiences of nurses undertaking care. In *Worlds of Illness*, A. Radley (Ed.). London: Routledge.

MacWhinney, B. 1991. *The CHILDES Project: Tools for Analyzing Talk.* Hillsdale, NJ: Erlbaum.

MacWhinney, B., and C. Snow. 1985. The Child Language Data Exchange System. *Journal of Child Language*, 12 (2): 271–296.

1990. The Child Language Data Exchange System – an update. *Journal of Child Language*, 17 (2): 457–472.

Mahon, J. E. 1996. Review of 'The Poetics of Mind' by R. Gibbs. *International Journal of Philosophical Studies*, 4: 202–203.

1997. Truth and Metaphor: A defence of Shelley. In *Metaphor and Rational Discourse*, B. Debatin, T. R. Jackson, and D. Steuer (Eds.). Tübingen: Niemeyer.

Mair, M. 1976. Metaphors for living. *Nebraska Symposium on Motivation.* Lincoln, NE: University of Nebraska Press.

Mandler, J. 1992. How to build a baby–2. *Psychological Review*, 99: 587–604.

Manly, B. F. J. 1986. *Multivariate Statistical Methods: A Primer.* London: Chapman and Hall.

Mann, W. C., and S. A. Thompson, 1988. Rhetorical structure theory: Towards a functional theory of text organisation. *Text*, 8 (3): 243–281.

Marchant, G. J. 1992. A teacher is like a ...: Using simile lists to explore personal metaphors. *Language and Education*, 6 (1): 33–45.

Marjanovic-Shane, A. 1989a. *Metaphor beyond Play: Development of Metaphor in Children*. University of Pennsylvania. Unpublished PhD thesis.

——— 1989b. "You are a pig": For real or just pretend? Different orientations in play and metaphor. *Play and Culture*, 2: 225–234.

Marr, D. 1982. *Vision*. New York: W. H. Freeman and Co.

Master, P. 1991. Active verbs with inanimate subjects in scientific prose. *English For Specific Purposes*, 10: 15–33.

Matic, M., and R. Wales. 1982. Creating interpretations for novel metaphors. *Language and Communication*, 2 (3) : 245–267.

McCarthy, M. 1990. *Vocabulary*. Oxford: Oxford University Press.

McGhee, P. 1985. From self-reports to narrative discourse: Reconstructing the voice of experience in personal relationship research. In *Accounting for Relationships: Explanation, Representation and Knowledge*, R. Burnett, P. McGhee and D. Clarke (Eds.). London: Methuen.

McKeon, R. (Ed.). 1941. *The Basic Works of Aristotle*. Translated by I. Bywater. New York: Random House.

McKeown, B., and D. Thomas, 1988. *Q Methodology*. London: Sage.

McNamara, T. P. 1994. Knowledge representation. In *Thinking and Problem Solving*, R. J. Sternberg (Ed.). San Diego, CA: Academic Press.

Meadows, S., and A. Cashdan. 1988. *Helping Children Learn: Contributions to a Cognitive Curriculum*. London: David Fulton.

Medin, D. L., and B. H. Ross. 1989. The specific character of abstract thought: Categorization, problem-solving and induction. In *Advances in the Psychology of Human Intelligence*, R. J. Sternberg (Ed.) (Vol. 5). Hillsdale, NJ: Erlbaum.

Mercer, N. 1995. *The Guided Construction of Knowledge: Talk Amongst Teachers and Learners*. Clevedon: Multilingual Matters.

Messick, S. 1980. Test validity and the ethics of assessment. *American Psychologist*, 35 (11): 1012–1027.

Miller, G. 1993. Images and models, similes and metaphors. In *Metaphor and Thought*, A. Ortony (Ed.). New York: Cambridge University Press.

Miller, S., and M. Fredericks. 1988. Perceptions of the crisis in American public education: The relationship of metaphors to ideology. *Metaphor and Symbolic Activity*, 5 (2): 67–81.

Mishler, E. 1986. *Research Interviewing*. Cambridge, MA: Harvard University Press.

Montgomery, S. L. 1991. Codes and combat in biomedical discourse. *Science as Culture*, 2 (3): 341–391.

Moon, R. E. 1987. The analysis of meaning. In *Looking Up*, J. Sinclair (Ed.). London and Glasgow: Collins.

Morson, G. S., and C. Emerson. 1990. *Mikhail Bakhtin: Creation of a Prosaics*. Stanford: Stanford University Press.

Moscovici, S. 1984. The phenomenon of social representations. In *Social*

Representations, R. Farr, and S. Moscovici (Eds.). Cambridge: Cambridge University Press.

Munby, H. 1986. Metaphor in the thinking of teachers: an exploratory study. *Journal of Curriculum Studies*, 18 (2): 197–209.

Murphy, G. 1996. On metaphoric representation. *Cognition*, 60: 173–204.

Murray, P. 1989. Poetic genius and its classical origins. In *Genius: The History of an Idea*, P. Murray (Ed.). Oxford: Basil Blackwell.

Nahm, M. C. (Ed.). 1950. *Aristotle on The Art of Poetry*. Translated by S. H. Butcher. New York: Liberal Arts Press.

Neisser, U. 1976. *Cognition and Reality*. New York: W. H. Freeman and Company.

Neisser, U. (Ed.). 1987. *Concepts and Conceptual Development: Ecological and Intellectual Factors in Categorization*. Cambridge: Cambridge University Press.

Newman, D., P. Griffin, and M. Cole. 1989. *The Construction Zone: Working for Cognitive Change in School*. Cambridge: Cambridge University Press.

Nias, J. 1989. *Primary Teachers Talking: A Study of Teaching as Work*. London: Routledge.

Niemeier, S. 1997. A didactic view on metaphor and metonymy. Paper presented at the Researching and Applying Metaphor II conference, University of Copenhagen.

OED. 1994. *The Oxford English Dictionary on CD ROM* (2nd edition). Oxford: Oxford University Press.

Ormell, C. 1996. Eight metaphors of education. *Educational Research*: 38 (1): 65–75.

Ortony, A. 1975. Why metaphors are necessary and not just nice. *Educational Review*, 2: 45–53.

1979a. Metaphor: A multidisciplinary problem. In *Metaphor and Thought*, A. Ortony (Ed.). New York: Cambridge University Press.

1979b. The role of similarity in similes and metaphors. In *Metaphor and Thought*, A. Ortony (Ed.). New York: Cambridge University Press.

1979c. Beyond literal similarity. *Psychological Review*, 86: 161–180.

(Ed.) 1979. *Metaphor and Thought*. New York: Cambridge University Press.

1988. Are emotion metaphors conceptual or lexical? *Cognition and Emotion*, 2: 95–103.

(Ed.) 1993. *Metaphor and Thought* (2nd and revised edition). New York: Cambridge University Press.

Ortony, A., M. Foss, R. Vondruska, and L. Jones. 1985. Salience, similes and the asymmetry of similarity. *Journal of Memory and Language*, 24: 569–594.

Oxford Advanced Learners' Dictionary. 1995. (5th edition), J. Crowther, K. Kavanagh, and M. Ashby (Eds.). Oxford: Oxford University Press.

Paine, L. W. 1990. The teacher as virtuoso: A Chinese model for teaching. *Teachers College Record*, 92 (1): 49–81.

Paine, L. 1992. Teaching and modernization in contemporary China. In

Education and Modernization: The Chinese Experience, R. Hayhoe (Ed.). Oxford: Pergamon.

Palmer, F. R. 1974. *Semantics: A New Outline*. Cambridge: Cambridge University Press.

Palmer, S. E. 1989. Levels of description in information-processing theories of analogy. In *Similarity and Analogical Reasoning*, S. Vosniadou, and A. Ortony (Eds.). Cambridge: Cambridge University Press.

Patthey-Chavez, G., L. C. and M. Youmans. 1996. Watery passion: The struggle between hegemony and sexual liberation in erotic fiction for women. *Discourse and Society*, 7: 77–106.

Pawley, A., and F. Syder. 1983. Two puzzles for linguistic theory: Nativelike selection and nativelike fluency. In *Language and Communication*, J. Richards, and R. Schmidt (Eds.). London: Longman.

Penrose, R. 1989. *The Emperor's New Mind*. London: Vintage.

Pepper, S. 1935. The root metaphor theory of metaphysics. *Journal of Philosophy*, 32: 365–374.

Perfetti, C., and M. Britt. 1995. Where do propositions come from? In *Discourse Comprehension*, C. Weaver, S. Mannes, and C. Fletcher (Eds.). Hillsdale, NJ: Erlbaum.

Perrine, L. 1971. Four forms of metaphor. *College English*, 33: 125–138.

Pettit, M. 1982. The demarcation of metaphor. *Language & Communication*, 2 (1): 1–12.

Piaget, J. 1952. *The Origins of Intelligence in Children*. New York: International Universities Press.

Pinker, S. 1994. *The Language Instinct*. London: Penguin Books.

Pollio, M., and H. Pollio. 1974. Development of figurative language in school children. *Journal of Psycholinguistic Research*, 3: 185–201.

Pollio, H., and M. Pickens. 1980. The developmental structure of figurative competence. In *Cognition and Figurative Language*, R. Honeck, and R. Hoffman (Eds.). Hillsdale, NJ: Erlbaum.

Pollio, H., and M. Smith. 1980. Metaphoric competence and complex human problem solving. In *Cognition and Figurative Language*, R. P. Honeck, and R. R. Hoffman (Eds.). Hillsdale, NJ: Erlbaum.

Ponterotto, D. 1994. Metaphors we can learn by. *English Teaching Forum*, 32 (3): 2–7.

Provenzo, E. F., G. N. McCloskey, R. B. Kottkamp, and M. M. Cohn. 1989. Metaphor and meaning in the language of teachers. *Teachers' College Record*, 49 (4): 551–573.

Quinn, N. 1991. The cultural basis of metaphor. In *Beyond Metaphor: The Theory of Tropes in Anthropology*, J. Fernandez (Ed.). Stanford, CA: Stanford University Press.

Quinn, N., and D. Holland (Eds.). 1987. *Cultural Models in Language and Thought*. Cambridge: Cambridge University Press.

Quirk, R., and S. Greenbaum. 1975. *A University Grammar of English*. London: Longman.

Quirk, R., S. Greenbaum, G. Leech, and J. Svartvik. 1985. *A Comprehensive Grammar of the English Language*. London: Longman.

Radley, A. 1993. The role of metaphor in adjustment to chronic illness. In *Worlds of Illness*, A. Radley (Ed.). London: Routledge.

Richards, I. A. 1936/1979. *The Philosophy of Rhetoric*. Oxford: Oxford University Press.

Ricoeur, P. 1978. *The Rule of Metaphor*. Translated by R. Czerny. London: Routledge and Kegan Paul.

1979. The metaphorical process. In *On Metaphor*, S. Sacks (Ed.). Chicago, IL: University of Chicago Press.

Rips, L. 1989. Similarity, typicality, and categorization. In *Similarity and Analogical Reasoning*, S. Vosniadou, and A. Ortony (Eds.). Cambridge: Cambridge University Press.

Risiott, R. 1997. "Can you really say that in English?" University of York, Dept. of Language and Linguistic Science. Manuscript.

Robson, C. 1993. *Real World Research*. Oxford: Blackwell.

Rogoff, B. 1990. *Apprenticeship in Thinking*. New York: Oxford University Press.

Rosch, E. 1978. Principles of categorization. In *Cognition and Categorization*, E. Rosch, and B. Lloyd (Eds.). Hillsdale, NJ: Erlbaum.

Rose, S. 1993. *The Making of Memory*. London: Transworld.

Ross, B. H., and T. L. Spalding. 1994. Concepts and categories. In *Thinking and Problem Solving*, R. J. Sternberg (Ed.). San Diego, CA: Academic Press.

Ross, H. A. 1993. *China Learns English*. Hew Haven: Yale University Press.

Russo, J. E., E. J. Johnson, and D. L. Stephens. 1989. The validity of verbal protocols. *Memory and Cognition*, 17 (6): 759–769.

Sacks, H., E. A. Schegloff, and G. Jefferson. 1974. A simplest systematics for the organisation of turn-taking for conversation. *Language*, 50 (4): 696–735.

Sacks, S. (Ed.). 1979. *On Metaphor*. Chicago, IL: University of Chicago Press.

Santos, T. 1989. Replication in applied linguistics research. *TESOL Quarterly*, 23 (4): 699–702.

Saussure, F. de. 1960. *Course in General Linguistics*. Translated by W. Baskin. London: Peter Owen.

Sayce, R. A. 1953. *Style in French Prose*. Oxford: Clarendon Press.

Schank, R. C. 1982. *Dynamic Memory*. Cambridge: Cambridge University Press.

Scheffler, I. 1960. *The Language of Education*. Springfield, IL: Charles Thomas.

Schegloff, E. 1984. On some questions and ambiguities in conversation. In *Structures of Social Action*, J. Atkinson, and J. Heritage (Eds.). Cambridge: Cambridge University Press.

Scheper-Hughes, N. 1984. Infant mortality and infant care: Cultural and economic constraints on nurturing in Northeast Brazil. *Social Science and Medicine*, 19 (5): 533–546.

Scheper-Hughes, N., and M. Lock. 1986. Speaking 'truth' to illness: Metaphors, reification and a pedagogy for patients. *Medical Anthropology Quarterly*, 17 (5): 137–140.

1987. The mindful body: A prolegomenon to future work in medical anthropology. *Medical Anthropology Quarterly*, 18 (1): 6–41.

Scheub, H. 1975. Oral narrative process and the use of models. *New Literary History*, 6 (2): 353–377.

Schoenhals, M. 1993. *The Paradox of Power in a People's Republic of China Middle School*. New York: M. E. Sharpe.

Schön, D. 1979. Generative metaphor: A perspective on problem-setting in social policy. In *Metaphor and Thought*, A. Ortony (Ed.). New York: Cambridge University Press.

1983. *The Reflective Practitioner: How Professionals Think in Action*. New York: Basic Books.

(Ed.). 1991. *The Reflective Turn: Case Studies in and on Educational Practice*. New York: Teachers College Press.

Schön, D., and M. Rein. 1994. *Frame Reflection*. New York: Basic Books.

Scollon, S. 1993. Metaphors of self and communication: English and Cantonese. *Perspectives* (City University of Hong Kong), 5 (2): 41–62.

Scott, M. 1994. Metaphors and language awareness. In *Reflections on Language Learning*, L. Barbara, and M. Scott (Eds.). Clevedon: Multilingual Matters.

Searle, J. 1979. Metaphor. In *Metaphor and Thought*, A. Ortony (Ed.). New York: Cambridge University Press.

Seedhouse, P. 1996. *Learning Talk: A Study of the Interactional Organisation of the L2 Classroom from a CA Institutional Discourse Perspective*. University of York. Unpublished DPhil thesis.

Shiff, R. 1979. Art and life: a metaphoric relationship. In *On Metaphor*, S. Sacks (Ed.). Chicago, IL: University of Chicago Press.

Shillcock, R. 1990. Lexical hypotheses in continuous speech. In *Cognitive Models of Speech Processing: Psycholinguistic and Computational Perspectives*, G. Altmann (Ed.). Cambridge, MA: MIT Press.

Sinclair, J. 1991. *Corpus, Concordance, Collocation*. Oxford: Oxford University Press.

Singer, M. 1994. Discourse inference processes. In *Handbook of Psycholinguistics*, M. Gernsbacher (Ed.). New York: Academic Press.

Slife, B., and R. Williams. 1995. *What's Behind the Research*. London: Sage.

Smith, F. 1987. *Misleading Metaphors of Literacy*. Victoria, BC: Abel.

Sontag, S. 1991. *Illness as Metaphor: AIDS and its Metaphors*. London: Penguin.

Soyland, A.J. 1994. *Psychology as Metaphor*. London: Sage.

Sperber, D., and D. Wilson. 1985/86. Loose talk. In *Proceedings of the Aristotelian Society*. Oxford: Blackwell.

1986. *Relevance: Cognition and Communication.* Oxford: Blackwell.

Steen, G. 1992. *Metaphor in Literary Reception.* Vrije Universiteit, Amsterdam. Unpublished PhD thesis.

1994. *Understanding Metaphor in Literature: An Empirical Approach.* London: Longman.

1996. Metaphor and discourse: Towards a linguistic checklist for metaphor. Paper presented at the BAAL/CUP seminar on Researching and Applying Metaphor. University of York.

1997. Du style et de la science littéraire empirique: Vers une stylistique de la métaphore en prose littéraire. In *Actualités de la stylistique*, M. B. van Buuren (Ed.). Amsterdam: Rodopi.

Stein, H. 1990. *American Medicine as Culture.* Colorado: Westview.

Sternberg, R. J. (Ed.). 1994. *Thinking and Problem Solving.* San Diego, CA: Academic Press.

Sternberg, R. J., R. Tourangeau, and G. Nigro. 1979. Metaphor induction and social policy: The convergence of macroscopic and microscopic views. In *Metaphor and Thought*, A. Ortony (Ed.). New York: Cambridge University Press.

Stratman, J.F., and L. Hamp-Lyons. 1994. Reactivity in concurrent think aloud protocols: Issues for research. In *Speaking About Writing*, P. Smagorinsky (Ed.). Newbury Park, CA: Sage.

Summers, D. 1996. Computer lexicography: The importance of representativeness in relation to frequency. In *Using Corpora for Language Research*, J. Thomas, and M. Short (Eds.). London: Longman.

Sutton, C. 1992. *Words, Science and Learning.* Buckingham: Open University Press.

1994. 'Nullius in verba' and 'nihil in verbis': Public understanding of the role of language in science. *British Journal of the History of Science*, 27: 55–64.

Sweetser, E. 1990. *From Etymology to Pragmatics: The Mind–Body Metaphor in Semantic Structure and Semantic Change.* Cambridge: Cambridge University Press.

Taylor, W. (Ed.). 1984. *Metaphors of Education.* London: Heinemann.

Thomas, J., and M. Short (Eds.). 1996. *Using Corpora for Language Research.* London: Longman.

Thornbury, S. 1991. Metaphors we work by: EFL and its metaphors, *ELT Journal*, 45 (3): 193–200.

Tourangeau, R., and R. J. Sternberg. 1981. Aptness in metaphor. *Cognitive Psychology*, 13: 27–55.

1982. Understanding and appreciating metaphors. *Cognition*, 11: 203–244.

Triandis, H. C. 1995. *Individualism and Collectivism.* Boulder, CO: Westview Press.

Turner, M. 1991. *Reading Minds: The Study of English in the Age of Cognitive Science.* Princeton, NJ: Princeton University Press.

1996. *The Literary Mind*. New York: Oxford University Press.

van Dijk, T., and W. Kintsch. 1983. *Strategies of Discourse Comprehension*. New York: Academic Press.

van Lier, L. 1994. Forks and hope: Pursuing understanding in different ways. *Applied Linguistics*, 15 (3): 328–347.

van Teeffelen, T. 1994. Racism and metaphor: The Palestinian–Israeli conflict in popular literature. *Discourse and Society*, 5 (3): 381– 405.

Verbrugge, R. R. 1980. Transformations in knowing: A realist view of metaphor. In *Cognition and Figurative Language*, R. P. Honeck, and R. R. Hoffman (Eds.). Hillsdale, NJ: Erlbaum.

Vosniadou, S. 1987. Children and metaphors. *Child Development*, 58: 870–885.

1989. Context and the development of metaphor comprehension. *Metaphor and Symbolic Activity*, 4: 159–171.

Vosniadou, S., and A. Ortony. 1983. The emergence of the literal–metaphorical–anomalous distinctions in young children. *Child Development*, 54: 154–161.

(Eds.). 1989. *Similarity and Analogical Reasoning*. Cambridge: Cambridge University Press.

Vygotsky, L. 1968. *Thought and Language*. Cambridge, MA: MIT Press.

1978. *Mind in Society*. London: Harvard University Press.

Waggoner, J. E. 1990. Interaction theories of metaphor: Psychological perspectives. *Metaphor and Symbolic Activity*, 5 (2): 91–108.

Wales, R., and G. Coffey. 1986. On children's comprehension of metaphor. In *Research Issues in Child Development*, C. Pratt, A. Garton, W. Tunmer, and A. Nesdale (Eds.). Sydney: Allen and Unwin.

Wang, Z. L. (Ed.) 1990. *ELT in China*. Beijing: Foreign Language Teaching and Research Press.

Weaver, C., S. Mannes, and C. Fletcher. 1995. *Discourse Comprehension*. Hillsdale, NJ: Erlbaum.

Wellek, R., and A. Warren. 1949. *Theory of Literature*. Harmondsworth: Penguin.

Weller, S. C., and A. K. Romney. 1988. *Systematic Data Collection*. Qualitative Research Methods Series, No. 10. London: Sage.

Wells, G., and G. L. Chang-Wells. 1992. *Constructing Knowledge Together: Classrooms as Centers of Inquiry and Literacy*. Portsmouth, NH: Heinemann.

Wertsch, J. 1985. *Vygotsky and the Social Formation of Mind*. Cambridge, MA: Harvard University Press.

Wheeler, C. 1987. The magic of metaphor: A perspective on reality construction. *Metaphor and Symbolic Activity*, 2 (4): 223–237.

Wheelright, P. 1968. *The Burning Fountain*. Bloomington, IN: Indiana University Press.

White, R. 1996. *The Structure of Metaphor: The Way the Language of Metaphor Works*. Oxford: Blackwell.

Williams, L. V. 1983. *Teaching for the Two-Sided Mind.* Englewood Cliffs, NJ: Prentice Hall.

Wilson, D., and D. Sperber. 1988. Representation and relevance. In *Mental Representations,* R. Kempson (Ed.). Cambridge: Cambridge University Press.

Winner, E. 1988. *The Point of Words: Children's Understanding of Metaphor and Irony.* Cambridge, MA: Harvard University Press.

Wittgenstein, L. 1953. *Philosophical Investigations.* Oxford: Blackwell.

Wolfson, N. 1976. Speech events and natural speech: Some implications for sociolinguistic methodology. *Language in Society,* 5: 189–209.

Wood, D. 1986. *How Children Think and Learn.* Oxford: Blackwell.

Wood, D., J. S. Bruner, and G. Ross. 1976. The role of tutoring in problem solving. *Journal of Child Psychology and Psychiatry,* 17: 89–100.

Woodward, T. 1991. *Models and Metaphors in Language Teacher Training.* Cambridge: Cambridge University Press.

Young, L. W. L. 1994. *Crosstalk and Culture in Sino-American Communication.* Cambridge: Cambridge University Press.

Yu, N. 1995. Metaphorical expressions of anger and happiness in English and Chinese. *Metaphor and Symbolic Activity,* 10 (2): 59–92.

Yum, J. O. 1988. The impact of Confucianism on interpersonal relationships and communication patterns in East Asia. *Communication Monographs,* 55: 374–388.

Index